# THE BIBLE IN WORLD CHRISTIAN PERSPECTIVE

# THE BIBLE IN WORLD CHRISTIAN PERSPECTIVE

Studies in Honor of Carl Edwin Armerding

Edited by
David W. Baker and W. Ward Gasque

REGENT COLLEGE PUBLISHING
*Vancouver, British Columbia*

THE BIBLE IN WORLD CHRISTIAN PERSPECTIVE
Copyright © 2009 Regent College
All rights reserved

Published 2009 by
REGENT COLLEGE PUBLISHING
5800 University Boulevard
Vancouver, British Columbia
V6T 2E4 Canada
www.regentpublishing.com

Cover image: "The Good Samaritan," by He Qi
www.heqiarts.com

All rights reserved. No part of this publication may be reproduced, stored in a retrieval system, or transmitted, in any form or by any means, electronic, mechanical, photocopying, recording or otherwise, without the prior permission of the publisher or the Copyright Licensing Agency.

Views expressed in works published by Regent College Publishing are those of the author and do not necessarily represent the official position of Regent College (www.regent-college.edu).

Library and Archives Canada Cataloguing in Publication

The Bible in world Christian perspective : studies in honor of Carl Edwin Armerding / edited by David W. Baker and W. Ward Gasque.

Includes bibliographical references.
ISBN 978-1-57383-432-2

1. Bible—Criticism, interpretation, etc. 2. Christianity andculture.
3. Evangelistic work—Biblical teaching. I. Armerding, Carl Edwin
II. Baker, David W. (David Weston), 1950– III. Gasque, W. Ward

BS540.B44538 2009    269'.2    C2008-906551-4

# Contents

Introduction ........................................................................................ 7

About Carl Edwin Armerding ......................................................... 11

Contributors ..................................................................................... 15

1. The Bible in the World and the World of the Bible ....................... 17
   *David W. Baker*

2. Exodus 22:1-4: A Case of Restitution vs. Retribution ................... 25
   *Robin J. DeWitt Knauth*

3. Eight Key Functions of Leadership ................................................ 51
   *Soo-Inn Tan*

4. Herodotus and Esther: A Second Look .......................................... 59
   *Robert L. Hubbard, Jr.*

5. Some Reflections on Paul's Understanding of Christ as Lord ....... 73
   *Gordon D. Fee*

6. Petitionary Prayer and the Nature of God ..................................... 83
   *Clark H. Pinnock*

7. The Reforming Agency of a Psalm in the Later Middles Ages ..... 93
   *James M. Houston*

8. Becoming the People's Book:
   A Brief History of the Bible in China ........................................... 109
   *Glen G. Scorgie*

9. What Evangelicals can learn from the Benedictines ...................... 125
   *Laurel Gasque and W. Ward Gasque*

10. Apologetics Today: Learning from a Master ................................. 151
    *Michael Green*

11. Old Testament Narrative and Christian Ethics ............................. 165
    *Jonathan R. Wilson*

12. Turning a Blind Eye: Emmanuel Levinas, John 9, and
    the Blindness of Responsibility ........................................................ 175
    *Jeff Keuss*

13. Mission as the Integrating Center of Theological Education .......... 193
    *Jeffrey P. Greenman*

14. Reading the Bible in the Global Marketplace ................................. 211
    *R. Paul Stevens*

15. The Heart of Leadership is Asking the Right Questions ................ 233
    *Peter Shaw CB*

16. The Named Human and the Question of 'Being' Christlike ........... 241
    *Darrell Cosden*

*Curriculum Vitae* .............................................................................. 265

# Introduction

## To Carl Edwin Armerding on the
## Occasion of his Return to Vancouver

The essays in this book have been written in honor of Dr. Carl Edwin Armerding—distinguished Bible scholar, teacher, writer, administrator, mentor, friend, and encourager of many—on the occasion of his return to Vancouver, British Columbia, Canada.

Carl is not retiring. As a biblical scholar, he knows that the word (or even the concept of) "retirement" is not found in Scripture. Even if it were, he would probably find some hermeneutical approach that would allow him special dispensation to continue doing what he has always loved—studying, teaching, and preaching the Word and inspiring, mentoring, and encouraging upcoming generations of Christian leaders to "go and do likewise." Rather, he is re-focusing.

Although Carl has never been career-minded, but rather service-oriented, we may think of his having had two careers to date. First was his career as a scholar-teacher at Regent College (1970–91). Having set an example of excellence in teaching and scholarship in the early days of this fledgling educational institution, he answered the call of the board of directors to serve as the CEO during the most crucial time of the school's financial and academic development. Having given exemplary leadership to the college for more than a decade, he stepped aside to pass the baton to an administrative leader with different gifts that seemed appropriate for the next phase of Regent's institutional development.

And so the door was opened for Carl's second career (1991–2006), giving leadership to the renewal of a strategic Christian educational center in Austria (Schloss Mittersill Study Centre) and also contributing to the academic development of the Oxford Centre for Mission Studies (UK). Through his ministry with these two institutions, he has contributed significantly to the strengthening of the scholarly resources of leaders of the global Christian movement outside of the West.

Returning to Canada opens the door to Carl's third career, serving as a roving ambassador for good theology and biblical scholarship to the global church. Carl and Betsy have returned to Canada to be near their children and grandchildren, but already Carl has been summoned back to Central and Eastern Europe to teach and to advise. And he has recently taught in China and has invitations to India and other Asian countries as well as elsewhere. Naturally, Regent College has asked him to teach at least one course per annum, and many of his students here are non-Westerners.

These essays by former students, colleagues, and friends of Carl Armerding are but a small token of his influence and interests, as well as the affection of his former students and colleagues. "The Bible in World Christian Perspective" would be an appropriate heading for his three careers. At Regent, the world came to Vancouver to study with a small band of risk-oriented scholars, to be equipped for ministries in the marketplace, the academy, and the churches. And through them Carl has made a significant impact on global Christian leadership. Two of the first six full-time students at Regent College are contributors to this volume, representing the UK (marketplace) and the USA (academy).

During Carl's time in Europe, he taught, advised, and mentored young scholar-leaders from all over the world. And this ministry is continuing as we move toward the second decade of the twenty-first century. Taking into consideration the longevity of his parents and

INTRODUCTION

their siblings, there are good reasons to suspect that Carl may have a longer ministry in his third career than he had in either of the first two. It is our prayer that that may come to pass, to the great benefit of God's people around the globe.

David W. Baker and W. Ward Gasque

# About Carl Edwin Armerding

Carl Edwin Armerding was born into the family of Grace Horsey and Howard Sherman Armerding on April 30, 1936 in Boston, Massachusetts. His parents had a long history among the Plymouth Brethren. His grandfather William M. Horsey was an itinerant Bible teacher, evangelist, and church planter across Canada and the United States (including Hawaii). His paternal grandparents were leaders among the Grant (Exclusive) Brethren in New Jersey and the two families were long-time friends. Among the Armerding family of ten children were Dr. Carl Armerding, missionary, pastor and long-term professor of Bible at Wheaton College (IL), regular visiting professor at Dallas Theological Seminary, and a leader in both Greater Europe Mission and Central American Mission. Carl Edwin's uncle George Armerding was for a time President of Christian Businessmen International; his uncle Ludwig was for many years Superintendant of Jerry McCauley Mission in New York City; his aunt Minnie Armerding was a missionary among the indigenous people of the Southwestern United States; and his father Howard was President of the Gideons International. The preachers who frequented the home included Robert J. Little, Brethren Bible teacher and later Radio Pastor of Moody Bible Institute, and Dr. Harry Ironside, who became the celebrated pastor of Moody Church and author of many popular Bible commentaries. The Bible was central to the life of the family, and young Carl grew up with a deep love for Scripture.

Carl's parents, along with their siblings and many of their friends, left the Exclusive Brethren around 1939 and became active in the Open (Christian) Brethren, where they remained for the rest of their lives. The Armerdings, including older brother Bill, moved to Lynnfield, Massachusetts from their home in Malden just after Carl was born, and he had his public school education in Lynnfield and Wakefield. His father Howard was a salesman until World War II, when he was employed to oversee the building of water and storage tanks as part of the war effort. Howard was away from the family during much of the war. Brother Peter was born in 1942. Carl graduated from Wakefield High School in 1953 and went on to attend Gordon College in Wenham, Massachusetts, where he was class president and graduated in 1957 with a degree in history. He spent several summers as a lifeguard at Bible camps in New Hampshire and Maryland during his college days.

Upon graduation from college Carl entered the US Navy Officer's Candidate School in Newport, RI, serving until 1961 as an officer in the National Security Agency at Ft. Meade, Maryland, where he made many friends among the Christian Brethren movement and among members of the Officers' Christian Union (OCU—now Officers' Christian Fellowship). Upon release from active duty in 1961, he was sent by the OCU to Europe as their travelling secretary, gaining ministry experience and an interest in and love for Europe. He later returned to the USA to pursue theological education, first at Covenant Seminary in St. Louis, then at Wheaton College Graduate School, and finally (completing his Bachelor of Divinity degree) at Trinity Evangelical Divinity School. In 1963 he met and married Betsy Jane Leonard, with whom he has four children: Calvin, Jennifer, Geoffrey and Elizabeth. Carl and Betsy moved back to Boston, to Brandeis University, where Carl completed his PhD (1968) in ancient Near Eastern languages and culture under Professors Cyrus Gordon and Harry A. Hoffner.

Following a post-doctoral year in Jerusalem at Hebrew Union College, Carl's teaching career in Old Testament began at Wheaton

INTRODUCTION

College Graduate School [1969–70] after which he became one of the founding faculty at Regent College in Vancouver, British Columbia. Carl rose through the ranks of Assistant, Associate and full Professor to became the second Principal (later President) of Regent College (1977–88) a role in which he oversaw Regent's emergence as a widely recognized center of Evangelical Christian higher education. He concluded his tenure by leading the development of Regent's beautiful campus 'under the Green Roof' at the entrance to the University of British Colombia. During those years, Carl helped to begin both the Institute for Biblical Research and a Northwest Section of the Society of Biblical Literature, serving as IBR's Secretary from 1977–82 and as President of the Region for SBL in 1975–76. He also continued as a Reserve Officer in the US Navy, retiring as a Captain in 1990.

In 1991 Carl left Regent College to become Director of the Schloss Mittersill Study Centre in Mittersill, Austria, where he led a cutting edge graduate theological educational program for a wide range of international students, especially from the newly open Central and Eastern European countries. During the following decade he also served as Senior Research Fellow at the Oxford Centre for Mission Studies in England. Carl retired from Oxford in 2002 and the Schloss in 2006, although he continues to serve both as requested. Carl and Betsy have now returned to their home in Vancouver, where they are active in the ministry of University Chapel and provide a strong encouragement to their children living in the area. Carl continues regularly to teach in Europe and Asia, as well as at Regent College and elsewhere. He spends much of his time mentoring and seeking to encourage numerous younger scholars and leaders of Christian ministries. Along the way, Carl has written all or part of various books, and a wide variety of articles, both scholarly and popular.

# Contributors

**David W. Baker**
Professor of Old Testament and Semitic Languages
Ashland Theological Seminary

**Darrell Cosden**
Associate Professor of Theology
Judson University, Elgin, Illinois.

**Robin J. DeWitt Knauth**
Assistant Professor of Religion, Lycoming College

**Laurel Gasque**
Team Leader, Religious and Theological Studies Fellowship, Canada
Sessional Lecturer in Christianity and the Arts, Regent College

**W. Ward Gasque**
English Ministries Pastor, Richmond Chinese Alliance Church, Canada
Founding Faculty Member, Regent College

**Michael Green**
Senior Research Fellow
Wycliffe Hall, Oxford, England

**Jeffrey P. Greenman**
Associate Dean of Biblical and Theological Studies,
Professor of Christian Ethics
Wheaton College, Wheaton, Illinois

**Gordon D. Fee**
Professor Emeritus of New Testament Studies
Regent College, Vancouver, BC, Canada

# THE BIBLE IN WORLD CHRISTIAN PERSPECTIVE

**James M. Houston**
Board of Governors' Professor Emeritus, Spiritual Theology
Regent College, British Columbia, Canada

**Robert L. Hubbard, Jr.**
Professor of Biblical Literature
North Park Theological Seminary, Chicago, Illinois

**Jeff Keuss**
Associate Professor of Christian Ministry
Seattle Pacific University, Seattle, Washington

**Clark H. Pinnock**
Professor Emeritus of Systematic Theology
McMaster Divinity College, Hamilton, Ontario, Canada

**Glen G. Scorgie**
Professor of Theology
Bethel Seminary, San Diego, California

**Peter Shaw CB**
Professor of Leadership Development, Newcastle University Business School;
Executive Coach, Praesta Partners, London, England

**R. Paul Stevens**
Professor Emeritus of Marketplace Theology
Regent College, Vancouver, British Columbia, Canada

**Soo-Inn Tan**
Director, Graceworks, Singapore;
Honorary Associate Pastor, Evangel Christian Church, Singapore

**Jonathan R. Wilson**
Pioneer McDonald Professor of Theology
Carey Theological College, Vancouver, British Columbia, Canada

1

# The Bible in the World and the World of the Bible

## On Learning Biblical Languages

DAVID W. BAKER

**Globalization and Diversity**[1]

A social reality at the start of the twenty-first century, whether for good or ill, is globalization, and its constituent element—diversity. This should not come as a surprise for Christians, since they are natural concomitants to faithfully fulfilling Christ's command to "make disciples of all nations" (Matt 28:19). Relationships have expanded greatly beyond small, relatively homogenous communities of many past generations. The expanding network of relationships has many strands, which affect not only the church, but also theological education. Most church bodies have allied missions organizations, and the accrediting body for institutions of theological education in North America (Association of Theological Schools,

---

1. This article is affectionately dedicated to Carl Armerding, who models not only the contemporary globalization of the Gospel through his life's work of educating the world, but also helped point me to the contextualization of the Old Testament in its own world.

ATS) devotes a 22-page chapter in its Handbook of Accreditation to globalization and diversity.[2]

During an ATS meeting over two decades ago, a description of globalization within theological education involved four elements: evangelization, ecumenical cooperation, dialogue between Christianity and other religions, and social action on behalf of disadvantaged people.[3]

Among many other aspects of this description, it is clear that knowledge, an increasing awareness of the "other," is a *sine qua non* to achieving globalization on any of the four levels mentioned. This is not a straightforward task, since too often lip service is given to diversity, but there is no thought as to how to live with difference which diversity brings. It is far easier to expect the different to become like us.

In many contexts, globalization is not realized only through geographic dislocation, though that is still a valid and valuable means of getting to know the other–going to where they are. Increasingly, demographic mobility, whether by choice or displacement, has brought the other to us.[4] Cross-cultural contact no longer means leaving one's home, but can be as easy as inviting the family next door into the home.

While there is a growing awareness of diversity in the church,[5] Martin Luther King's words spoken at Western Michigan Univer-

---

2. "Guidelines for Evaluating Globalization in Commission Schools," in *Handbook of Accreditation* (Pittsburgh: The Association of Theological Schools, 2005), section 7.

3. Don S. Browning, "Globalization and the Task of Theological Education in North America," reprinted in *Theological Education* 30 / Supplement 1 (1993): 15-16.

4. It is too easy for most North Americans to forget that the ethnic-cultural majority of the America of today is also the product of demographic displacement, since most were the "other" who found their way from elsewhere.

5. See, e.g., Ibrahim A. Gambari, "The Challenges of Globalization and the Role of The United Methodist Church," 2004 Willson Lecture accessed at http://www.gbhem.org/atf/cf/%7B0BCEF929-BDBA-4AA0-968F-D1986A8EEF80%7D/Pub_GlobalizationGambari2004.pdf, May 1, 2008.

sity in 1963 still hold true: "We must face the fact that in America, the church is still the most segregated major institution in America. At 11:00 on Sunday morning when we stand and sing and Christ has no east or west, we stand at the most segregated hour in this nation. This is tragic. Nobody of honesty can overlook this."[6] While steps have been made in opening up the church to this problem so it may be addressed,[7] the issue has not gone away during the almost half-century since King spoke.

Institutions of theological education are an important cog in the apparatus of globalization for the church, since they produce its future leaders. If they model an adequate response to the issue for their students, these students in turn are more likely to instigate reform in their parishes. Toward this end, among other reasons, schools have long sought to attract minority and international students, with varying success. One of the hurdles in encouraging such diversity, however, has been faculty composition, since "half of the [ATS accredited] schools have no racial/ethnic person on the faculty."[8] Students find it difficult to find a home in a location where they are alone.[9] Additionally, schools have not adequately addressed the issue of what actually constitutes cross-cultural understanding. Proximity does not necessarily equate with appreciation. That is, commuting students sitting next to those with different backgrounds during a three-hour lecture class but then immediately returning to

---

6. Accessed at www.wmich.edu/library/archives/mlk/q-a.html on April 29, 2008.

7. Among many resources available, see Spencer Perkins and Chris Rice, *More Than Equals: Racial Healing for the Sake of the Gospel*, revised (Downers Grove: InterVarsity Press, 2000) and George Yancey, *Beyond Racial Gridlock: Embracing Mutual Responsibility* (Downers Grove: InterVarsity Press, 2006).

8. "Two Association venues address race and ethnicity in theological education," *Colloquy* 10/3 (January/February 2002), 3.

9. Homogenous churches must also take this phenomenon into consideration when seeking to become more diverse. They are presented with a "chicken-and-egg" problem of wanting to bring outsiders into its world which is foreign since there are no outsiders in it.

their respective homes do not by doing so enter into a cross-cultural experience. Thought and planning on the part of the lecturer and the institution as a whole must take place to provide opportunity for students to turn from facing the podium to facing each other in some sort of dialog if meaningful encounters are to take place and walls of separation are to come down.

**A Place for Language Study: Walls and Bridges**

One of the most direct means of producing awareness of both the "other" and of one's self as "other," encountering that which is different, and impelling a movement toward bridging differences, is foreign language study. One is immediately confronted with an ordering of reality which is different to one's own, a wall between two world-views. In order to effectively communicate, or even to understand, one must therefore search for hooks, threads of contact between the familiar of one's own language world and the new language world of the dialogue partner which can bridge the two worlds. One is forced, almost on a visceral, rather than simply on a cognitive level, to participate in one of the foundational elements of andragogical education, moving from the known to the unknown, with the concomitant realization that what was previously understood as "known" itself was only a partial comprehension of reality.

This awareness of the other can be achieved to some extent for the world of the Bible through exposure to various translations different from that which is most familiar, so opening up other possible understandings. It is more powerfully accomplished, however, when encountering Scripture in the original languages of enscripturation.

Study of biblical languages can also effect critical theological reflection when the student realizes that God originally addressed his creatures in neither King James' nor contemporary English. God did not actually say "Let there be light" (and possibly not even the Hebrew *yehi 'or*; Gen 1:3).[10] A common cultural chauvinism, thinking that God is like me even in language and so surely also in ethnicity and gender, takes an immediate blow. One now has to pay attention in a new way to words which too often have become mute, losing any real meaning through familiarity.

Textual encounter in the original languages also provides an opportunity for "close reading" par excellence. Pioneered for English literature by I. A Richards and developed by the New Critics,[11] this modern supplement to the venerable tools of exegesis and commentary, also called "total interpretation,"[12] is marked by careful analysis of a text even to the level of words. While eschewing the New Critics' claim that understanding can be attained through study of the text alone, without resort to study of its literary or historical context, their approach did a good thing by reviving interest in the study of the text itself. The study of a text in its original drives the reader to look at each constituent element, not only analyzing morphology and syntax, but also seeing how the piece works on a discourse level, shining new light on what might have become stale from its over-familiarity in English. One is forced to make every level of the text to some extent one's own, grappling with valid available options of interpretation and coming to appreciate the truth of the old Italian adage *Traduttore, traditore* ("to translate is

---

10. This is not the place to enter into a discussion of the interesting, and ultimately unanswerable, question as to what language God actually spoke at creation. I tell my Hebrew students that they will be greeted at the Pearly Gates with the greeting "*Shalom! Mah shelomchah?*" If they can answer in Hebrew, they will be ushered straight in. If not, they will have to learn Hebrew to gain entry, which is the source of the concept of purgatory.

11. See, e.g., J. C. Ransom, *The New Criticism* (Norfolk: New Directions, 1941). For a brief survey of the approach as used in Old Testament studies, see Tremper Longman, III, *Literary Approaches to Biblical Interpretation*, Foundations of Contemporary Interpretation 3 (Grand Rapids: Zondervan, 1987), 25-27.

12. Meir Weiss, *The Bible from Within: The Method of Total Interpretation* (Jerusalem: Magnes Press, 1984).

to betray"). Language study should not drive one to the cynicism which this phrase could elicit, thinking that we face an impossible task. Rather, it engenders excitement at the rich pregnancy of words and phrases which the new wineskins into which it is placed are not able to adequately contain. It drives the language student to say, "This endeavor at translation is well and good, but now let me tell you the rest of the story." This excitement is not as forcefully garnered by relying solely on translations of others.

Language study also inculcates an appreciation of the culture of the other in a more direct manner than can be attained through a simple explanation; one sees reality through their eyes. For an example from a non-biblical language, even without learning Sumerian, the earliest, non-Semitic language formerly used in what is now Iraq, one can see that the same symbol is used for "heaven" and "god." The importance of astral deities in that part of the world, which later gave rise to the zodiac and astrology, becomes strikingly apparent through one's own observations rather than simply being told who early inhabitants of Mesopotamia worshipped.

Breadth of vocabulary on a topic sheds light on what is important to a society or a subsection of it. Specialized vocabularies develop for those for whom it is important to describe subtle differences between types of snow (for the Inuit), sandpaper grades (for finish carpenters), or colors of the palette (for painters). In the Bible, a clear example is the numerous Hebrew words which are part of the semantic field of "sin,"[13] showing that holiness, or its lack, looms large in the awareness of God's people. A preliminary study of Hebrew allows one to notice the number of these terms, while further study clarifies some of the distinctions between the terms but also indicates that, without any native speakers to use as informants, some of the subtler nuances are, and probably always will

---

13. See Willem van Gemeren, *New International Dictionary of Old Testament Theology and Exegesis* (Grand Rapids: Zondervan, 1997) 5: 155, 175, 198, 211, 215.

be, inaccessible to us. Language study thus brings us closer to an accurate understanding, while at the same time closer to a realization that complete understanding is impossible.

Language study thus helps bridge walls built by time and geographic distance. It fosters an attitude toward Scripture in some ways similar to that which the inhabitants of Narnia developed toward Aslan, the lion: he could be a valiant and valuable companion, but he could never be domesticated. So God's word, spoken in dialects of which there are no living native speakers, is a guide to which we can draw closer through study of the languages, but one which allows us to see ultimate reality only as through a fog, sometimes with more clarity, but often dimly. May serious students of Scripture continue diligently to lessen the dimness and expand the clarity not only for themselves, but for readers across the globe.

2

# Exodus 22:1-4 (21:37-22:3)
## *A Case of Restitution vs. Retribution*

### ROBIN J. DEWITT KNAUTH

*¹If a man steals an ox or a sheep, and slaughters it or sells it, five cattle he shall restore in place of the ox, and four of the flock in place of the sheep. ²If during the tunneling the thief is found, and he is struck and he dies, there is no bloodguilt for him. ³But if the sun has risen upon him, there will be bloodguilt for him. Surely he will make restitution; if he has nothing, then he will be sold on account of his theft. ⁴If, surely, what he stole is found alive in his possession, whether ox or donkey or sheep, he shall restore double.*

*Exodus 22:1-4*

**Introduction**

Scholarly understanding of the theft laws in Exodus 22:1-4 (21:37-22:3 in the Hebrew Masoretic Text) in the Covenant Code, deemed by most scholars to be the oldest collection of laws in the Bible, seems to have reached a rare state of consensus. This comfortable scholarly consensus, however, obscures some difficulties which further investigation could clarify. The present study addresses two long-recognized difficulties within the passage and reinterprets the law, yielding significant implications for wider trends of the legal traditions of Israel during its early history as a society. The first difficulty is a minor issue regarding the differing levels of compensation prescribed as restitution. The second is a more major issue having to do with the continuity and integrity of the unit. To resolve this issue of continuity, the intended context of the verses is reexamined and an entirely new interpretation is proposed. This new interpretation, then, carries wider implications for the character of Israelite law and its connection with other ancient Near Eastern legal traditions.

**Five, Four, Two...**

The differing levels of compensation prescribed here have long been an object of speculation. Specifically, the problem lies in understanding why initially the penalty for stealing an ox is five-fold restitution while for a sheep it is only four-fold, and then a couple verses further on a blanket rate of two-fold restitution is mandated. No explanation for the initial difference between oxen and sheep is given in the text. The laws of the Hittites make similar distinctions between levels of restitution for the theft of various animals, though, again, no explanation is given.[1] Exod 22:3 then reduces the

---

1. The system of restitution attested in the Hittite laws is as follows: # 45 = three-fold for unreturned lost property, # 57-59 = formerly thirty-fold but now ten-fold for plain livestock theft, # 60-62 = seven-fold for removing the brand of a straying animal, # 63-65 = formerly fifteen-fold but now ten-fold for theft of various animals, # 67-69 = formerly twelve-fold but now six-fold for various other animals, #110 = double for stealing plaster from a bin, # 81-83, 91-97, 101-103, 108-109, 119-143 = various monetary fines for stealing pigs, bees, grain, articles in a house, fruit, wood, plants, birds, plows, carts, water troughs, whips, emblems, spears, copper nails, curtains, doors, bricks, leather reigns, chariot wheels, copper knives and various other articles.

The Code of Hammurabi, although calling for the death penalty in an overwhelming majority of theft cases, also allows for multiple restitution in two: #8 (thirty-fold to the state or ten-fold to a private citizen, though if the thief were unable to pay then the

penalty to only two-fold restitution regardless of the type of animal, but specifies a condition that the animal is found still alive in the thief's hand, whereas the first clause had been conditioned upon the animal having been already slaughtered or sold. Various explanations have been offered for these differences, some more satisfying than others.

Among these, the most innovative is put forth by Daube (89, 94-95). He suggests that the two-fold restitution provision represents an historical development within the law in which the penalty for theft was reduced generally at such time as possession became an acceptable proof of theft. Such a view finds some support within the explicitly stated reduction of penalty for theft within the Hittite corpus (# 57-69). This explanation is also attractive in that it makes some sense of the second difficulty of the passage concerning the ordering of the verses. Namely, if 22:3 is a later addition to the law of theft, it would be justifiable to place it at the end of the already existing law on the topic.

The obvious problem with this explanation is that the verses themselves make a clear distinction between the two cases on the basis of whether or not the original animal is recoverable. Moreover, if the second provision is meant to supersede the first, then one would expect either that the first would have been deleted or that, as with the Hittite laws, some explicit statement of the change would be given in order to avoid confusion. This theory also fails to address the distinction made in the first clause between oxen and sheep, versus the lack of such distinction in the later law. In the end, it remains both

---

sentence reverted to death), and #265 (ten-fold for an entrusted animal). Note also the biblical references in Exod 22:7-9 (double restitution for any stolen property found in the thief's hand), 2 Sam 12:6 (four-fold restitution for a stolen sheep, already slaughtered; the LXX version reads seven-fold), Proverbs 6:30-31 (seven-fold restitution, likely to indicate 'perfect' or 'full' restoration—de Vaux p. 160), Lev 6:1-7 (restitution in full plus one-fifth added to its value) and Luke 19:8 (four-fold).

unproven and unnecessary, since other solutions, based upon simple common-sense reasoning, are perfectly plausible.

The most convincing of these offers that the first distinction between oxen and sheep is based upon the loss not only of future value (the labor of the ox, the wool of the sheep) but also, in the case of the ox, of past labor—namely the substantial investment involved in training the ox for its labor (Cole 171). If the original animal is recovered, however, such a distinction is no longer necessary since neither the past training nor the future labor/value is lost. The double restitution is then merely punitive in nature, acting as a deterrent against crime, since the owner's loss was only temporary and minimal. Such an understanding seems entirely plausible and satisfactory in accounting for the differing levels of compensation. It still, however, leaves a major problem with the ordering of the verses—that the logical progression of laws of compensation for theft seem to be interrupted by other laws concerning bloodguilt for intruders.

**Order**

Standard commentaries by Noth (183), Childs (474), Sarna (130), Cassuto (282) and others all agree that verses 1-2a are a later interpolation or parenthetical addition. They are secondarily inserted into the middle of this law concerning theft of livestock because they have generally to do with theft and housebreaking, even though their main thrust regards whether or not the property owner incurs bloodguilt if the thief is fatally injured during a break-in. In fact, some major translations (the NEB, RSV and NRSV) as well as many commentators (e.g. Ellison 119, Davies 179) actually reorder the verses at this point in order to make sense of them.

Such an approach fails to appreciate the continuity which exists between these various provisions. If verses 1-2a are indeed a later addition, then someone, at least, thought they belonged there. Current scholarship does not account for the editor's motivation in placing them at precisely that point. If it were only the general theme of 'theft' which connects them, then why not place it at the end of the unit instead of in the middle?

Part of the problem in understanding the current ordering of the verses lies in one's interpretation of the scenario envisioned, and the distinctions being made. In this respect it seems to be widely assumed that the interior verses (22:1–2a) concern the more general problem of theft involving housebreaking, and that the major distinction being made depends on whether the theft occurs at night or during the day. This well-accepted understanding of things is, however, unsatisfactory on several counts. Firstly, it is likely that these interior verses, like the exterior verses (21:37, 22:3), are concerned mainly with livestock theft. More importantly, this universally assumed night/day distinction lacks a solid basis in the text. The nighttime context of the first clause is never explicitly stated, but only assumed as the natural opposition to 'if the sun has risen upon him' in the second clause. However this phrase itself is a strange idiom, apparently unique to this context. Its supposed meaning here of 'during the day' is highly questionable. A closer study of the language involved is necessary, among other things. First, however, we turn to a specific issue of continuity in context; namely that the context of the entire passage is one of livestock theft.

**House-Breaking and Livestock Theft**

Perhaps part of the reason that the natural connection existing between these provisions is missed by the modern reader is that he does not appreciate the connection between housebreaking and theft of livestock. We live in an age of private, fenced in land where most of the natural predators of livestock have been eliminated, and animals are kept either outside or in barns and outbuildings separate from the house, while the house itself is centrally heated and richly endowed with a wide assortment of valuable objects. House-breaking is therefore naturally assumed to involve the theft of all sorts of valuables, but not animals.

The average Israelite, however, would not have owned many 'valuables' as we would classify them. His main assets would consist of land and livestock.[2] A few farming tools, some pottery and a set of clothes per person would generally round out the belongings. Meanwhile, in his article on "The Archaeology of the Family in Ancient Israel," Lawrence Stager has made a convincing case that the average Israelite dwelling included a stabling area for animals on the ground floor, built to accommodate sheep, goats, donkeys and even cows inside, with an upper story providing sleeping quarters for the people.[3] Such an arrangement would insure protection of the animals from predators and from straying during the night, and would offer an added benefit of extra shared warmth during the cold winter rainy season. In view of these two considerations, it seems reasonable to make the connection that the house-breaking here implies theft of livestock, and thus fits well in its context.

Also of possible interest in this regard is the story of Jephthah in Judges 11:30-31, 34-40. His vow to sacrifice to God whatever first

---

2. Cf. Gen 12:16, 26:14, 30:43, 46:32; Deut 3:19; 1 Sam 25:2; and Job 1:3ff where an equation of wealth = livestock is made. Note the use of *bāqār* in Hebrew for both 'cattle' and 'acquired property,' from *bāqar* 'to acquire.'

3. Stager's evidence for asserting this model of a typical Israelite home as including two stories with a stable area inside on the ground floor is quite impressive. In addition to citing biblical references to 'upper rooms' as sleeping quarters (Josh 2:15-18, Judges 3:24, 2 Sam 19:1-5, 1 Kings 17, 2 Kings 1:1-6, 2 Kings 4:10, Acts 1:13, 9:36-41, 20:8) and 'stall-fed calves' (1 Sam 28:24, Psalm 50:9, Amos 6:4, Jer 46:21, Mal 3:20, Luke 15:23-27) which were 'kept inside the house' (1 Sam 28:24), he amasses a considerable amount of archaeological evidence, from a number of different sites all over Israel, both for the existence of an upper story and for the presence of indoor stabling areas for animals. Among the tell-tale features cited for this were the low height of ceiling beams, flagstone flooring (for better drainage) in that specific area while the rest of the floor was nicely plastered, the absence of hearths, ovens or cisterns in this area, unmistakable feeding troughs or mangers built into the walls, and compartments or stalls between pillars of appropriate size for the accommodation of various animals (Stager 11-17).

came out of his house upon his return, and the resultant sacrifice of his daughter, has long been problematic in view of clear prohibitions against (and condemnations of) child-sacrifice in the Bible (e.g. Lev 18:21, Deut 18:10, 2 Kings 16:3, 17:17, 21:6). The obvious solution is that he fully expected some animal to be the first to come out, and certainly not his daughter (the pronoun used is masculine, whereas his family members—wife and daughter—are only feminine). The incidental implication behind this is that animals had a normal place inside the house.

One final piece of supporting evidence for these internal verses being also concerned primarily with theft of livestock is a grammatical one. As argued by Jackson (1972, 49), the definite article in 22:1 must necessarily refer to some previously introduced subject—namely the cattle-thief already mentioned in 21:37. A new topic would have been introduced by an indirect formulation.

## Night and Day

Now we turn to an investigation of the primary emphasis of the interior verses, seeking to determine what the intended point of distinction actually was. As stated above, the vast majority of commentators understand the verses as primarily distinguishing between day-time and night-time theft. The explanation given for this, basically, is that a thief must expect to encounter resistance from the occupants of the house during the night, since they all would be there asleep, and therefore he is more likely to have murderous intent, whereas during the day he might have expected all of the occupants to be out and about their business (Cassuto 282, Sarna 130, etc.).

Rabbinic interpretation in the *Mekilta de Rabbi Ishmael*, Tractate Nezikin (Lauterbach 102), and the *Babylonian Talmud*, Sanhedrin 72a-b, proposes a slightly different nuance, allowing for two possible distinctions. One is based on a principle derived from Deut 22:23-27 about the availability of help. The other is based on an allegorization of the risen sun as representing peaceful intent (as opposed to murderous intent) on the part of the thief, or perhaps clarity of intent. Both of these are again connected to the timing of the theft—whether it takes place at night or during the day.

The deciding factor is agreed by all to be in the timing. If the break-in occurs at night then the use of lethal force in self-defense is justified for a number of reasons. In the dark, with no readily available lights to see by (no flashlights, electricity or even matches), it would have been impossible to determine whether the thief was armed and dangerous with intent to murder, or even at what point he has been rendered harmless (Cole 171). Moreover, as noted above, the fact that the thief must have known that the residents of the house would all be there asleep during the night creates a certain presumption of deadly intent. If, however, the break-in occurs during the daytime, then it would be easier to gage the appropriate level of force necessary. So the argument goes.

However, if the concern were mainly one of distinguishing accidental killing in a context of self-defense from intentional killing, then there are other laws in the Covenant Code covering this (Exod 21:13, 18-21). This seems a strange context to bring such a thing up again. Furthermore, daylight is no guarantee that an intruder could not have murderous intent, or that a fight might not ensue in which the intruder would be struck and then die. It seems that this interpretation requires altogether too much 'reading-in' to the law. A simpler and more straightforward understanding should be sought.

First on the agenda for further investigation of this point must be the often-cited parallels from the lawcode of Eshnunna (CE) # 12 and 13, which make a clear distinction between daytime and nighttime in determining the penalty for trespass (theft *per se* is not mentioned). This is the strongest evidence on the side of the traditional interpretation of the Exodus law as discussed above. Again, commentators have been unanimous in connecting these laws, and the meaning of the Eshnunna provisions is entirely unambiguous as to the day/night distinction. Some significant differences, however,

## EXODUS 22:1-4: A CASE OF RESTITUTION VS. RETRIBUTION

should be acknowledged. Not only does the Eshnunna law mention nothing about theft or thieves, but, in fact, none of the language used there corresponds in any way to the language used in Exodus.

CE #13 reads: "A man who is seized in the house of a commoner, within the house, at midday, shall weigh and deliver 10 shekels of silver; he who is seized at night within the house shall die, he shall not live." (Roth 61)

Exodus 22:1-2a reads: "If in the tunneling the thief is found, and he is struck and he dies, there is no bloodguilt. If the sun has risen up him there is bloodguilt for him. Surely he will restore…"

Upon close examination, one can see first of all that the ordering of the clauses with regard to night and day is reversed. Secondly, while Exodus refers specifically to a thief, CE uses the general word for a man. CE specifies that the man is seized (N of *tsbt*) in the house at night, while Exodus uses a conditional '*im*- followed by a participial temporal clause ('if during the tunneling') and the verb 'he is found' (N of *mts'*), making no explicit mention of either 'house' or 'night.' CE assigns a specific fine for the daytime intruder; this Exodus law (depending upon the specific delimitation assigned by the particular scholar) either says nothing of any penalty for a daytime thief, specifying only that his life is protected by the normal sanctions of blood-vengeance, or else it specifies restitution—but if (as is usually supposed) he was caught in the act during the day before the theft was accomplished, then what restitution could be made? Restitution cannot be the penalty for a thief apprehended in the act, daytime or not. Further, while restitution comprises the main context for the Exodus law here, if not being an actual part of it, there is nothing about restitution in the context of the CE law since nothing was actually stolen. Exodus concerns itself primarily with blood-guilt (*dāmîm*); this concern is entirely absent from CE. In fact, the *only* cognate vocabulary in the entire pericope is the common verbal root *mwt*, which, owing to its high frequency in Semitic usage generally, should not be assigned a great deal of weight.

More fundamentally, these verses in Exodus are mainly concerned with whether or not the householder is guilty of murder if the thief gets killed, while the Eshnunna laws are concerned with assigning a penalty to the intruder. Exodus allows the death of the thief without sanctions of blood-vengeance against the householder; Eshnunna prescribes death to the thief as his punishment. Thus, while the biblical law allows no blood-vengeance for the thief who is killed in 22:1, it is not because this is the penalty for theft but only because it was a matter of self-defense for the householder. Such may well not be the case at Eshnunna. CE #13, regarding an intruder found inside someone else's house, would seem to be the direct parallel of the biblical law here as traditionally interpreted, with the night-time intruder subject to death while the day-time intruder pays only a comparatively nominal fine of 10 shekels. One might easily envision the distinction as relying upon the reasoning proposed above, namely, a higher probability of intent to murder during the night. The same may not be so easily supposed, however, with regard to the preceding law in CE #12 about trespassing in a field, which has exactly parallel wording with respect to both the distinction in timing and the resultant penalty. In this case the same distinction of penalty is made, but there can be little question of intent to murder or self-defense out in the field at night.

Although it is impossible to be certain, since the penalty for theft is not stated elsewhere in the extant laws of Eshnunna, one may suppose from this that death was merely the standard penalty for theft, and that the nighttime setting provided a presumption of guilt in this regard, whereas a daytime trespasser might have had some more innocent motive (or at least a less systematic and therefore less harmful method) and is thus assigned only a fine as warning. In any case, the salient condition here, clearly emphasized by the syntax (in that it is syntactically repetitive and unnecessary, since *ina eqel* = 'in the field' has already been specified), is that the man is 'in the

## EXODUS 22:1-4: A CASE OF RESTITUTION VS. RETRIBUTION

*crop*' or 'among the sheaves' (*ina kurullim*).[4] Other proposals for the meaning of this word include 'inside the fence/enclosure' or 'with the (stolen) sheaf.' In any case, the point is that it is simply theft, and not any concern for intent to murder, that is indicated here. A similar trespassing law in the Lipit-Ishtar lawcode #9 assigns the same fine to a man seized in an orchard for stealing (no mention of night-time or day-time setting is made). While stealing is the explicit charge here, presumably it would be the relatively minimal and harmless theft of only a few pieces of fruit. Biblical law, far from punishing the hungry trespasser, explicitly requires landowners to allow poor people, travelers and neighbors to pick and eat whatever they want, and even to harvest from the edges and corners of the field, as well as from the leftover gleanings (Lev 19:9-10, Deut 23:24-25).

Another significant difference here lies in the very unambiguity of the statement of a day/night distinction in Eshnunna (*ina mūtslālim, ina mūshim*). If, indeed, the biblical law in the Covenant Code generally is a direct heir of these legal traditions from Eshnunna, as many would argue based not only upon content but also upon such things as literary structure and even precise terminology,[5] then one might well expect the biblical law to be equally unambiguous in its distinction, if, in fact, the same distinction is intended. Compare, for instance, the wording found in Genesis 31:39—'whether stolen by day or stolen by night,' with its explicit use of *'yôm'* and *lāylāh* here and also in 31:40, which adds the preposition (*'bayyôm'* and *'ballāylāh*). These verses clearly exhibit the unambiguous syntax normally used in biblical Hebrew to indicate occurrence during daytime or nighttime.

In Genesis 31:39 the immediate reference seems to be to animals stolen by wild beasts, for which the shepherd is nevertheless held responsible. Meanwhile, other passages such as Job 24:13-17,

---

4. I follow here the work of Roth and Yaron.
5. E.g. the use of an exact cognate verb in the laws of the goring ox, as argued by Malul. Cf. the detailed analyses offered by Otto.

Jeremiah 49:9 and Obadiah 5 make it clear that nighttime is the assumed setting for theft (and indeed for criminal activity in general). Job 24:16, in particular, seems precisely parallel to the situation in Exodus 22:1, with the use of the exact same verbal root (*khtr*) for the breaking in of the thief. The passage in Job makes it explicitly clear that the thief is definitely *not* expected to be out during the day, but only works at night.[6] Likewise, in Akkadian literature, one can cite the Tale of the Poor Man of Nippur: "In the middle of the night like a thief he arose."

The only other participial usage of this verb (Jeremiah 2:34) is even more significant. The exact same form (*bammakhteret*) is used here as a temporal modifier for the exact same verb (*mts'*). Furthermore, the Jeremiah passage is also concerned with bloodguilt (*dam*). Specifically, Jeremiah accuses God's people, declaring that: "On your clothes is found the lifeblood of the innocent poor, though you did not catch them in the act of breaking in (lit: 'find them during the tunneling')." The Jeremiah passage assigns bloodguilt to the one who kills a thief despite not having caught him *bammakhteret*. There is no evidence to suggest that the phrase here primarily implies 'at night,' since no mention of the sun rising or of daytime parallels it as a contrast. Rather, it is clearly a simple matter of his not being caught in the act of breaking in. The nighttime setting is merely implied by the activity of theft. This accusation can only be a direct reference to the law as we have it in Exodus 22:1. Jeremiah asserts that the thief was only stealing because he was poor and hungry (cf. Proverbs 6:30-31, 30:8-9), and should not have been killed except

---

6. This correspondence is given greater weight by the fact that it is a relatively uncommon root in the Bible, with only two occurrences in its participial form, and eight other verbal uses, one of which (Jonah 1:13, where it refers to rowing) is unrelated in meaning, while five others are found in two contexts in Ezekiel. The only other verbal usage of this root in Amos 9:2 contains no involvement of a thief, nor do the Ezekiel passages, but the three uses in Ezekiel 12 (where an escape into exile is symbolized) do involve an explicit night-time context for sneaking away.

in self-defense. Rather (as stated in Proverbs 6:30-31),[7] although a thief may not be despised for stealing to satisfy his hunger when he is starving (again note the implication of theft of livestock), he must make full restitution ('seven-fold' here is meant to convey 'perfect' or 'complete') in accordance with the law. The implication, as will be discussed below, is that instead of being satisfied with restitution, the rich property owners were going out after the fact and killing the destitute thieves, considering themselves guiltless of their blood.

It is the precise meaning of the phrase *'im zārkhāh hashemesh 'ālāyw* which is the crucial point. Does it really mean only 'if during daylight,' or might it better be interpreted as referring to the passage of time—with the thief being discovered only the following day, after the actual theft had already taken place? Only in this case can the following provision of restitution make sense. According to BDB, the primary meaning of the verbal root *zrkh* is 'rise, come forth.' A meaning closer to 'break out, break through' may catch the nuance of the verb a bit better, and would make an interesting word play within the Exodus passage, with 'if during the breaking through' being parallel to 'if it has broken out' (cf. its usage in 2 Chron 26:19 for the sudden breaking out of leprosy upon the forehead of the king, as well as its usage in Psalm 112:4 and Isaiah 58:10, 60:1-3 for light breaking through into the darkness). Its derivative noun *mizrākh* means not 'daylight' but 'sunrise, dawn.' A quick surv*ey of other occurrences* of the root *zrkh* reveals no other instance of the use of the exact idiom found here (the closest is in 2 Kings 3:22). Nor does it seem to appear in any context that could arguably force it to indicate a daytime setting generally. On the contrary, with 'the sun' as its object, it would seem usually to

---

7. I prefer a translation here of "Men do not despise a thief" (NIV) or "Thieves are not despised" (NRSV), as over against the RSV's "Do not men despise a thief?" since it makes better sense of what follows as a contrastive phrase. So JPS: "A thief is not held in contempt for stealing to appease his hunger; Yet if caught he must pay sevenfold; He must give up all he owns."

indicate an active rising of the sun in the morning (often found in conjunction with words like *babbōqer* 'in the morning,' *lammākhorāt* 'on the next day,' *hashākhar* 'dawn'), in contexts involving passage of time—i.e. referring to the following morning (see, for example, Gen 32:25, 32, Judges 9:33, 2 Samuel 23:4, 2 Kings 3:22, Psalm 104:19-23, Eccl 1:5, and Jonah 4:7-8). One significant exception to this is in Nahum 3:17. This passage involves an opposition which explicitly excludes an interpretation of the phrase as indicating merely a daytime setting. Specifically, Nahum 3:17 opposes *byom qārāh* / 'in a day of coldness' (a cold day when the sun is presumably hidden by clouds) to *shemesh zārkhāh* (when the sun breaks through the clouds). Since it is clearly already daytime, the significance of *shemesh zārkhāh* must be something else, and not a mere reiteration of its being daytime. Such an understanding would be clearly contradictory since the verse sets up a contrastive circumstance in which different things happen.

As all would agree, *'im shemesh zārkhāh* stands in obvious opposition to the phrase *'im bammakhteret*—'if in/during the tunneling.' As Sarna (130) points out, such a laborious mode of entry (by digging through the wall) must imply a nighttime setting, since by day it would be immediately obvious to any bystander what was going on. The emphasis here, however, would seem to be not on the implied timing of the theft, but on the timing of the finding (*mts'*) in relation to the theft—i.e. whether the thief is discovered while in the act of tunneling into the house, or not until the following day after the theft has already been successfully accomplished. All of this is not to say that the first clause does not have a nighttime setting or the second a daytime setting. They obviously do. However this is only happenstantially true. It is not the point of main distinction. Moreover, it is not the timing of the tunneling which is at stake either, which applies only to the first clause. Rather, it is the timing of the *finding* which is at issue (*mts'*) being the active verb which governs both clauses).

EXODUS 22:1-4: A CASE OF RESTITUTION VS. RETRIBUTION

Guilt could be established in Israel only by a limited number of means: by the testimony of two witnesses, by catching him in the act, or by possession—if the stolen property was 'found in his hand' (cf. 1 Sam 12:3-5; cf. Jackson 1972, p. 48). The direct contrast to this finding 'during the tunneling,' then, would be if the thief were found out later—the next day—rather than being caught in the act. Furthermore, it is interesting to note that this clause is then followed by a provision relating to the case where the stolen animal is found alive in the thief's hand (the very situation here proposed)—that only double restitution must be made. This interpretation also makes better sense of the perfective form of *'im zārkhāh*—'if it has risen.'

**Self-Defense or Retributive Justice, Old and New**

Another alternative is thus proposed here for the point of distinction in this clause. It is a distinction between killing a man in self-defense under immediate threat when a thief is caught in the act versus purposive retribution the next day. In other words, the second clause here envisions that the following day after the theft, the property owner discovers who the thief was and goes out after him to find and kill him as retribution for the theft. The law specifies that if he does this he is guilty of murder, and subject to the normal sanctions of blood-vengeance. He is not guilty of murder, however, if he kills the thief in the act that night, because his own life might have been in danger.

The primary motivation for this interior clause, in light of this new interpretation, is then made obvious. An older legal convention had prescribed the death penalty for house-breaking and theft. Such is clearly the law in the Code of Hammurabi (CH # 6-11, 22, 25 re theft; #21 re making a breach in a house). This provision in Exodus 22 stands in conscious opposition to the older tradition, making it clear that any attempt to apply the older penalty, aside from a case of self-defense, would be considered murder and would be subject to the normal procedures of blood-vengeance by the next of kin. This same conclusion is propounded by Cassuto (281-282): that we have here a direct polemic against the opposing law as it stands in the Code of Hammurabi. Cassuto interprets these verses, and makes sense of their current context, as propounding a fundamental Torah principle regarding the sanctity of human life, given in direct opposition to Hammurabi's lower valuation of life as demonstrated by assignment of the death penalty for a property offense.

**Wider Implications**

This new interpretation of the law has some wider implications for the nature of Israelite law and its possible connection with other ancient Near Eastern law codes—that its relationship is more complex than simple "borrowing," that it is likely to reflect actual real-life practices and concerns, and that it demonstrates a fundamental principle of the sanctity of human life in the Torah.

The likelihood of a direct or indirect literary connection between the Covenant Code in the Bible and various other ancient Near Eastern law collections such as those of Hammurabi and Eshnunna has been convincingly argued by Malul, Otto, Fensham and others. The most common method of making such an evaluation usually takes similarities as evidence for a connection, while differences must either be explained away as insignificant or be counted as evidence for the absence of a connection. However, in the laws at hand, as well as in certain places elsewhere, it is the very differences which seem to be most revealing as evidence for a direct connection. For example, directly preceding the verses considered here in Exod 21:28-36 is the classic test case of the goring ox, for which strikingly similar laws are found in both Hammurabi and Eshnunna. More significant than the parallels, however, is one point where the biblical law appears intentionally and pointedly to contradict an alternative legal tradition as found in Hammurabi. Namely, as Greenberg points out, Exod 21:31 explicitly applies the same law

EXODUS 22:1-4: A CASE OF RESTITUTION VS. RETRIBUTION

of criminal negligence to a case involving the death of a son or daughter (that the owner must be killed or pay a ransom) in contrast to the corresponding principle for negligent homicide in Hammurabi #229-230 that it is the negligent man's son or daughter that should be killed. Although this solution does not come up in Hammurabi's treatment of the goring ox (CH #250-252), but rather in a case of the collapse of a poorly constructed building, the same principle of negligence would seem clearly to be present. The principle of vicarious punishment is likewise present in CH #210. This specific conflict over vicarious punishment may also be behind the prohibition in Deut 24:16 that "fathers shall not be put to death for their children, nor children put to death for their fathers; each is to die for his own sin." In the same way, a direct and conscious opposition to the theft law as it stands in Hammurabi (where the death penalty is assigned for theft) may be evident in Exod 22:1-4.[8]

One need not, with Cassuto, rely entirely upon Hammurabi for this tradition however. A number of narrative stories within the Hebrew Bible itself, set in the patriarchal period and the early monarchy, seem to imply death as an accepted penalty for theft, or at least indicate some conflict over the issue. For example, when Laban pursues Jacob after his departure from Haran and complains that he has stolen his household gods, Jacob immediately declares that whatever person in whose possession the teraphim are found shall not live (Gen 31:32—usually assigned to E). Likewise, when

---

8. While there is ample evidence for some connection generally between these traditions (whether positive or negative in influence), it should be noted that Malul's methodological principles for determining a direct connection between laws also demands a test for uniqueness. This test fails with regard to an established death penalty for cattle theft and house-breaking, since such laws also abound in numerous unrelated cultures. In addition to the Code of Hammurabi and other collections from Semitic societies such as the Middle Assyrian Laws (# A:3-5, but contrast C+G:5,8 and F:1), evidence of application of the death penalty for theft is also found among the Greeks, Saxons, and the British under Henry I (Mendelsohn 41), not to mention its being a common custom in the American Old West.

Joseph sends out a party to pursue his brothers with the complaint that someone has stolen his cup, again the brothers unanimously declare that whoever is found to have the stolen article should die (Gen 44:9—usually assigned to J, or possibly to some special source). Despite the fact that both of these cases involve cultic objects (the teraphim and a cup used for divination), it is nevertheless significant that both of the epic sources contain reference to death as a penalty for theft.[9]

The case of Joseph's cup is even more interesting in that it directly juxtaposes two possibilities for punishment—death and slavery. The brothers declare that the person in whose sack the cup is found should die, and the rest would become slaves, but the Egyptian official replies by saying that only the one who has stolen the cup shall become a slave (Gen 44:10). Thus the principle propounded here is not death, but slavery. Of further possible interest here is the fact that in the Code of Hammurabi #8, there was some provision for making restitution, but it was at the impossible rate of thirty-fold to the state or ten-fold to a private citizen, and if the thief was unable to make that restitution then, again, punishment reverted to the death penalty. It is interesting, then, that here in Exodus, the clause about blood-guilt for killing the thief is directly followed by a provision providing that if the thief were too poor to make the required restitution then he would be sold into slavery for his theft (but in no case killed). This specific contrast makes the juxtaposition of these two possibilities (death or slavery) in the Joseph story all the more significant.[10]

---

9. It should, perhaps, be noted that when Achan breaks the ban by stealing a robe and some gold, he and all his house are first stoned and then burned. This, however, as Greenberg (1986, pp. 8-9) rightly points out, is related to the contagious nature of ritual impurity with regard to the breaking of the ban, and therefore is not relevant here.

10. Incidentally, Josephus interpreted this provision to mean that the thief would be handed over as a slave to the person he had robbed (*Antiquities* IV.8.27).

EXODUS 22:1-4: A CASE OF RESTITUTION VS. RETRIBUTION

Similarly, within the Deuteronomistic History, we find David's pronouncement concerning Nathan's parable about the man who stole his neighbor's ewe: "As the LORD lives, the man who did this should die!" (literally: 'is a son of death'—2 Sam 12:5). Again, one may argue that it was a case involving extenuating circumstances, and that David spoke too quickly in his outrage, but then this pronouncement of death is followed immediately (corrected perhaps?) by a statement of the actual law as given here in Exodus: "He shall restore the lamb four-fold" (2 Sam 12:6; LXX = seven-fold). Note, also, Samuel's defense of his leadership at the institution of the monarchy, declaring publicly that he had not taken anything from anyone, and that if anything were 'found in his hand' that witnesses should be produced and that he would make restitution (1 Sam 12:3–5).

It would seem from all of these that there was some precedent in Israel, as well as in Hammurabi, for punishing theft with the death penalty,[11] and also that there was considerable tension between this and the alternative punishment of multiple restitution or slavery as given in the law here. Such a reduction in penalty, even from a penalty of death to one of restitution, is found explicitly stated in a number of the Hittite laws (# 57–69 reduce the ratio of payment; #123 actually substitutes a monetary fine for what was formerly a capital offense; #166 likewise, though not a case of theft, substitutes a substantial payment of property for what was formerly punished by death).

That biblical laws may reflect real-life practices and concerns in Iron Age Israel is demonstrated by an ostracon discovered in 1960 by Naveh at Mes ad O Hashavyahu near Yavneh Yam, which mentions a legal dispute in which a worker complains that his garment was forcibly (and wrongfully) appropriated (lines 8, 9,

---

11. See Daube (94), who speculates that probably all kinds of theft 'were at some time punishable by death' in earlier Hebrew legal tradition. Also see Jackson (1972, pp. 164-166).

12), using language highly similar to language found in the laws of Exod 22:25-26 (requiring garments taken in pledge to be returned by nightfall) and Deut 24:17 ("do not...take the cloak of the widow as a pledge"), as well as prophetic accusations in Amos 2:8 ("they lie down beside every altar on garments taken in pledge"). There was evidently a real-life problem of garments being appropriated. Likewise with the theft law, there appears to be a reflection here of a real-life problem where violated property-owners were going out and killing thieves, in accordance with former customary practices. The new law, as formulated in Exodus, anticipates resistance to the proposed change and therefore specifically addresses this issue as a potentially continuing problem.

The scenario envisioned here is that the new law of restitution sought to be more humanitarian and constructive in its approach, but had to fight against the tenacious older convention (death) as well as against doubts as to this new law's enforceability. Specifically: any person rich enough to be able to restore five-fold would not have stolen in the first place; anybody desperately poor enough to resort to stealing would certainly be unable to pay the prescribed restitution. Under such inescapable circumstances, reversion to the older system of retributive justice seems justified and necessary. This is, in fact, precisely the solution offered in Hammurabi #8: if the thief is too poor to make the exorbitant thirty- or ten-fold restitution (and what thief wouldn't be), then he is to be killed. It is this problem that the Exod 22:2 clause seeks to address, as it stands, in specifically this context. Theft is no longer a capital offense, and anyone going out and killing a thief, aside from self-defense, is guilty of murder and subject to blood-vengeance. Instead, one is to wait for restitution, and if the thief is too poor to make restitution immediately, then, rather than reverting to the death penalty as in Hammurabi, the thief is to work off the debt as an indentured servant. This clause is the assurance to the property owner that justice will be done under the new law—one way or another—without his having to resort to the old system of retributive justice. The higher valuation of human life represented here, that specifically rejects the death penalty for property offenses, demonstrates an important principle of the Torah in distinction from the ancient Near Eastern legal tradition that was its inheritance from the surrounding culture (Greenberg, Cassuto).

**Summary**

In summary, the entire law in Exod 21:39-22:3 concerns mainly theft of livestock, in which nocturnal house-breaking is involved, and envisions three possible scenarios corresponding with the three possible modes of proof mentioned earlier.

I. The first is the general case where the thief is found out after he has already sold and/or slaughtered the animal, presumably proven with the help of two witnesses providing testimony with regard to the sale or slaughter of the animal and positive identification as to its rightful ownership. The verdict here is four- or five-fold restitution. There is no issue of the landowner taking matters into his own hands in this case, since the guilt is not immediately obvious and must be proven at court by the witnesses.

II. The second is where the thief is caught in the act. There is no restitution to be made since he was unsuccessful in his theft, but if there is a struggle and he is killed by the property owner at that point, there is no bloodguilt for him since it was in self-defense.

III. The third is where the thief is found out the next day with the stolen animal still alive in his possession. In this case the property owner is guilty of murder if he takes matters into his own hands and kills the thief according to the older legal tradition. The thief, rather, must make restitution or be sold into slavery for his theft. The rate of restitution, meanwhile, is only two-fold since the original animal is restored quickly with little loss to the owner.

## Conclusion

Scholarly tradition concerning the interpretation of this passage is that Exodus 22:1-2a distinguishes between daytime and nighttime house-breaking in determining the bloodguilt of a property owner for killing a thief, and is intrusive in its current context of laws concerning restitution for theft of livestock. It has been the thesis of this paper that the house-breaking laws are likewise concerned primarily with theft of animals (which are kept inside the house at night), and assume a nighttime setting for the theft. The distinction being made here is between self-defense in the face of immediate threat, and purposive retribution after the fact. This different understanding of the verses then allows them to make better sense in their current context. They are not intrusive, but necessary correctives supporting a newer process of restitution in the face of an older legal convention of retribution wherein housebreaking and livestock theft was a capital offense. This older convention is evidenced in several biblical narratives as well as in the Code of Hammurabi. The existence of similar penalties in other, unrelated cultures however, means that while the law may well be taken as evidence for the direct influence of Mesopotamian laws upon biblical law, such a conclusion is not entirely necessary. It is, however, further evidence for a similarly harsh penalty for theft being in force in Israel during an earlier period.

So here we see played out a significant transition in the principles underlying the application of justice in Israel. This fundamental change is what lies behind the present provision where the thief is protected from conventional ancient Near Eastern retributive justice in favor of a more constructive and humane solution

## EXODUS 22:1-4: A CASE OF RESTITUTION VS. RETRIBUTION

involving service and restitution for property offenses.[12] It should not be thought, however, that such a conception is somehow unique to Israel or to biblical law. As seen above, Hittite laws of theft are entirely based upon principles of multiple restitution and monetary fines (although the ratio of payment is often somewhat harsher). Here, too, we find a process of mitigation going on within the laws themselves, with explicit statements of older penalties being substantially reduced. In two of the laws we even find explicit reference to offenses formerly punished by death now having only pecuniary penalties. Even in the Code of Hammurabi, where the overwhelming majority of theft cases prescribe death, there are two in which multiple restitution are allowed. The biblical law here does, however (as Greenberg, Cassuto and others have argued), reflect the high value placed on human life in Israel as over against the value of property. This high valuation of life, though not unique to Israel, is noteworthy as a fundamental motivating principle lying behind much of biblical law.

### Bibliography

Cassuto, Umberto. 1967 *A Commentary on the Book of Exodus*. Jerusalem: Magnes Press.

Childs, Brevard. 1974 *The Book of Exodus*. Old Testament Library. Philadelphia: The Westminster Press.

Cole, R.A. 1973 *Exodus*. London: Tyndale Press.

Cross, Frank M. 1973 *Canaanite Myth and Hebrew Epic*. Cambridge: Harvard University Press.

Danby, Herbert. 1933 *The Mishnah*. Oxford: Clarendon Press.

Daube, David. 1969 *Studies in Biblical Law*. New York: KTAV.

---

12. Compare the 'victim-offender reconciliation program' sponsored by the Mennonite church as a more constructive alternative (involving mediation, dialogue, service and restitution) to incarceration and imprisonment within the normal justice system.

Davies, G.H. 1967 *Exodus*. London: SCM Press.

Ellison, H.L. 1982 *Exodus*. Philadelphia: Westminster.

Epstein, I., ed. 1935 *The Babylonian Talmud*. London: The Soncino Press.

Fensham, F.C. 1978 "Extra-biblical material and the hermeneutics of the Old Testament with special reference to the legal material of the Covenant Code." *Aspects of the Exegetical Process*. Old Testament Society in South Africa Congresses 20-21. Ed. W.C. van Wyk, pp. 53-65. Pretoria: NHW Press.

———. 1980 "Das Nicht-haftbar-sein im Bundesbuch im Lichte der altorientalischen Rechtstexte." *JNSL* 8:17-34.

———. 1988 "The Book of the Covenant." *The International Standard Bible Encyclopedia*. G.W. Bromiley, ed. Grand Rapids: Eerdmans.

Gibson, John. 1971 *Hebrew and Moabite Inscriptions*. Textbook of Syrian Semitic Inscriptions, v. 1. Oxford: Clarendon Press.

Gnuse, Robert. 1985 *You Shall Not Steal: Community and Property in the Biblical Tradition*. Maryknoll: Orbis Books.

Greenberg, Moshe. 1960 "Some Postulates of Biblical Criminal Law." *Yehezkel Kaufmann Jubilee Volume*, pp. 5-28, ed. M. Haran. Jerusalem: Magnes Press.

———. 1986 "More Reflections on Biblical Criminal Law. *Studies in Bible*, ed. S. Japhet. *Scripta Hierosolymitana* 31:1-17. Jerusalem: Magnes Press.

Jackson, B. 1972 *Theft in Early Jewish Law*. Oxford: Clarendon Press.

——— 1975 "Reflections on Biblical Criminal Law." *Essays in Jewish and Comparative Legal History*. Studies in Judaism in Late Antiquity 10. Leiden: Brill. Pp. 25-63

——— 1975 "Principles and Cases: The Theft Laws of Hammurabi." *Ibid*, pp. 64-74.

Jung, Moses. 1929 *The Jewish Law of Theft, with comparative references to Roman and English Law*. Philadelphia: Dropsie College.

Lauterbach, Jacob, trans. 1935 *Mekilta de Rabbi Ishmael*, v. 3. Philadelphia: Jewish Publication Society.

Lewy, Immanuel. 1957 "Dating the Covenant Code Sections on Humaneness and Righteousness (Exod 22:20-26; 23:1-9)." *Vetus Testamentum* 7: 322-326.

Malul, Meir. 1990 *The Comparative Method in Ancient Near Eastern and Biblical Legal Studies*. Alter Orient und Altes Testament, Bd. 227. Kevelaer: Butzon & Bercker.

Marx, Alfred. 1988 "Sacrifice de Reparation et Rites de Levee de Sanction." *ZAW* 100:183-98.

Mendelsohn, S. 1968 *The Criminal Jurisprudence of the Ancient Hebrews, compiled from the Talmud and other Rabbinical writings, and compared with Roman and English Penal Jurisprudence*. New York: Hermon Press.

Naveh, Joseph. 1960 "A Hebrew Letter from the Seventh Century B.C." *Israel Exploration Journal* 10: 129-139.

Neufeld, E. 1951 *The Hittite Laws*. London: Luzac & Co.

Neusner, Jacob. 1988 *Mekhilta According to Rabbi Ishmael: An Analytical Translation*, v. 2. Atlanta: Scholars Press.

Noth, Martin. 1962 *Exodus*. Old Testament Library. Philadelphia: Westminster Press.

Otto, Eckart. 1987 "Rechtssystematik im altbabylonischen 'Codex Ešnunna' und im altisraelitischen 'Bundesbuch': eine redaktionsgeschichtliche und rechtsvergleichende Analyse." *Ugarit-Forschungen* 19:175-97.

―――. 1989 *Rechtsgeschichte der Redaktionen im Kodex Ešnunna und im 'Bundesbuch': eine redaktionsgeschichtliche und rechtsvergleichende Studie zu altbabylonischen und altisraelitischen Rechtsüberlieferungen*. OBO 85. Göttingen : Vandenhoeck & Ruprecht.

―――. 1993 "Korperverletzung oder Verletzung von Besitzrechten? Zur Redaktion von Ex 22,15f. im Bundesbuch und #55; 56 im Mittelassyrischen Kodex der Tafel A." *ZAW* 105:153-65.

Pardee, Dennis. 1982 *Handbook of Ancient Hebrew Letters*. SBLSBS 15. Chico: Scholars Press.

Paul, S. 1970 *Studies in the Book of the Covenant in the Light of Cuneiform and Biblical Law*. VTSupp 18; Leiden: Brill.

Pohl, A. 1949 "Neue Ausgrabungen in Iraq (Die Gesetze von Ešnunna)." *Orientalia NS.* 18:124-128, pl. x-xx.

Roth, Martha. 1995 *Law Collections from Mesopotamia and Asia Minor.* SBLWAW 6. Atlanta: Scholars Press.

Sarna, Nahum. 1991 *Exodus.* JPS Torah Commentary. Philadelphia: Jewish Publication Society.

Smith, Morton. 1978 "East Mediterranean Law Codes of the Early Iron Age." *Eretz-Israel* 14. H.L. Ginsberg Volume. Jerusalem: Israel Exploration Society.

Speiser, E.A. 1967 "Early Law and Civilization." *Oriental and Biblical Studies*, ed. J. J. Finkelstein and M. Greenberg, pp. 534-555. Philadelphia: University of Pennsylvania Press.

Stager, Lawrence. 1985 "The Archaeology of the Family in Ancient Israel." *Bulletin of the American Schools of Oriental Research* 260:1-35.

Thackeray, J., trans. 1930 *Josephus Antiquities* IV. Loeb Classical Library. Cambridge/London: Harvard University Press.

de Vaux, Roland. 1961 *Ancient Israel: Its Life and Institutions.* London: McGraw-Hill.

Westbrook, Raymond. 1985 "Biblical and Cuneiform Law Codes." *RB* 92:247-264.

———. 1988 *Studies in Biblical and Cuneiform Law.* CahRB 26. Paris: Gabalda.

———. 1992 "Punishments and Crimes." *Anchor Bible Dictionary* 5:546-556

Yaron, Reuven. 1969 *The Laws of Eshnunna.* Jerusalem: Magnes Press.

3

# Eight Key Functions of Leadership
## Meditations on Leadership from the Book of Nehemiah

SOO-INN TAN

*My parents taught me to always thank people who have blessed me. Therefore I am grateful for this opportunity to contribute an article for this Festschrift for Dr. Carl E. Armerding because it gives me an opportunity to thank him for a number of ways he has blessed me. I first met Dr. Armerding in the '80s when I was a student at Regent College. I appreciated the way that he went out of his way to interact with me as an individual, to get to know me better, and to encourage me in my life and my studies. And I will never forget his course, Introduction to the Old Testament. For the first time I had a handle on how the different parts of the Old Testament functioned and how they fitted together. The framework on the Old Testament that he gave us continues to guide my understanding of Scripture till today. I hope this article on leadership from the book of Nehemiah helps in some way to honor his many years of faithful service as an Old Testament scholar and as a leader.*

## Introduction

There is a growing recognition in contemporary leadership literature that leadership is more a function than a position. Walter C. Wright summarizes this growing recognition in his book *Relational Leadership* (Carlisle, U.K.: Paternoster, 2002):

> If by leader we mean one who holds a position of authority and responsibility, then every Christian is not a leader. Some are—some are not. But if by leader we mean a person who enters into a relationship with another person to influence their behavior, values or attitudes, then I would suggest that all Christians should be leaders. Or perhaps more accurately, all Christians should exercise leadership attempting to make a difference in the lives of those around them.

If leadership is more function than office, a number of liberating consequences follow. First, it should discourage people from pursuing leadership for the wrong reasons, for example desiring leadership with the mistaken belief that a leader is someone better than his or her peers. More importantly, if leadership is more function than office, it frees everyone to function as leaders. Everyone has the potential of influencing others to move toward God-given goals. But what does leadership entail?

There are at least eight key functions associated with the exercise of leadership. These functions appear in the leadership of Nehemiah from the book that carries his name. A leader must:

Have vision.
Be able to communicate vision.
Persevere in the pursuit of the group's vision.
Mobilize the group to pursue its vision.
Genuinely care for people.
Work together with other leaders.
Understand that he/she leads to the degree that he/she follows the leadership of God.
Trust in God.

## Eight key leadership functions

### 1. A leader must have vision.

If leading a group somewhere, you must know the destination. Leaders have a picture of a hoped-for future of the group they are influencing. Jerusalem's city wall was in ruins, but Nehemiah had a picture of the wall of Jerusalem rebuilt and strong (Neh 2). He had a vision of what should be. Leaders must be seers, people who see a picture of what should be. Only then can they lead others to actualize that future. Jesus gave his disciples a vision of making disciples in every ethnic group (Matt 28:18-20). Moses had a vision of a land flowing with milk and honey (Exod 3).

The leader's vision must be a God-given one. Nehemiah's vision of the wall of Jerusalem arose from his understanding of the purposes and the promises of God. Many leaders are driven by dreams of their own making, visions that serve the leader's ego. The true leader will have a vision, but the vision will be rooted in God and His purposes.

Key question: What is God's vision for your group?

### 2. A leader must be able to communicate vision.

The second key leadership function is communication. After all, if a leader has a vision, it is only the leader's vision until communicated to the group. If the group catches the vision and takes ownership of it, it becomes their vision too. Nehemiah takes pains to explain his vision to the leaders of the Jewish community at Jerusalem (Neh 2: 11-18). And perhaps he communicated best by his personal example—how he continually gave himself to the task before them.

Many associate communication with public speaking, and therefore feel themselves poor communicators because they can't speak well in public. But public speaking is only one communication form, and not always the most effective. In the New Testament, Paul communicates in numerous ways, including informal chats, public teaching, debates, small group discussions, and letters. A leader need not be a good public speaker, but a leader must know how to communicate.

Key question: Are you effectively sharing your vision with the group?

### 3. A leader must persevere in the pursuit of the group's vision.

It can be argued that perseverance is more an attitude than a function. Whatever it is, a leader must have it. No worthy vision will be realized easily. As Nehemiah discovered, there will be opposition from without (Neh 4) and problems from within (Neh 5). Therefore a leader cannot be easily discouraged. The true leader must persevere in the face of discouragement and setbacks. Often that means a leader must be willing to go it alone until others begin to truly believe in the viability of the work.

The leaders in the Bible understood this. Paul, for example, paid a heavy price in pursuit of his God-given ministry (2 Cor 4:8-10). Like Nehemiah, he pressed on till his work was done (2 Tim 4:7). The practice of leadership is costly, but there is no other way. Indeed, it is only when others see that you are in it for the long haul that they choose to.

Key question: Are you persevering in the pursuit of your group's vision?

### 4. A leader must mobilize the group to pursue its vision.

The primary difference between a doer and a leader is that doers work on their own but a leader mobilizes others, working with them to get the job done. The wall of Jerusalem was successfully rebuilt because Nehemiah mobilized all sorts of different people to work on it (Neh 3). Nehemiah deployed people to work on sections of the wall near their own homes, a strategic decision to boost morale and motivation. Nehemiah also encouraged the people when they were tired and discouraged (Neh 4:10-14).

The leader as a mobilizer of others is a principle that is expounded elsewhere in Scripture. Ephesians 4:11-13 makes it clear that God's work is to be done by all of God's people. The responsibility of leaders is to equip people for service. Leaders must be able to mobilize others for ministry by deploying them correctly, by equipping them, and by encouraging them.

Key question: What are you doing to ensure that your group members have the equipping necessary to work towards their vision?

**5. A leader must genuinely care for people.**

What sort of leaders do people follow? People follow leaders who know where they are going. People also follow leaders who genuinely care for their welfare. In the midst of the program to rebuild the walls of Jerusalem, Nehemiah took pains to address a serious matter of social injustice (Neh 5). He was genuinely concerned with the poor being exploited by their fellow Israelites. He wasn't so obsessed with the rebuilding of the wall that he was blind to the real needs of his people. Instead he took concrete and sacrificial steps to help those who were suffering.

A true leader cares for goals, but also cares for people. The apostle Paul was always focused on his mission, yet truly loved those under his care (2 Cor 2:4). Some leaders are task oriented. Others are people oriented. The true leader will work at being both.

Key question: Do you know where your people are hurting?

### 6. A leader must work together with other leaders.

The reconstruction of Jerusalem needed the rebuilding of the wall. It also needed a fresh recommitment to the Law. For this the people needed Ezra, the priest and scribe (Neh 8). Ezra and Nehemiah were both leaders playing key roles in the reconstruction of post-exilic Israel. Nehemiah was willing to work with other key leaders in the mission to rebuild Israel. Earlier he had worked with the local leaders in Jerusalem (Neh 2:16-18). Nehemiah understood that a true leader must be committed to team leadership. No one can go it alone.

It is instructive that when Ephesians 4:12 spells out the principal duty of leaders, it refers to leaders in the plural—apostles, prophets, evangelists, pastors and teachers. There is no hint here of one super-leader doing it all. The true leader will recognize personal strengths and limitations. He or she will actively seek to work with others in teams of people with different strengths. This is not always easy, but it is necessary.

Key question: Do you really believe you need other leaders to get the job done?

### 7. A leader must understand that he or she leads to the degree that he or she follows the leadership of God.

Current discussions on leadership give the impression that the burden of leadership initiative rests primarily on the shoulders of the human leader. Nehemiah, however, embarked on his mission out of a concern for the honor of God (Neh 1). He acted in response to a call that God had placed in his heart (Neh 2:12b). And the prayer of the Levites in Chapter 9 shows that the people understood the sovereign leadership of God in Israel's history. The true leader understands that leadership has legitimacy only when it follows the leadership of God.

EIGHT KEY FUNCTIONS OF LEADERSHIP

Paul states clearly in places like 1 Corinthians 3:5–4:5 that all Christian leaders are at best co-workers with God, who is the senior and indispensable partner. Effective leadership is not just a result of mastering leadership principles. Effective leadership results first and foremost from faithful obedience to the primary leadership of God.

Key question: If you are functioning as a leader under God, who is the senior-partner in your leadership?

**8. A leader must trust in God.**

Nehemiah is a great book to teach about leadership. It is also a great book to teach on the subject of prayer. This should be a clear sign that the two subjects are inextricably linked. Nehemiah's first response to the news of the sorry state of the wall of Jerusalem was to pray (Neh 1). When risking his life by asking the king's permission to rebuild the wall he first prayed (Nehemiah 2:4b). Faced with opposition, he prayed (Neh 4:4,9; 6:14). The completed wall was dedicated with elaborate thanksgiving prayers (Neh 12:27-43). Nehemiah was a highly capable leader and manager, but clearly believed that ultimately, success could only come from God (Neh 2:20). And so he prayed.

Psalm 127: 1b declares: "Unless the LORD builds the house, the builders labor in vain" (NLT). Unfortunately, few actually live as though they really believe this. The true leader knows it to be true and that is why he or she is a person of prayer.

Key question: What role does prayer actually play in your practice of leadership?

**Conclusion**

There is a desperate need for leadership in today's fast-changing world. This is true in the marketplace, and is definitely true in the church and church-related organizations. Increasingly, both church and marketplace are moving away from a model of the leader as some heroic, bigger-than-life individual. There is a growing recognition that potentially everyone can help provide leadership, and that leadership is more function than title or office.

This means that we must have some clarity as to what constitutes the practice of leadership. Our study of the book of Nehemiah reveals that leadership requires at least eight key functions. There will be few individuals who will be equally adept at all eight, which is why the true leader must be committed to team leadership. A leadership team has a greater chance of having individuals with complementary strengths who together will be able to include the eight functions in their leadership practice.

Still, in a period of such interest in leadership, we need to say that a Christian leader is finally one whose trust is ultimately in the Lord. While we must continue to cull both Scripture and the best management literature for leadership wisdom, there must be a fresh return to the centrality of God in all things and therefore a fresh recommitment to prayer.

4

# Herodotus and Esther
## *A Second Look*[1]

### ROBERT L. HUBBARD, JR.

*"Herodotus fascinates: he is the father who must
ever be evoked or invoked, the phantom who must
be exorcised, the ghost who must be banished."*[2]

So wrote classical scholar François Hartog concerning the author whose remarkable literary achievement, The Histories, still sparks both fawning adulation and fierce criticism. The work provides biblical scholars a rare extra-biblical glimpse of the Ancient Near East during the Persian Period (i.e., contemporary to the Hebrew Bible's post-exilic books) and has energized a lively discussion of biblical historiography.[3] In part it led Adele Berlin to suggest

---

1. It is a great personal privilege to extend warmest congratulations to this volume's honoree, a good friend, academic colleague, and former shipmate. I've always admired his deep love for God, his exemplary character, his model leadership, and his love for people. Our life-paths intersected doubly since we're both Old Testament scholars and Navy Chaplains. So, Carl, I pray that God may grant you both *berachot rabboth* and the proverbial "fair winds and following seas" in the years ahead.
2. F. Hartog, *The Mirror of Herodotus* (Berkeley: University of California Press, 1988), xvi.
3. E.g., P.V. Niskanen, *The Human and the Divine History: Herodotus and the Book of Daniel* (JSOTS 396; Edinburgh: T & T Clark, 2004); S. Stott, "Herodotus and the

59

recently that Esther and Greek writings emerge from the same literary context and share the same conventions.[4] But biblical scholars still tend to invoke Herodotus as if citing an authoritative modern historian to render judgment on Esther but invoke Esther's wonderful literary artistry to characterize it as fiction and, hence, of lesser, if not little, use for matters of history.[5] If Berlin is right, however, a reassessment of both books would seem in order if they, indeed, share the same playing field.

This essay seeks to contribute to this larger discussion by surveying the recent consensus among classical scholars concerning the literary nature and sources of The Histories. It comes not to bury Herodotus but to appraise him, assessing, first, his social location and literary influences and, second, his Persian linguistic skills and sources for things Persian. It will then suggest implications for how to read both Herodotus and Esther.

---

Old Testament: A Comparative Reading of the Ascendancy of King Cyrus and David," *SJOT* 16/1 (2002): 52-78 (with bibliography); F.A.J. Nielsen, *The Tragedy in History: Herodotus and the Deuteronomistic History* (JSOTS 251; Sheffield: JSOT Press, 1997); J. Van Seters, *In Search of History: Historiography in the Ancient World and the Origins of Biblical History* (New Haven; London: Yale University Press, 1983).

    4.    A. Berlin, *Esther* (JPS Bible Commentary; Philadelphia: The Jewish Publication Society, 2001), xxviii. For a comparative study of nine motifs, cf. I. Hofmann and A. Vorbichler, "Herodot und der Schreiber des Esther Buches," *Zeitschrift für MIssionswissenschaft under Religionswissenschaft* 66 (1982): 294-302.

    5.    E.g., the skepticism of M.V. Fox, *Character and Ideology in the Book of Esther* (2nd ed.; Grand Rapids: Eerdmans, 2001), 131-39; but cf. the more moderate approach of D.J.A. Clines, *Ezra, Nehemiah, Esther* (NCB; Grand Rapids: Eerdmans, 1984) 256-61. John Bright's venerable history lists Esther only twice, once as a source for the early development of Judaism (the section title), and once with "cf. Esther" in parenthesis as a point of comparison to the need for post-exilic Jews to stick together against their enemies. But Esther plays no role in his discussion of Israel under the Persians; cf. J. Bright, *A History of Israel* (4th. ed.; Philadelphia: Westminster, 2004), 431-32, 444, 515 (the index).

## Herodotus: His Social Location

Little is known about the life of Herodotus of Halicarnassus.[6] In The Histories he claims to have traveled extensively around the Mediterranean, including Asia Minor, Phoenicia, Palestine, and Egypt.[7] As Byrskog notes, his travels enabled him—a non-participant in the events he reports—"to confirm and supplement what he had heard [via oral sources] with what he had himself seen (2:99, 147)."[8] Popular parlance may call Herodotus "the father of history," but classical scholars carefully nuance what "historian" means in his case.[9] Following in the tradition of earlier Greek epic poets (especially Homer), Herodotus probably was a logios—a collector and public oral performer of historical logoi or stories. His aim was "to keep alive the memory and glory of great deeds of the past."[10] Besides the epic poetic tradition, another important influence was what Oswyn Murray calls "a moralizing tradition" among Ionian

---

6. For what follows, cf. J. Marincola, "Introduction," *Herodotus: The Histories* (New Edition, tr. A. de Sélincourt; New York: Penguin Books, 1972), ix-xiii; and *idem.*, *Greek Historians* (New Surveys in the Classics 31; Oxford/ New York: Oxford University Press, 2001), 19-25.

7. He reports personal consultations in Egypt with various priests at Memphis (ii. 3, 112, 153), Heliopolis and Thebes (ii. 2, 2), and Saïs (ii. 130 ["as the priests in the city of Saïs told me"]). Their information derived from both oral tradition and written texts preserved by literate clergy there. For discussion of Herodotus' onsite visit to Egypt, See J.A.S. Evans, *Herodotus: Explorer of the Past* (Princeton, NJ: Princeton University Press, 1991), 134-39.

8. S. Byrskog, *Story as History—History as Story* (WUNT 123; Tübingen: Mohr Siebeck, 2000), 99. I am grateful to Professor Richard Bauckham of the University of St. Andrews, Scotland for pointing me to this important volume.

9. Evans, 143, 145-46. For the evidence that he was the first historian to use himself as an "autopsy" (Gk. *autoptes* "eyewitness"), see Byrskog, 53-57.

10. Evans, 94, 107-108, 129. Evans proposes another early influence, an emerging phenomenon of "prose memorialists," a hypothesis he supports by careful review of the Greek evidence (122-29).

storytellers. This tradition sought to discern a moral pattern in the workings of history.[11] So, in Murray's view, the latter tradition ...

"...created Herodotus as a historian, and ... moulded his attitudes towards the patterns of history, the narrative techniques of his art, and the roles of creativity, accuracy, and invention. For we must recognize that ultimately truth in Herodotus is a question of aesthetics and morality, as much as of fact."[12]

The public expectations of Herodotus as a logios merit brief mention here. He would have held public performances that included rigorous interaction with the audience. The public expected the logios to take on the professional persona of "a savant who possessed expert knowledge of past events," perhaps even implying that he had direct access to more local oral sources than was in fact true.[13] Indeed, notes John Marincola, Herodotus seems preoccupied with dispelling the doubts of his audience about his authority and with avoiding inquiry about his sources. He writes as if driven to answer in advance the audience's question, "How do you know?"[14] Now, such dialogues during public presentations probably produced two important results: the subtle alignment of Herodotus' original materials with the perceptions of his hearers[15] and the production of

---

11. O. Murray, "Herodotus and Oral History," in N. Luraghi, ed. *The Historian's Craft in the Age of Herodotus* (Oxford: Oxford University Press, 2001), 17-44, esp. 24-34.

12. Murray, 33-34 (quote 33). He reckons Delphi as the only place on the Greek mainland to evidence this second tradition. But cf. Marincola, *Greek Historians*, 20: "A desire to preserve great deeds and search out causes of human events puts Herodotus into a category different from his Ionian predecessors. Herodotus is distinguished by the monumentality of his work (which is longer than either Homeric poem) and by his universality (his treatment of the deeds of Greeks and non-Greeks)."

13. Evans, 112.

14. Marincola, *Greek Historians*, 8.

15. Cf. Evans, 97-98. Very little is known, however, about Herodotus' fifth-century audience, how long his performances lasted, and what "practical" purpose his work served; cf. John Marincola, *Authority and Tradition in Ancient Historiography* (Cambridge: Cambridge University Press, 1997), 20. For Thucydides' criticism of oral

long passages of oral history that later became parts of the written Histories.[16]

**Herodotus and the Near East: The Language Issue**

As a native-speaker, Herodotus could visit sites around Greece, read inscriptions himself, and interview informants and witnesses. But what were his sources for Persia and Media? All evidence suggests that he had not personally visited either place,[17] so his knowledge of the latter—including the names of Persians, the details of events, quotations of words, etc.—must derive from second- or third-hand sources.[18] In such cases, the historical reliability of Herodotus hangs upon the reliability of those sources. But the quest for his sources raises another question: Could he speak and/or read Persian, or was he dependent on translators and/or translations? The evidence makes it likely that he had, at best, a kind of Berlitz Phrase-Book knowledge of Persian.[19] Herodotus nowhere claims nor demonstrates fluency in any oriental languages or a reading knowledge of any foreign documents.[20] At one point Herodotus describes a pillar inscribed for Darius as "filled with the Assyrian [not specifically Persian] letters" (iv. 87), a general

---

performers, including Herodotus, as seeking glory rather than historical accuracy, see *Thuc.* 1.20.3-21.1.

16. Evans, 99.

17. P. Högemann, *Das Vorderasien und die Achämeniden: Ein Beitrag zur Herodot-Analyse* (Beihefte zum Tübingener Atlas des Vorderen Orients, Reihe B 98; Wiesbaden: Dr. Ludwig Reichert, 1992), 50. The earlier thesis of Fehling that Herodotus' explicit citations of sources are fictional has recently fallen out of favor; cf. D. Fehling, *Die Quellenangaben in Herodot* (Untersuchungen zur antiken Literatur und Geschichte 9; Berlin; New York: de Gruyter, 1971), 60.

18. Evans, 112.

19. Evans, 139, n. 203.

20. Cf. D. Lateiner, *The Historical Method of Herodotus* (Phoenix Supplementary Volume 23; Toronto/Buffalo: University of Toronto Press, 1991), 101 ("He could not consult Persian or other written sources because he did not know the languages").

reference simply to its use of cuneiform signs to write Persian (cf. i. 199).[21] Two statements, however, confirm that he did not know Persian well, if at all. First, he proudly claims to have made a linguistic discovery—that all Persian names without exception end in the same letter (s).[22] In reality, only proper names in the i- and u-stems nominative singular end in s (actually š), so it seems likely that Herodotus based his observation either on their form in written or spoken Greek (i.e., Greek names commonly end in s) or perhaps on his hearing of Persian names pronounced by oral sources.[23] It is known that Xerxes employed Greek master craftsmen at Susa and that Greek physicians, scholars, and masters of art contributed to upper class Persian society.[24] Thus, probably centuries of Greco-Persian contacts had already standardized Greek transliterations of Persian names and important terms, a treasury on which Herodotus may have drawn.

In the statement (vi. 98), he comments on the meanings of the names Darius, Xerxes, and Artaxerxes.[25] Clearly, Herodotus

---

21. W.W. How and J. Wells, *A Commentary on Herodotus*, Vol. 1 (Oxford: Clarendon Press, 1961) at iv. 87. 1: "H. uses 'Assyrian' (*Assuria*) any cuneiform (here for Persian), which of course he could not read").

22. He even claims that the Persians themselves have missed this observation: "Here is another matter that is true of the Persians, and, though they have not noticed it themselves, I have. Their names, which express their bodily powers or their magnificence, all end in the same letter, the one the Dorians call 'san' and the Ionians 'sigma.' On searching the matter out, you will find no exceptions to this among their names" (i.139).

23. E. Meyer, *Forschungen zur Alten Geschichte* (Halle: M. Niemeyer, 1892), 1, 194; R. G. Kent, *Old Persian* (American Oriental Series 33; 2nd ed. ; New Haven: American Oriental Society, 1953), §178, 181.

24. For the evidence, see M. A. Dandamayev and V. G. Lukonin, *The Culture and Social Institutions of Ancient Iran* (Cambridge: Cambridge University Press, 1989), 294-97.

25. "In Greek, the name Darius means the Doer [*erxeies*], Xerxes means the Warrior [*areios*], and Artaxerxes means the Great Warrior [*megas areios*]. And that is what the Greeks would correctly call these kings in their own tongue." The translation is

assumes Artaxerxes to be a composite form of the name Xerxes in Persian, an assumption apparently based on their Greek forms. But his claims run aground at two points: Xerxes and Artaxerxes in fact derive from different Persian roots, and none of the names bears the meaning he suggests.[26] The two linguistic comments discussed above clearly imply that Herodotus was dependent on others for information he gleaned about Persia. As François Hartog observes, except for the tyrannical Persian puppet, Histiaeus of Miletus, who occasionally seems to speak (and perhaps write) a few words in Persian (vi. 4, 29; cf. v. 11, 23-24, 106), Greco-Persian conversations in The Histories occur through interpreters (iii. 38, 140).[27]

**Herodotus and the Near East: The Sources**

So, given the language barrier, what were Herodotus' sources for Persian matters? The short answer is that, despite careful probing of The Histories, the sources simply elude precise identification. Occasionally, he cites his informants by name,[28] claims personal knowledge of Persian customs (i. 131, 140), or reports what he has heard personally from others (i. 95, 133; iii. 1, 105; vii. 12). He twice quotes inscriptions by Darius (iii. 88; iv. 91; cf. iv. 87 [two pillars, "on the one Assyrian, on the other Greek"]) but fails to identify how he obtained the quotations.[29] Often he makes claims without citing any source (e.g., iii.1; iv. 1; v. 1; vii. 1; ix .84). His opening references in

---

from Herodotus, *The History* (trans. David Grene; Chicago: University of Chicago Press, 1987), 448.
26. Meyer, 1, 194-195.
27. Hartog, 239; K. H. Waters, *Herodotus the Historian* (London: Croom Helm, 1985), 77.
28. E.g., the three priestesses at Dodona (northwestern Greece) whom he interviewed concerning the origin of its oracle (i. 46; ii. 52; ix. 93); cf. Evans, 110.
29. Herodotus mentions three stele inscriptions erected by Darius, one in Persia (iii. 88) and two in Thrace (iv. 87, 91), one of whose inscriptions had both cuneiform ("Assyrian") and Greek texts (iv. 87); cf. the discussion in P. Lecoq, *Les inscriptions de la Perse achéménide* (Paris: Gallimard, 1997), 19-21.

Books 1-5 to Persian experts (perseon ... hoi logioi, i. 1-v. 2) might imply the use of Persian written sources, but classical scholars are virtually unanimous that he primarily drew on oral ones.[30] Even scholars like Detlev Fehling who believe that Herodotus invented his material whole-cloth or drew on actual written sources concede that he represents his sources as being oral rather than written.[31]

Besides, even if he could read Persian (in my view, unlikely), to date there are in fact no known written Persian chronicles to consult and only a few available inscriptions to study had he had access to them (also, unlikely).[32] The only sections of The Histories thought possibly to draw on written sources are the list of satrapys (iii. 89-97), the description of the Persian royal road (v. 52-3), and the roster of Persian army and navy contingents massed at Dorsicus (vii. 61-98).[33] Comparison of the satrapy list with lists from Darius' inscriptions confirms the accuracy of Herodotus' information but not whether its source was written or oral.[34] But can one identify his sources more

---

30. Murray, 16; Evans, 140; Lateiner, 101-102; cf. Waters, 77, who notes that the common formula "there is a *logos* [for something]" probably refers to an oral source and almost certainly does so with foreign language material. From Herodotus' own reports, Waters (76-77) calculates that oral sources outweigh written ones by a five-to-one ratio. Cf. also Lateiner, 101, who avers that the five-fold reference to sources in the proem "certainly was not to persuade by authority, but to amuse by a parody of appeals to (bad) evidence."

31. For the former explanation, see Fehling, *Die Quellenangaben in Herodot*; for the latter, see, H. I. Immerwahr, *Form and Thought in Herodotus* (Philological Monographs 23; Cleveland: Press of Western Reserve University, 1966), 6 ("throughout the Histories Herodotus maintains the fiction that his work is an oral account, even where we know or surmise it to be based on written sources").

32. Lateiner, 102.

33. Murray, 35-56; Evans, 140; Lateiner, 102; Waters, 86; W. Aly, *Volksmärchen, Sage und Novelle bei Herodot und Seinen Zeitgnossen* (2nd ed.; Göttingen: Vandenhoeck & Ruprecht, 1969), 163-64.

34. Grene, 252, n. 12, who contrasts his accuracy here with the inferior quality of his information in describing the empire's far eastern boundary (iii. 97ff.). On the other hand, the author's sources, not his own bias, probably account for his failure consistently

precisely? As a starting point, Murray isolates two potential sources apparently not available to Herodotus. First, unlike his situation in Egypt, Herodotus had no access to members of a Persian priestly class and its tradition (whether oral or written).[35] Second, his portrait of eastern peoples in general shows no influence of their written literary or historical genres (e.g., inscriptions, priestly chronicles, law codes, or religious texts). Thus, while Herodotus' account of Egyptian history mirrors his contact with priests there, his account of eastern history lacks the influence of available oriental literary and historical techniques.[36] Further, rather than credit written records for the satrapy list, royal road description, and military lists, Murray plausibly traces them instead to a kind of "documentary orality" (i.e., the tendency to compose detailed information in tables or lists) that would be typical of Greeks within the Persian imperial bureaucracy.[37] And that is the important point: his information came either through Greeks or Greek-speakers.

Can one further clarify their identity? Lateiner boldly proposes a single individual—Zopyrus, a Persian noble whose desertion from the Persians to the Athenians Herodotus reports (iii. 160)—as

---

to name many women featured in minor episodes (e.g., the tragic wife of Masistes) ; cf. Waters, 128-29.

35. Murray, 35-36. In this view, Herodotus' understanding of Persian religion and superficial treatment of the Magi (e.g., i.101-140; iii.61-80) betray the lack of contact with Persian religion and it leadership. For discussion of his Egyptian sources, see B. A. Strawn, "Herodotus' *Histories* 2.141 and the Deliverance of Jerusalem: On Parallels, Sources, and Histories of Ancient Israel," in B. E. Kelle and M. B. Moore, eds., *Israel's Prophets and Israel's Past : Essays on the Relationship of Prophetic Texts and History in Honor of John H. Hayes* (New York/ London: T & T Clark, 2006), 220-25.

36. Murray, 36.

37. Murray, 37-38; cf. Evans, 140. Here Murray has in mind the hypothesis of David Lewis that the latter was one of Herodotus' sources; cf. D. Lewis, "Persians in Herodotus," in M. H. Jameson, ed. *The Greek Historians: Literature and History* (Saratoga: ANMA Libri, 1985), 101-117), calling it a useful "way forward" that "postulates a type of tradition which is likely to possess a relatively high level of detailed factual accuracy."

the source for Herodotus' account of specific events, if not for the Persian history as a whole.[38] Most scholars eschew named individuals in favor of social groups as informants, although their suggestions vary considerably. So, P. Högemann credits Persians living in Greece who were unhappy with an Achaemenid policy they saw as blatant militant expansionism,[39] while Waters traces Herodotus' source for the Persian invasions to the personal recollections of Greek informants, possibly Greek expatriates the storyteller met in Ionia.[40] According to Grene, the materials derive from somewhere in the east, either from Greeks living there or local people who spoke Greek (there were many).[41] Finally, careful study of the Persian narrative's two main sections leads Murray to conclude that both draw on variants of the official imperial version current among Persia's non-royal, high aristocracy or leading families.[42]

In sum, for Persian matters, the most likely sources are located in either Greece or Persia. In Greece the possible candidates include disgruntled Persian opponents of the Achaemenid regime (Högemann) or—for the invasion, specifically—Greek expatriates in Ionia (Waters). In Persia the choices are either Greeks there (e.g., in the royal bureaucracy) or Greek-speakers (Grene), or perhaps leading Persian families (Murray). In the absence of a consensus, for the present one must remain open to all the suggestions. Perhaps Herodotus drew on "all of the above."

---

38. Lateiner, 101-102. For dissent from this view, see Murray, 39.
39. Högemann, 60-61.
40. Waters, 80-81. This view rests on Waters' observation that Herodotus treats "exotic lands or Eastern history" differently from the Persian invasions; cf. his full discussion of Herodotus' main sources for the Persian side of the war (80-89).
41. Grene, 2.
42. i. 1; cf. Murray, 38-40. In his view, these are the people whom Herodotus identifies as "the chroniclers among the Persians" (i. 1). What he calls the "two great blocks" are a Median account of the fall of the Median empire and the rise of Cyrus (i.73-4, 95-130), and a more Persian one about the Magian usurpation and Darius' revolutionary rise to power (iii.30, 61-88).

## Herodotus and Sources: Two Cautions

Finally, two cautions require mention in assessing Herodotus' sources. First, one must distinguish authentic Persian stories from ones said to be Persian by Greeks. According to Murray, compared to Greek tales, Persian stories bear two unique literary marks. They lack "the religious or moral dimensions" of their Greek counterparts, and they use "a pure form of the Novelle"—i.e., "a short story" told regardless of whether or not any "historical" reality lies behind it.[43] The Persian stories in Herodotus seem to meet both criteria. Like the cruel episode in which Queen Amestris avenges Xerxes' infidelity (ix. 108-113), they present court novels replete with typical elements and stock situations absent in Greek stories (e.g., palace intrigues, bedroom scenes, vengeance and treachery, women with power equal to that of men, etc.).[44] In Murray's words, they "may not be reducible to our sort of history," but in Herodotus they nevertheless offer "a genuine expression of Persian traditions about the past."[45] Of course, as Murray warns, one must always reckon with the tricky possibility that Persian and Greek traditions influenced the other—that Herodotus' own historical imagination drew on both the Persian court novel and on Greek storytelling to present "a plausible Persian version of events...."[46]

Second, the caution requires us also to reckon with the so-called mirror-phenomenon first explored by Hartog.[47] To introduce oriental life to the Greeks Herodotus had to translate it into terms already

---

43. Murray, 41, citing the definition of K. Reinhardt. For Reinhardt's earlier discussion of what is "Persian" and what is "Greek" in Herodotus, see K. Reinhardt, *Vermächtnis der Antike* (Göttingen: Vandenhoeck & Ruprecht, 1960), 133-74.

44. Murray, 41-2. Other Persian traditions, however, might report them differently, including casting them as "instances of divine protection of the king and the triumph of righteousness" (quote 42).

45. Murray, 42.

46. Murray 43-44; cf. A. Momigliano, *Alien Wisdom: the Limits of Hellenization* (Cambridge/ New York: Cambridge University Press, 1975), 131.

47. Hartog, 61-111.

familiar to them. His strategy was to find mirror images of common Greek phenomena—i.e., customs among non-Greek peoples opposite those of Greece—in order to aid Greeks in understanding the Persian data. This approach, of course, risks tainting The Histories with a decidedly Greek slant, but Waters rightly counsels that our modern hindsight easily spots most unreliable sources, partisan interests, and authorial prejudice.[48] One must also acknowledge that his portrait of characters, especially Persian kings, draws on the motifs and style of the Greek folktale (and perhaps on the epic as well) in order to win credibility with the audience by appealing to a popular Greek archetype.[49] Finally, his hyperbolic count of the size of the Persian force draws on the Greek tradition's tendency to exaggerate military numbers, as if to say, "the bigger they are, the harder they fall."[50]

## Herodotus and Esther: Concluding Observations

So what have we learned about Herodotus from classical scholars? First, Herodotus was an ancient *logios*—one who collected and publicly performed logoi (or stories) in order to keep alive memory of the past. The fingerprints of the epic poetic tradition of Homer probably left their imprint on his work, as did an Ionian moralizing tradition of prose storytelling (Murray). His sources were oral informants who told what they had heard or seen, speaking either in

---

48. Waters, 89, 92.
49. Evans, 43; cf. his comment (61) that the Xerxes whom Herodotus presents as announcing the ill-fated invasion of Greece more closely resembles the brash, arrogant, and gullible young king of Aeschylus than anything else.
50. Evans, 64 ("Its size flouted the human condition. It did not know how to be flexible, a flaw that contributed to its own downfall"). In my view, stains of that same hyperbole also taint some of more strident recent criticism of Herodotus and undermine its own credibility; cf. B. Shimron, *Politics and Belief in Herodotus* (Historia Einzelschriften 58; Stuttgart: Franz Steiner Verlag Wiesbaden, 1989), 113; J. Wiesehöfer, *Das Antike Persien. Von 550 v. Chr. bis 500 n. Chr.* (München/ Zürich: Artemis & Winkler, 1993), 84.

Greek or in Persian through a Greek interpreter. The latter case, of course, inevitably ran the risk of losing something in the translation. Behind the finished written Histories lay a long process of repeated public performances, the author's projection of authority based probably on fewer actual sources than his presentation implied, and the subtle alignment of Herodotus' material with public perceptions of reality. As Murray says, in Herodotus' historiography, truth had as much to do with aesthetics (i.e., good storytelling) and morality (i.e., history's inner workings) as with "facts."[51] The result is a marvelous literary masterpiece but one that is less a "history" in a modern sense and more—in Murray's words—"a genuine expression of Persian traditions about the past."[52]

This brings me, finally, to propose that this nuanced understanding of the historiography of Herodotus narrows the literary gap between Herodotus and Esther. It relativizes the typical history-fiction dichotomy that regards the two books as polar opposites—Herodotus as "history" and Esther as "fiction." It opens the possibility for their comparison and for a reading of Esther as "history" in the same sense as Herodotus. Through the dress of comedy Esther offers—to paraphrase Murray slightly—"a genuine expression of Jewish traditions about the Persian past." If so, the question is: what ancient memories shaped the content of Esther and find their voice in its pages? Whose voices are they, and what is their audience? Limits of space require us to content ourselves with only a brief sketch of some preliminary possibilities.

Unlike Herodotus, the Hebrew version of Esther remembers the Persian king by the name Ahasuerus not Xerxes. Granted, both names derive from the same Persian original, but among Jews the name Ahasuerus would evoke a set of connotations drawn from the book of Esther, not from Greek literature as would the name,

---

51. Murray, 34.
52. Murray, 42.

Xerxes. (The name Artaxerxes in LXX would evoke its own set of recollections). Among its memories of Ahasuerus are his enormous wealth, luxurious palace, appetite for—but problematic relationships with—women, inattention to administrative detail, and dangerous dependence on advisors. In my view, the book remembers him not with disdain, disgust, or dismay but with gentle, sarcastic amusement at the "emperor with no clothes on."

Further, while Persia's failed conquest of Greece preoccupied Herodotus, Hebrew Esther's focus falls on life in the Persian capital city of Susa over nearly a decade. It remembers life under Ahasuerus as problematic for Jews: Esther was not to divulge her Jewishness once she entered the road to royalty. Jewish life in Susa apparently demanded a low profile. A widespread undercurrent of antipathy toward Jews seems to surface in Haman's vicious scheme (7:6) and his title as "the enemies of the Jews" (8:13; 9:1, 16, 22). He may personify a wider hatred of Jews in some quarters of Susa and perhaps elsewhere in the empire. Finally, the book recalls that Jewish cleverness and bravery spared the Jews—an escape whose memory the feast of Purim perpetuates. These, of course, merely illustrate how Esther might be "a genuine expression of Jewish traditions about the Persian past"—how one might consider it to be "historical" in some sense. If my appraisal and proposal convince, details concerning ancient historiography will need to be further nuanced and a new biblical partner welcomed occasionally into the conversation.

5

# Some Reflections on Paul's Understanding of Christ as Lord

## GORDON D. FEE

While writing to native Greek-speakers, the Apostle Paul finds occasion three times in his letters to use two Aramaic words/ phrases, *Marana tha* (1 Cor 15:22 ["Come, Lord"]) and *Abba* (Gal 4:6; Rom 8:15 ["Father"]). These words appear to be part of early Christian devotion, since they are assumed to be well-known to the varied recipients of these three letters. Significantly, these two words/phrases also reflect the heart of Pauline Christology: Christ as Lord and Son of God, the latter because *Abba* is language used by Jesus himself. The purpose of this essay is to point out the significance of the Paul's use of the first of these, his understanding of Christ as *Kyrios* ("Lord"). I propose to do this in two ways: first, by examining two key texts (1 Cor 8:6; Phil 2:10); and, second, by pointing out, on the basis of what Paul does with the Greek version (the LXX) of the Jewish *Shema* in these two texts, how consistently he uses this title as a referent to Christ when he is echoing other Old Testament passages. Here I limit myself to what are probably the earliest of Paul's letters (1 and 2 Thess), to demonstrate how fixed this usage had become at such an early point in Christian history. I begin with some statistics.

Of the three primary referents to Christ in Paul's letters (Lord, Jesus, Christ), the most common is the title-turned-name, "Christ," which occurs alone some 211 times and 165 more in some form of combination with the others. That is followed by the title "Lord," which occurs 176 times alone and 86 more in combination. What is significant about the latter is that, except for twelve instances where Paul is actually citing the Septuagint and no point is made as to who "the *Kyrios*" of the passage is,[1] this title is otherwise used exclusively to refer to Christ. Here, then, is the christological significance of this feature

## I. Jesus as *Kyrios* in 1 Corinthians 8:6

Some of the Corinthians had apparently asserted their rights to attend meals in pagan temples, on the basis that since there is only one God, no god exists in the temples. In response Paul reminds them of the many "gods" and "lords" in the world, whom he will later define as demons (1 Cor 10:19-22). In contrast to them, Paul reasserts the most fundamental doctrine from his Jewish heritage, now taken over and thus assumed among early Christians: absolute monotheism. But in this case, Paul does a truly remarkable thing; he reworks the fundamental Jewish statement of faith, the *Shema* of Deuteronomy 6:8, by expanding the Christian understanding of the one God to include the one Lord, Jesus Christ. That this is so can be easily demonstrated by a close look at the two texts. In nicely balanced clauses Paul affirms:

---

1. See Rom 4:8; 9:28, 29; 10:16; 11:34; 15:11; 1 Cor 3:20; 14:21; plus the "says *Kyrios*" formula apparently added by Paul to the citations in 2 Cor 6:17, 18; Rom 11:3; 12:19.

## PAUL'S UNDERSTANDING OF CHRIST AS LORD

(1) But for us     One *theos*     the Father,
from whom     all things
and we for him,

(2) and     One *Kyrios*     Jesus Christ
**through whom**     all things
and we **through him**

Deut 6:4 (LXX):
Listen Israel,     *Kyrios*     our *theos*
*Kyrios* One is

What Paul has done seems plain enough. He has kept the "one" intact, but divided the *Shema* into two parts, with the Greek word *theos* (God) now referring to the Father, and *Kyrios* (Lord) referring to Jesus Christ the Son. Because Paul's interests here are pastoral, he identifies the "one Lord" as none other than the historical "Jesus Christ," the one who died for all, especially those with a weak conscience (v. 11).

Thus, over against the "gods many" of paganism, the *Shema* rightly asserts—as the Corinthians themselves have caught on—that there is only one God; and typical of Paul's Jewish monotheism, the one God stands over against all pagan deities at two crucial, interrelated points: as *Creator* of all that is; and concomitantly as the one *Ruler* of all that he has created. Nothing—absolutely nothing—lies outside the realm of the one Creator-Ruler God. Thus God the Father is *from* and *for* in relation to everything that exists; that is, he is its source and goal (or purpose) of being—although the final phrase ("we for him"), noticeably Pauline, moves easily from creation to redemption, where God is the goal of his people in particular.

The surprising moment comes in line 2. Over against the "lords many" of paganism, there is only *one Kyrios*, Jesus Christ, whose relation to creation is that of effective agent. Thus the Father has created all things through the agency of the Son, who as the one *Kyrios* is also—and now Paul's second point is being established—the agent of their redemption ("and we through him"). The whole therefore, typically for Paul, encloses the work of the Son within that of the Father; that is, the two "through"-phrases regarding the one Lord's role as agent of creation and redemption are (logically) framed by the *from* and *for* phrases regarding the Father as the ultimate source and goal or purpose of all things—both creation and redemption.

It needs hardly be pointed out that this second line is a plain, undeniable expression of Paul's presuppositional conviction about Christ's *preexistence* as the Son of God: preexistence, because of the assertion that "through him are *all things*," with creation in view; *Son of God*, because of Paul's identity of the "one God" as "the Father."

All of this seems deliberate on Paul's part. That is, he is reasserting for the Corinthians that their theology has it right—there is indeed only one God, over against all other "gods many and lords many." But at the same time he insists that the identity of the one God also includes the one Lord; and ultimately he does so because (1) this is the now shared Christian perspective about the one God, and (2) it is the inclusion of Christ as Lord in God's identity that will give Paul the leverage to forbid attendance at pagan festive meals. Not only does it lack love toward those for whom Christ died (8:10-13), but also their own sacred meal is eaten in honor of/in the presence of the one *Kyrios* (10:16-22). Furthermore, they have radically misunderstood the nature of idolatry. That the idols are not "gods" is a given; what the Corinthians have failed to reckon with is that the idols are in fact the habitation of demons (see e.g., Deut 32:17). And Paul's final point in this argument is that because there is only one *Kyrios*, and because the idols are the habitation of demons, they may not under any circumstances sit at both tables. For that is in fact a denial of the one Lord (10:19-22). Hence the reason for this elaboration of the *Shema* at the very beginning of Paul's attempt to correct their behavior—and theology—on this matter.

## II. The Bestowal of "the Name": Philippians 2:10

The "biblical" explanation as to how this came about is found in the divine vindication portion (vv. 9-11) of the Christ-story in Philippians 2:6-11. Here Paul asserts that Christ's exaltation following his incarnation and crucifixion consisted of the bestowal on him of "the Name." The "Name" bestowed, of course, is not "Jesus," as the text is so often read, since for Paul that is the name given to him regarding his earthly life. Rather, this is a play on the Tetragrammaton (YHWH), the divine "Name," whose significance runs throughout Deuteronomy (5:11; 12:11, 21; 14:23-24, etc). By a piece of divine providence, Yahweh became the *unpronounceable* name of God, which somewhere in the Second Temple period had ceased to be used at all, lest one do so in vain and thus break the third commandment. Though it appeared in the Hebrew text, and early on was carried over into the Septuagint without translation, at some early point the word *Adonai*, "the Lord," was used as a substitute for the YHWH; and this in turn finally made its way into the Septuagint for the divine Name itself—so that one got such strange locutions as Psalm 110:1 (109:1 LXX): "*Kyrios* said to my *kyrios*."

In this passage, the result of the exaltation of Jesus is thus expressed in two coordinate clauses taken directly from the Septuagint of Isaiah 45:23, both of which stress that the whole creation shall offer him homage and worship, presumably at his Coming. Thus the present narrative covers the whole gamut of Christ's prior existence as God, his incarnation for the sake of us humans and our salvation, and his subsequent exaltation at the Father's right hand. Thus our passage begins in eternity past with Christ's "being in the 'form' of God," then focuses on his incarnation, and finally expresses his exaltation as something already achieved (v. 9), thus presupposing resurrection and ascension; now it concludes by pointing to the final future event, when all created beings shall own his lordship.

First, Paul says that *at the name of Jesus*, the *Kyrios*, *every knee should bow*. "Bowing the knee," of course, is a common idiom for doing homage, sometimes in prayer, but always in recognition of the authority of the god or person before whom one is kneeling. What Paul does is full of import: for the "to me" of Isaiah 45:23, which refers to Yahweh, he substitutes *at the name of Jesus*. In this stirring oracle (Isa 45:18-24a) Yahweh, Israel's Savior, is declared to be God alone, over all that he has created and thus over all other gods and nations. In verses 22-24a Yahweh, while offering salvation to all but receiving obeisance in any case, declares that "*to me* (Yahweh = *Adonai* = *Kyrios*) every knee shall bow." Paul now asserts that at Christ's exaltation God has transferred this right of obeisance to the Son; he is the *Kyrios* to whom *every knee* shall eventually *bow*.

But notice, second, what Paul does with the second line of the doublet in Isaiah 45:23: every tongue (of every person on bended knee) shall express their homage in the language of the confessing—but currently suffering—church: *Kyrios is Jesus Christ*. This confession, which comes by the Spirit, according to 1 Corinthians 12:3, is the line of demarcation between believer and non-believer according to Romans 10:9. And here lies the ultimate triumph and irony in the passage. Those responsible for the suffering in Philippi proclaim that "the lord is Caesar." But at the end, when all creation beholds the risen Jesus, both they and their "lord Caesar" will join with all others to declare that *Kyrios* is none other than the Jesus whom the Romans crucified and whom Christians worship. But the confession will not then be one of conversion, but of final acknowledgement that "God has made this Jesus, whom you crucified, both Lord and Christ" (Acts 2:36).

One can scarcely miss the christological implications. In the Jewish synagogue the appellation "*Kyrios*" had long before been substituted for God's "name" (Yahweh). The early believers had now transferred that "name" (*Kyrios*) to the risen Jesus. Thus, Paul says, in raising Jesus from the dead, *God* has *exalted him to the highest place* and bestowed on *him* God's own name—in the Hebrew sense of *the Name,* referring to his investiture with God's power and authority. At the same time, Paul's monotheism is kept intact by the final phrase, *to the glory of God the Father.* Thus, this final sentence begins with God's exalting Christ by bestowing on him "the name" and concludes on the same theological note, that all of this is to God the Father's own glory.

### III. Paul's Use of *Kyrios* in Thessalonians

Once one sees how carefully Paul avoids using *Kyrios* to refer to God the Father, one is also struck by how much and how often *Kyrios* (= Yahweh) language from the Septuagint has been taken over by Paul and used with reference to Christ. And this from the very beginning, for in 1 and 2 Thessalonians alone there are at least twelve of these.

The place to begin is at the very outset of 1 Thessalonians, where Paul uses *Kyrios* exclusively to refer to Christ, while *theos* refers exclusively to the Father, a usage that finds explanation in the two (later) passages already examined. This is made certain in the present case by the related facts that in the opening greeting Paul speaks of the church of the Thessalonians as "in God (*theos*) the Father and the Lord (*Kyrios*) Jesus Christ," which language he picks up again in verse 3. When in the immediate context he uses both of these words individually, the *theos* in verse 2 clearly refers to God and the *kyrios* in verse 6 clearly refers to Christ; and so it goes throughout 1 Thessalonians, and the entire corpus.

1. So when we encounter the phrase ὁ λόγος τοῦ κυρίου ("the word of the Lord") in verse 8 (and again in 4:15 and 2 Thess 3:1), we have no reason to think other than that the genitive "of the Lord" here refers to Christ. But this, of course, is an Old Testament term, found frequently in the prophets, now being appropriated by Paul to refer to Christ.

2. In 1 Thessalonians 3:13 we have an even more remarkable bit of intertextuality. In what is a clear echo of Zechariah 14:5, where the Septuagint of Zechariah reads: *And my Lord God shall come and all his holy ones with him.* Paul changes "shall come" to

*parousia* (Coming) and omits "my God," so that the whole reads, "at the *parousia* of our *Kyrios* Jesus *with all his holy ones.*" Here Christ is clearly seen as taking the role once attributed to God.

3. In 1 Thessalonians 4:6, Paul says that "*Kyrios* will punish all who commit such sins," using a combination that occurs in the Septuagint in Psalm 94:1, as "*Kyrios* (= Yahweh) is a God who avenges." Again, language that in the Old Testament refers to Yahweh, now is used to refer to Christ.

4. In 1 Thessalonians 5:2 Paul picks up the familiar phrase "the Day of Yahweh (= Adonai = *Kyrios*)," which emerges first in the Old Testament in Joel 1 and 2, and now applies it directly to Christ as *Kyrios*. Thus the Day of Yahweh has for Paul become the Day of our *Kyrios*, Jesus Christ.

5. In the Old Testament, "swearing" or "charging" someone to some action is done in the name of *Kyrios* = Yahweh, who is then sometimes further designated as the God of heaven and earth. In 1 Thessalonians 5:27 Paul appropriates this language with reference to Christ.

When we turn to 2 Thessalonians we find that this clear intertextual phenomenon has increased in even more remarkable ways.

6. It begins at 1:9-10. First, the phrase "shut out from the presence of *Kyrios* and from the glory of his might" is a direct borrowing from Isaiah 2:10, where the Old Testament Yahweh = Adonai (the LORD) is applied directly to Christ. So also with the phrases "on the day he comes to be glorified in his holy people" and "to be marveled at among all those who believe." The first of these phrases echoes Psalm 89:7, while the second is a direct borrowing from Isaiah 52:15. And what in both of these passages were references to Yahweh under his "name/title" LORD, now refer to Christ as *Kyrios*.

7. This phenomenon continues with the prayer report that follows in verse 12, where the phrase, "that the name of *Kyrios* Jesus might be glorified in you" is a clear echo of the same language in Isaiah 66:5, referring to Yahweh.

8. So also again in 2:8, where the clause *"Kyrios* Jesus will overthrow with the breath of his mouth and destroy by the splendor of his coming" is largely picking up the language used in Isaiah 11:4. And this is the one clear instance among these many texts where the first referent is not Yahweh himself, but Yahweh's messianic servant. The difference, of course, is that the present referent is to the exalted Lord and refers to his *final* judgment.

9. On three occasions in later letters (1 Cor 1:9; 10:13; 2 Cor 1:18), Paul has reason to appeal to God's faithfulness in the laconic language, "God is faithful." But in 2 Thessalonians 3:3 he does a most remarkable thing, by asserting that *"Kyrios* is faithful"; and the context makes it clear he now means Christ.

10. One of the more remarkable uses of *Kyrios* in Paul is his willingness to direct prayer to him, a strictly divine prerogative for a passionate monotheist like Paul. But in these letters Paul regularly prays to God the Father and Christ the *Kyrios* (see 1 Thess 3:12-13; 2 Thess 2:16-17). In 2 Thessalonians 3:5 he directs prayer to Christ alone and does so by means of deliberate intertextual use of 1 Chronicles 29:18, "May *Kyrios* direct your hearts into the love of God."

11. The final two instance of such intertextual use of *Kyrios* = Yahweh occur in the benediction (3:16) at the end of 2 Thessalonians. In other letters Paul refers both to "the peace of God" and "the God of peace" (see how these come close to each other in Phil 4:7 and 9). In a most remarkable moment, Paul concludes 2 Thessalonians without mention of God the Father at all. He starts with a blessing, "May *Kyrios* of peace himself give you peace at all times and in every way. *Kyrios* be with you." And the final grace, as in most of his letters, reads: "The grace of our *Kyrios*, Jesus Christ be with you all."

12. I note finally that the "May *Kyrios* be with you" in the preceding benediction is the final moment of intertextuality in these letters. In a singular moment in all of his letters, Paul dips into his Jewish heritage with the blessing, *"Kyrios* be with you"; only in

this case, given the nature of the letter, it becomes, "*Kyrios* be with *all* of you." In so doing he appropriates language that in the Old Testament was seen as evidence of faithfulness to Yahweh, as the author of Ruth is keen to point out. Thus Boaz greets his workers with: "The LORD be with you"; to which they respond, "The LORD bless you!" (Ruth 2:4). Paul's greeting once again reflects the (in this case verbless) text of the Septuagint.

What needs to be emphasized as a concluding word to this rehearsal of Paul's use of *Kyrios* in 1 and 2 Thessalonians is twofold. First, to point out how thoroughgoing this phenomenon actually is; and related to that, second, to point out how theologically unselfconsciously, what might be described as nearly off-handedly, Paul does this. Here is a man not trying to *assert* a high Christology, but a man who simply *assumes* it in every way. It is not at all difficult to see how Paul was used along with John by the orthodox to express their trinitarianism a couple of centuries later.

For whatever else was true for Paul, he is a thoroughgoing monotheist all the way through. Yet at the same time both his devotion to Christ and his way of speaking about Christ is such that Paul attributes to Christ Jesus his Lord very many of the divine prerogatives. Thus at the end I note again the substantial reality that Paul's devotion to Christ is that reserved by his Jewish heritage for God alone. Early Christian Christology hardly gets any higher than that.

It is a distinct pleasure to offer these musings regarding Paul's use of the Old Testament in honor Carl Armerding, a dear friend and sometime Old Testament colleague at Regent College, Vancouver.

6

# Petitionary Prayer and the Nature of God

## CLARK H. PINNOCK

I am pleased to be part of a volume honouring Carl Armerding, who is a good friend and a colleague of former days. In my essay I have chosen to write on petitionary prayer and certain implications arising for the doctrine of God. Believers are more than "objects" of redemption; they are also "subjects," children of God, covenant partners, and co-workers with God. God loves it when we walk with him and converse with him. God values such interaction and conversation. Even though he can act alone without us, he delights to do things in consultation with us. And God even allows our praying to influence what he does and the very course of history.[1]

Prayers come in many different forms. They include prayers of praise, confession, intercession and contemplation. Each kind of praying has its own reasons and its own appropriateness. Of special

---

1. Help is available for our understanding in Vincent Brummer, *What are We Doing when We Pray?: A Philosophical Inquiry* (London: SCM Press, 1984), in Robert Ellis, *Answering God: Towards a Theology of Intercession* (Carlisle: Paternoster Press, 2005), and in David Crump, *Knocking on Heaven's Door: A New Testament Theology of Petitionary Prayer* (Grand Rapids: Baker Academic, 2006).

interest to us here in this essay is "petitionary prayer," the kind in which we ask God for specific things such as a healing or a word of knowledge. Some people are sceptical about such prayer. Why would God, they wonder, who is a being of infinite intelligence, take account of such requests? Why ask God for something he already knows we need? Would he not do it without being asked? Do we want to say that God would forego doing something important just because a creature forgot to mention it in his or her prayers? What then are we to make of petitionary prayer, and what does it tell us about the nature of God?[2]

**Part One: The meaning of Petitionary Prayer**

From my reading of the scriptures, it seems to be the case that God responds to our petitions sometimes and grants us benefits just because we asked him for them. The biblical evidence is strong. James informs his community in blunt terms that they had not gotten some benefit "because they did not ask for it" (Jas 4:2). Consider the story of the unjust judge who did not intend to give the poor widow any justice, but who did so because she "persisted" in her petitions (Luke 18:5). Remember the fellow who did not want to rise from bed to help a friend but who did so, because of the "persistence" of his asking (Luke 11:8)? In some mysterious way, prayer moves God's hand. In Revelation 8:1, the heavenly host is silenced so that God might listen to the prayers of the saints and act accordingly upon them. Our God is not a God whose will is fixed in each detail from all eternity but a God who responds to his people's

---

2. Other authors reflect on these issues too. Consider Clark H. Pinnock *et al.*, *The Openness of God* (Downers Grove: InterVarsity Press, 1994), 156-62; Terrance Tiessen, *Providence and Prayer: How does God Work in the World?* (Downers Grove: InterVarsity Press, 2000); John Sanders, *The God Who Risks: A Theology of Providence* (Downers Grove: InterVarsity Press, 1998); Clark H. Pinnock *Most Moved Mover: A Theology of God's Openness* (Grand Rapids: Baker Academic, 2001); and John Polkinghorne, *The Work of Love: Creation as Kenosis* (Grand Rapids: Eerdmans, 2001).

praying. Prayer can change the world, because it can change God and what is possible for God.

Consider Abraham's conversation with God respecting Sodom and Gomorrah and how God altered his plans in regard to them because the patriarch interceded for them (Gen 18:32). Consider Moses at whose request God "changed his mind" and did not destroy the people of Israel on account of prayer (Exod 32:14). Remember King Hezekiah and how he was given longer to live because he prayed (2 Kgs 20:1–6). God responds when we pray and even does things because we prayed. Jesus gives us an open invitation: "Ask, and it will given you; search, and you will find; knock, and the door will be opened for you. For everyone who asks receives, and everyone who searches finds, and for everyone who knocks, the door will be opened" (Matt 7:7–8). What a motivation we have to prayer we have to pray knowing that our prayers can change the future!

It is true, of course, that God is free to respond or not to respond. God is not at our beck and call. But, at the same time, he is a God who has decided not to be alone and not to act alone. Being triune by nature, God is himself a community who uses his freedom to create more communion in the context of a significant creation. God has decided not to be the only subject which exists, but to be here for us and with us and to be our God for ever. God wishes to bless us by letting us share in the richness of his own being and to have a part in his rule. In fact, petitionary prayer is a way of our participating in God's acting in the world. Had creatures not prayed, things would have turned out differently. In a certain way, God makes himself dependent on our praying. He certainly can do things without our approval and without our asking, but the fact remains that God likes to do things with us and not always alone. God likes partnerships and relationships which prayers symbolise. Our lives matter to God and therefore matter ultimately. Faith in God is not existentially repugnant because our prayers matter and our entire lives matter to God. God is the ground in reality itself of the final worth of our existence and our prayers matter, just as does everything else that we do matters. One could say that prayer is God's way of giving creatures the dignity of causality.

Evidently, God wants us to ask him to bring about states of affairs through prayer. Of course, God is not obligated to do exactly what we ask and may not do it if our requests are beyond the bounds of what is suitable, etc. The point is that prayer can make a difference to the world. Prayer can be a way of getting things done in the world because God likes to carry out his purposes along with human. Petitionary prayer is more problematic when it comes to classical theism because, in that way of thinking, God cannot "respond" to anything or do anything because we asked. That would make God dependent on the creature. God is unchangeable and wholly independent and his cannot be altered or thwarted in any way. Therefore, petitionary prayer cannot play a real role in the outcome of events. One cannot change God's will by anything that one does, even in small ways. Praying is just another item that is predetermined and which changes nothing. How discouraging it would to be called to prayer and to realise that our prayers cannot change anything because everything is fixed. In order for them to be meaningful there has to be flexibility in the system.[3]

---

3. I am generally in agreement with David Crump, *Knocking on Heaven's Door*, in his conviction that God is influenced by what we ask of God but I am puzzled as to why he does not draw out certain conclusions that seem to follow: such as divine temporality, libertarian freedom, and dynamic omniscience (p. 290). It may just be (and this is a surmise) that, given the hostility one experiences when "coming out of the closet" as an open theist, he prefers not to deal with certain issues right away. After all, to make it clear that one is an open theist is to invite fire at point blank range, so why do it? If one wishes to remain in good standing in the evangelical community one would be wise not to promote open theism. I can testify to this.

## Part Two: Petitionary Prayer and the Nature of God

1. Petitionary prayer is evidence of a personal relationship with a personal God. This is why prayer is so central to Christianity. It gives expression to that fact. Because God is a personal God and not an absolute substance, God is able to get involved in a changing world. This would not be possible for a deity with the classical attributes such as immutability and impassibility, unless the definitions were considerably modified. How could God (for example) be immutable in a strong sense and (at the same time) be able to respond to a changing world. Petitionary prayer is most intelligible in the context of relational theism. We must be able to change in relation to God, and God must be able to change in relation to us.

The tradition has experienced difficulty in finding a place for petitionary prayer in its thinking. In Thomism, they have to be thought of as factored into God's complete control through the category of second causes. In Calvinism, petitionary prayers are possible in the sense that God has determined to accomplish some things in answer to them. But the prayers themselves are predetermined. A personal and relational God can handle petitionary prayer best because only a personal and relational God can handle the interactive relationships that prayer involves.

2. Petitionary prayer brings to light the divine self-limitation. It reveals God who allows himself to become vulnerable in relationships because he cares about us. Like a parent, God carries us in his arms and speaks tenderly to us (Hos 11:3–4). He is a husband to his people. He does not give up on them even when they are unfaithful to him and inflict pain upon him. God perseveres in the hope that the relationship will develop into something better and become more mutual.

But how, we ask, can "a being greater than which cannot be conceived" be anything other than all-determining and unconditioned? How can God open himself to change and temporality? Is this not the realm of the creature? Yes it is, but in creation, God steps back (as it were) in order to bring a world into being alongside of himself. God retreats to make room for us even in our rebellion. God limits the use of his own power in order to enjoy fellowship with significant others. God shares his power with us. In becoming flesh, God renounces earthly power and allows himself to become victim. It seems as if God does not to want to be almighty apart from us. God involves himself with us in history for the sake of community. He hides his superior power and presents himself as weak to give us room to become all that we were meant to be. By grace, God opens himself up to the world. "He who was rich for our sake became poor so that we through his poverty might be rich" (2 Cor 8:9). God has chosen to be God in such a way as to be affected and conditioned by the world. Ours is a God whose foolishness is wiser than human wisdom and whose weakness is stronger than human strength (1 Cor 1:25).

3. Petitionary prayer also reveals the temporality of a God who experiences time with us. If he were a timeless being, who dwells in a non-temporal realm, God could scarcely handle prayers which arise out of the rough and tumble of history. If timeless, God could not interact with or be affected by temporal events because he would be existing outside a temporal series. But scripture gives us a narrative where God is a historical agent. It narrates God's story. Petitionary prayer makes sense best if God is temporal. In that case, he can deal with history and temporarily related to us, God experiences time, otherwise, he could not be with us in history. God is not timeless—God is everlasting and his life is one of endless duration. It is not biblical to think of God as timelessly existing since God is plainly involved in our history.

4. Petitionary prayer brings out passibility in God. He is willing to be moved by what the creature says. God cannot be coerced, but he can be affected. As a loving God, God can experience both rapturous delight and the precariousness of having his love spurned. Suffering is almost inevitable in loving relations because the lover cannot control the beloved. Love may be accepted or rejected. Therefore

one who loves makes himself/herself vulnerable. In dealing with our prayers, God experiences vulnerability and fragility. Although the tradition has seldom seen it, the pathos of God is close to the very heart of our gospel. A God of love and mercy cannot be impassible. In this context theologians worry about God changing in any way even though this "changing" is for our benefit. God can indeed be touched by the feelings of our infirmities. We celebrate God's changing for our sake. God is truly transcendent but is also involved in the world most passionately. He reigns over the world but is also affected by what happens. His people when they betray him make him weep. The cross is God's true glory.

5. Petitionary prayer effectively displays the wisdom of God. Had God taken the route of pancausality, had he decided to do everything in regard to creation all by himself, and not delegated any important function to the creature, well then everything would flow exactly as planned. Running the world would be a cinch. But that is not what God did. He did delegate important functions to human beings with significant freedom, with the result that matters in the universe became much more complex and challenges much greater and more numerous. My point is that in such a situation God is required to be more intelligent and resourceful. In a dynamic world, God is required to be very wise and resourceful. This is why wisdom becomes more a central attribute than it has been in traditional theism. If everything has been settled before creation, what is there to be wise about? What challenges are there really to puzzle over? What challenges are there to threaten total control? But in the world as God made it, many obstacles stand in the way of God's project and many problems need to be solved. In prayer we join God in pondering the way forward. In prayer we cry out "Lord, how long?"

6. Petitionary prayer speaks to our understanding of God's omniscience as well. If God knew the future exhaustively and as something definite in all respects, petitionary prayer would be vain and pointless. Why ask for things that are settled already?

God's omniscience, like his omnipotence, is geared to the kind of universe he made and not about God's ability to know everything. God does know everything that can be known but, because there is real freedom the future is not "there yet" to be known exhaustively. It would be jumping the gun to know what every person will do before they even do it. How could anyone know what the future free choices will be, if they actually are free choices? Given the nature of creation, God cannot determine the future without calling off the free will project. It is consequent on God's decision to create such a world as this. God knows the future as future and as open. If God were to infallibly fore-know every event before it happens, petitionary prayer and most of what matters in life, would be meaningless. It would mean that creation is after all a determined order. God knows everything that can be known but that this does not include everything about the future insofar as it contains as yet unrealised possibilities. God could have made a deterministic order, but it does not appear that he did so. God created a truly temporal order with an open future.[4]

## Conclusion

We are dealing nowadays with new horizons in our thinking about God. Traditionalists resist much of it, but many are being helped by it. Fresh winds are blowing and theological reform is continuing. Some of the baggage of classical theism is being set

---

4. Steven Roy has challenged the position of dynamic omniscience or present knowledge in *How Much does God Foreknow? A Comprehensive Biblical Study* (Downers Grove: IVP Academic, 2006). The tone is calm and fair. He can be positive as well as negative. Unfortunately he cannot dispose of the impression that, in many places, it seems plausible to read the Bible as saying that (for example) God tests people to see what they will do (Gen 22:12). Or that God changes God's mind in response to what people do (Jonah 3:9). Roy offers an impressive case for reading the Bible in a Calvinist manner, but he does not prove that the openness approach is everywhere implausible—far from it. Open theism is a hermeneutical option for evangelical free will theists.

aside to make room for a more relational doctrine of God. What is being proposed is not a God/world dependency in which God is dependent on the world. We are thinking rather of a dynamic world order where God allows himself to be affected by what goes on in the world voluntarily in a stunning manner.

7

# The Reforming Agency of a Psalm in the Later Middles Ages

JAMES M. HOUSTON

As his colleagues and friends, we are delighted to celebrate Carl Armerding's seventieth year with this Festschrift. I still remember visiting his home in Wheaton, Illinois, when we invited him to join the early faculty of Regent College. Betsy, his wife, had been challenged in her morning reading that day, "without faith it is impossible to please God..." (Heb 11:6). This settled their decision to step out in faith, to embark on a new venture indeed! Two years earlier, Carl had completed his dissertation from Brandeis University on "The Heroic Ages of Greece and Israel: Literary-Historical Comparison."[1] His concern was "to show Israel had a heroic age," as well as Greece. His focus was therefore upon the book of Judges.

The intrinsic nature of "the heroic" is its boundlessness, its indeterminacy in distinguishing between the human and the divine. "Heroes" then are viewed as demi-gods. The porosity of "the self," which lasted throughout the Homeric and later Graeco-Roman world, was challenged however by the prophet Samuel, as indeed against Saul, the last of the biblical heroic archetypes. Saul had all

---

1. Carl E. Armerding, *The Heroic Ages of Greece and Israel: Literary-Historical Comparison* (Ann Arbor: University Microfilms, 1968).

the traits of the "hero": aristocratic birth, natural beauty, military prowess, and wealth. What he lacked was "the fear of the Lord", as encompassing humility, prayerfulness, obedience to God's word. At the command of "I AM" or Yahweh, David while still a young shepherd boy—the youngest of Jesse's sons—is to the surprise of all concerned, anointed as Israel's exemplar of true kingship. The simple story of young David challenging the heroic society, represented by Goliath, is a profoundly polemic narrative, against those tempted with the primordial fantasy, "you shall be as gods" (Gen 3:4).

Yet at the same time, the whole history of Christian culture from the early Church until after the Middle ages was a "figural" world.[2] This was first developed in Jewish *Midrash,* where the rabbis believed new meanings would continue to be found in the scriptures with succeeding generations.[3] But the culture of metaphor, allegory, prophetic fulfillment, apostolic teaching of the unity of Old and New Testament, and the on-going commentaries of the Fathers maintain this figural consciousness. Abraham, Moses, David, continue to live on in the teachings of Jesus. Indeed, the early church fathers' apologetic against the pagans was that they were Jews first, and then in becoming Christians afterwards. Thus Justin Martyr, himself a gentile, makes his apologetic of Christianity, by referring all his points to the Old Testament first of all.[4] The Psalms as the miniature Bible, encapsulate in the figure of "David," the anticipation of "great David's greater Son." Heaven, earth and hell are all a present reality in Christian medieval consciousness, where miracles are the miracles of the Bible, and history is the history of God's people.

---

2. Erich Auerbach, *"Figura,"* in *Scenes from the Drama of European Literature,* trans. Ralph Manheim (New York: Meridian Books, 1959), 54, 61.

3. *Jewish Encyclopaedia, s.v.,* "Midrash" (trans. H. Freedman and M. Simon; London: Soncino Press, 1961).

4. Justin Martyr, *Dialogue with Trypho,* Works, A Library of Fathers of the Holy Catholic Church, vol. XL, Oxford, 1961.

## THE REFORMING AGENCY OF A PSALM

Allegory is the Christian world, preached from the pulpit, worshipped in the liturgy, symbolized in stained glass windows, and dramatized in the Nativity plays. For example, in sculpture, there are at Strasbourg cathedral two statues of ladies, similar in beauty but one is blindfolded with a broken lance in her right hand while from her left hand have fallen the broken tables of the law; she is the Synagogue. The other lady, the Church, wears a crown and holds in her right hand a cross, while in her left hand is a chalice.[5] Yet did not the apostle Paul himself describe Biblical children, Sarah and Hagar in Galatians 4:21-31, as the legitimacy for all later Christian allegory? However, the translucence of "biblical" reality makes it vulnerable to its misuse in the cult of the "heroic." This is why the character of David is the richest in paradox and the most difficult to grasp.

### David as the Prophet-King of God's People

It is not a subject much scholarly attention has been given to, but it is apparent the Psalter is radically anti-heroic. As Israel's hymnal and prayer book, as well as the Christian manual of moral life, no biblical book has had more profound moral influence throughout history until modern times. The contemporary scholarly interest in the history of its commentaries is an encouraging sign of a possible renaissance of Biblical studies.[6] John Eaton has pioneered in his emphasis that the kingship of Yahweh is the key theme of the Psalter.[7] Not all the psalms focus upon the king, for they are interspersed with focus upon the word of God, as well as upon the existential condition of his people. But God's Kingship and God's Word are

---

5. This was developed by Pseudo-Augustine, *Disputatio Ecclesiae et Synagogae*, in Edmond Martene and Ursin Durand, *Thesaurus Novus Anecdotum* (Lutetiae Parisorum: Sumptibus Florentini Delaulne, 1717), cols. 1497-1506.
6. Brian E. Daley, S.J., "Is Patristic Exegesis still Usable?: Reflections on Early Christian Interpretation of the Psalms," *Communio* 29 (Spring 2002): 185-216.
7. John Eaton, *Kingship and the Psalms* (SBT 32; London: SCM Press, 1976).

intrinsically inter-related, as the kingship law of Deuteronomy 17:14-20 testifies:

> "Be sure to appoint over you the king the I AM your God chooses .... When he takes the throne of his kingdom, he is to write for himself on a scroll a copy of this law, taken from the Levitical priests. It is to be with him, and he is to read it all the days of his life so that he may learn to revere the Lord his God and follow carefully all the words of this law and these decrees and not consider himself better than his fellow Israelites and turn from the law to the right hand or to the left".(Deut. 17:15,18-20)

The human king is called upon to be the exemplar of Yahweh's faithful people, who should wholly depend upon I AM, and who would obey the *Torah*.[8] Biblical kingship and proper piety go together. The unity of Psalms 1 and 2, as the introduction to the Psalter makes this clear: delight in the law of the Lord is a kingly act, and Yahweh's kingship is an invincible reality over all the nations, and indeed over the cosmos. Through such bi-focal lenses, the whole of the Psalter can be visualized, understood, and celebrated. When the risen Lord tells his disciples that all that is written of him "in the law of Moses and the Prophets and the Psalms must be fulfilled"(Luke 24:44), we may wonder why he did not cite the threefold way the Israelites had accepted their biblical canon, as the Law, the Prophets, and the Writings. This becomes more understandable if the traditional claim of what is 'Davidic', is considered; not of all the psalms but as their exemplar and inspirer, together with the 450 songs, noted in 1 Kings 5:12, and with the 1,005 songs of Solomon and his 3,000 proverbs.

---

8. Jamie A. Grant, *The King as Exemplar: The Function of Deuteronomy's Kingship Law in the Shaping of the Book of Psalms* (Society of Biblical Literature Academia Biblica 17; Leiden: Brill; Atlanta: Society of Biblical Literature, 2004).

## THE REFORMING AGENCY OF A PSALM

In the intertestamental period of the second and first centuries C.E., the Qumran community understood 'David's utterances in the psalms as being prophetic, and in some sense an extension of the prophetic writings.[9] They added another psalm to the 150 of our canon, entitled "A Hallelujah of David the Son of Jesse.[10] This is included in the Anglo-Saxon Eadwine Psalter. It purports David making confession:

> Smaller was I than my brothers
> And the youngest of the sons of my father,
> So he made me shepherd of his flock
> And ruler over his kids.
>
> My hands have made an instrument
> And my fingers a lyre;
> And [so] have I rendered glory to the Lord,
> Thought I, within my soul.

This is a poetic *midrash* of 1 Samuel 16:1-13, with the theme of v. 7, "the I AM looks upon the heart", and so the fourth stanza ends with the awareness that "Everything has God seen/, everything has He heard and He has heeded". The poem ends, "And He made me leader of His people/ and ruler over the sons of His covenant."[11] For David stated his purpose was "Let me render glory unto the Lord"—not merely the human instinct of fear, to kill Goliath. Later in the High Middle Ages, the ten-stringed harp is depicted in glossaries of the Psalter, as being ten-stringed, to allegorize the ten

---

9. Craig A. Evans, "The Dead Sea Scrolls and the Canon of Scripture in the Time of Jesus," in *The Bible at Qumran: Text, Shape and Interpretation,* ed. Peter W. Flint (Grand Rapids / Cambridge: Eerdmans, 2002), 76-77.
10. As J. A. Sanders has suggested in his book, *The Psalm Scroll of Qurâm Cave 11 (11QPsa)* (DJD, 4; Oxford: Clarendon Press, 1965).
11. Ibid., 55-56.

commandments, or as the ten human fingers that are submissive to the service of God.[12]

The iconography of David reveals many changes of the role David is interpreted to play within changing cultural situations. In the Vespasian Psalter of the eighth century, David is dressed in imperial robes, playing a contemporary harp, with musicians and dancers playing at his feet. He is God's *psalmista*, or "psalm maker," the regal poet of Israel.[13] In this Anglo-Saxon culture, psalmody is monastic, and liturgical. But in the thirteenth century Psalter of Isabel of France, here David is kneeling, in self-effacement of contrition and prayer, alone before God, while below, the religious figures are in an imitative posture of worshipful devotion. This age now recovers the homilies or *enarrationes* of Augustine, which are primarily exhortations to live a godly life. Poetic diction now becomes a diction for a virtuous life, and David is the voice of inspired *propheta*, whose 'prophecy' is more expressive of the Deuteronomic definition of a covenantal 'king', as the moralist *par excellence,* who is living as a *'torah'* person. For he has a double *persona*, representing Christ, the Word, as He proclaims the Sermon on the Mount, and also as the Church, living out the commanded life that is 'blessed' in the first Psalm. Medieval commentators continue to see both Christ and the Church as the initial *figura* of the introduction to the Psalter. As Richard Rolle concludes his *Prologue* to the first English vernacular commentary on the Psalter, "the matter of this book is Christ and his Spouse, that is the holy kirk… to conform men that are defiled in Adam, now [living] in Christ in newness of life". Iconically, Rolle wishes to act as David's mouthpiece, as David was God's prophet.

---

12. Martin van Schaik, *The Harp in the Middle Ages: the Symbolism of a Musical Instrument* (Amsterdam: Rodolpi, 1992).

13. See plate 1, from the British Museum, in Michael P. Kuczynski, *Prophetic Song: the Psalms as Moral Discourse in Late Medieval England* (Philadelphia: University of Pennsylvania Press, 1995), 3.

THE REFORMING AGENCY OF A PSALM

*The Use of Psalm 15 in Late Antiquity*

But in the period of the thirteenth–early fourteenth century, which we are selecting, the call for church and social reform is strong, It is also significantly selective of psalm 15 (14 in the Vulgate), because of verse 5, which praises the righteous "who lend money to the poor without interest, and do not accept bribes against the innocent".

Yet as early as the mid-fourth century, Basil the Great in his homily on Psalm 15(14), speaks only about the vice of usury. He notes that Ezekiel rates usury as "among the greatest of evils...and the law expressly forbids it" (Ezek. 22:12). He thinks it "reveals the greatest inhumanity, that the one in need of necessities seeks a loan for the relief of his life, and the other, not satisfied with the capital, contrives revenues for himself from the misfortunes of the poor man and gathers wealth."[14] He notes how Christ condemned usury in Matthew 5:42. This indictment continues throughout his homily, with no other reference to the rest of the psalm. About the same time, Hilary of Poitiers gives a more holistic commentary, stating the brevity of the psalm "summarizes all the instructions and commandments of the Old and New Testaments;"[15] yet again usury is high-lighted. Theodore of Mopsuestia focuses only on the second clause of the verse, the taking of bribes, which he sees as prevalent in the city of Antioch where he lived.[16] But the end result for both sins is the same, that one party "is made unjust and the other wretched".

---

14. Saint Basil, *Exegetical Homilies* (trans. Sister Agnes Clare Way, C.D.P.; Washington, D.C.: The Catholic University of America Press, 1963), 181-182.

15. Hilary of Poitiers, *In Psalmos 1-XCI, Sancti Hilarii Pictaviensis Tractatus super Psalmos* (ed. J. Doignon; Corpus Christianorum Series Latina, 61; Turhout: Brepols, 1977), 91.

16. Theodore of Mopsuestia, *Commentary on Psalms 1-81* (trans. Robert C. Hill; *Writings from the Greco-Roman World*, no. 5; Atlanta: Society of Biblical Literature, 2006), 179.

Again the Lombard commentator, Cassiodorus, returns to the sin of usury, but he interprets Psalm 15 following Hilary, as a simple summary of the Decalogue. Rhetorically, he suggests the figure of speech, *erotema,* is illustrated, in the psalm where an apt reply is being given to a questioner. "Who shall ascend unto the hill of the Lord?" This he interprets as, who is worthy to belong to the Church? Clearly only Christ is without blemish, who alone has fulfilled the Law. So he sees the psalm's focus upon Christ, Law-Giver, and Law-Fulfiller, who is described by ten virtues outlined in the psalm. So he concludes: "this is the great divine decalogue, the spiritual psaltery of ten chords. Here is the crowning number which only He could fulfill, who with His Father laid low the sins of the world."[17]

Both Origen and Gregory the Great had been the great masters of tropology, in applying the mystery of Christ to the Christian moral way of life. But in the twelfth century Bernard of Clairvaux (1091?-1153) took Scriptural moral application or "tropology" to a new level, or indeed a new "depth." He associated it with "conversion", implying the change of life from feudal knighthood to the simple and obedient life of a monk. Literally it was a new form of "monastification". For the traditional Benedictine model of accepting children to grow up unreflectively within the monastic community, was now being replaced by the Cistercian reform of recruiting youths as volunteers. These postulates now needed "conversion"—consciously and radically so—from their worldly ways, to become true monks. So a Cistercian commentary on Psalm 15 would be very illuminating. But since early Cistercian theology "ruminated" rather than gave an "exposition," we find literally hundreds of echoes to the Psalter within their homilies, but not a straightforward textual exposition.

---

17. *Cassiodorus: Explanation of the Psalms* (trans. and annotated by P. G. Walsh, vol. 1; New York: Paulist Press, 1990), 156-160.

## THE REFORMING AGENCY OF A PSALM

Significantly, the only commentary of a selected psalm which Bernard composed, was his seventeen sermons on Psalm 91. But everywhere, Bernard is quoting and using the psalms tropologically for this intent of "conversion."[18] In his seventh sermon on Ps. 91, he does quote Psalm 15:4, that the converted monk will despise the reprobate and honor those who fear the Lord.[19] As Bernard puts it, everything that the Gospel history contains can therefore be interpreted "according to tropology, so that what has preceded from Christ as 'the head' may consequently also be acted out morally within 'the body'."[20]

The twelfth century is indeed a turning point or "hinge period" of history. Its greatest spokesman, Bernard, is both "the last of the Fathers", and "the first of the moderns". For he follows Origen, Augustine and Gregory, and yet he promotes a new self-consciousness in his theology of love, that marks "the rise of the individual" within the twelfth century. If *conversio* was basic for his Cistercian monastic theology, it was also confronted by the new cultural challenge of incipient commerce. This was associated with the growth of the new urban centers of northern Italy and the lower Rhine lands, and also with their new secular schools of theology. All this gave a new freshness to Bernard's exegesis. However, it was not so much with Bernard as the "new monk", but with the later lay use of the Psalter, that brought Psalm 15 more prominently into focus for the moral reform movements of the next centuries.

Another significant event of the twelfth century was the introduction of Jewish merchants into England by William the Conqueror, in 1070, four years after his conquest of England. Jews became a counterpoise to Christian scholarship, instructing them in Hebrew for their exegesis of the psalms. Common ground was the allegori-

---

18. Bernard of Clairvaux, *Sermons on Conversion*, trans. and introduction by Marie-Bernard Saïd (Kalamazoo: Cistercian Publications, 1981), 11-25.
19. *Ibid*, 159.
20. Quoted by Henri Lubac, *Medieval Exegesis, vol. 2, op. cit.,* 135.

cal and historical treatment of the Psalter. Christian scholars like Robert Grosseteste (1175-1253), bishop of Lincoln, were favorable to the Jews, who reasoned on their behalf that the Church has grown out of the synagogue, as indeed Sarah was consort with Hagar. Later William Langland (late 14th century) is to also reason: since the Hebrews " know the first clause of our creed, *Credo in unum Deum*, [teach them] little by little [to believe also] in *Jesum Christum filium* and in *Spiritum Sanctum*."[21]

In the tranquility of an Oxford college, this spirit of tolerance was fair-minded, but in the market place, life was very different. For there, usury became personified with Jewry. Lacking civil status in a feudal society, the Jews remained outsiders to military obligations, legal and every civic tie. They were simply the personal property of the kings, like so many milking cows, to be taxed when their usury had fattened them sufficiently for the use of king's treasury. By 1187, the Jews were reckoned to have one-fourth of the moveable wealth of the kingdom, and one Jew alone, Aaron of Lincoln, kept Henry II solvent. Then the populace began riots, to rob the money-lenders, and to burn the records of indebtedness. After Grosseteste's death in 1255, crowd violence erupted in Lincoln, Jews were imprisoned *en masse* and a number were killed. Edward I tried to carry out the ideals of Grosseteste, who had argued it was a Christian charge to convert the Jews, not to kill them. Edward banned all usury in 1275, and all taking of interest, but the economic change of climate was too sudden and the legislation failed. In 1290, Edward expelled all Jews from England.[22]

The end result was that in scholarly commentary on the Psalter, a new literal/historical component was brought into the exegesis of the psalms, such as we find in Richard of St. Victor and Herbert of Bosham. But in popular appeal to the laity, Psalm 15 began to have

---

21. Ruth M. Ames, *The Fulfillment of the Scriptures: Abraham, Moses and Piers* (Evanston: Northwestern University Press, 1970), 35.
22. *Ibid*, 36.

special interest, simply because of verse 5, praising the righteous ". . . who lend money to the poor without interest and do not accept bribes against the innocent. Whoever does these things will never be shaken."

Meanwhile in 1246, the Council of Toulouse had re-iterated that the Psalter could be translated into vernacular languages. The precedent had originated with the lay movement of the Desert Fathers, who at least since the fourth century, had practiced daily recitation of the Psalter.

Then early in the fourteenth century, Richard Rolle wrote in Middle English the first lay commentary on the whole Psalter. It was widely used, as the numerous extant copies attest.[23] Since a layman had composed it, it was outside the jurisdiction of the church officials to prevent its circulation. He is indebted to Augustine, Cassiodorus, Peter Lombard, and Gilbert of Poitiers. From the latter he adopts the analogy of the psalms being 'verbal medicine", for the cure of the sick soul. He sees also the unique role of the Psalms, as the Bible in miniature, which Athanasius had first pointed out in the early fourth century.[24] Now this had become increasingly significant for the laity, who still had no direct access to the Latin Vulgate of the clergy. Humbly, however, Rolle still acknowledges the Latin text has authority over any English version, as if in deference to David himself. As we have already noted, Psalm 15 was significant as the summary of the Decalogue. David's role as the moral teacher *par excellence* now takes on new prominence under Rolle and later commentators. For his intent is to be the voice of David to the common people, as David had been God's prophet to Israel. Yet the psalms are "ful derke," with many obscure passages, so his own text

---

23. There are at least thirty eight extant copies of his vernacular commentary, mainly in private homes and university colleges.

24. Athanasius, *The Letter to Marcellinus,* trans. and introduction by Robert C. Gregg (New York: Paulist Press, 1980), 101-147.

is intended both to clarify the reader, as well as to stir up deeper devotion, in teaching God's ways to sinners.

Richard Rolle (c. 1300-1340), educated at Oxford, he remains a layman, spending over thirty years as a hermit. Because he remains independent of the church hierarchy or even local priests, he becomes the most influential and popular English commentator of the psalter. For the following two centuries, his is the only authorized translation of part of the Bible into English, which does not need diocesan permission for its use. He may be described as "the Franciscan lay reformer of England," whose mystical writings influences the rise of the Lollards and of Wyclif's teaching, as well as gives stimulus to later English mystics.[25] He breaks the Psalter loose both from its long monastic way of life as well as from the much shorter period of Christian/Jewish scholasticism, to put it into the hands of "the ploughman," as indeed William Langland epitomizes in the next generation, when Christ is now depicted as "Piers the Plowman." Both Richard Rolle and William Langland now address the common people, to see the whole universe as expressive of the mystery of the Trinity.[26]

Rolle inherited two devotional sources in Anselm and Bernard of Clairvaux. From Anselm he was directed to appreciate the personalized expressions of prayer, as Anselm composed prayers as expressive of the character and needs of particular individuals. While from Bernard, he was inspired by his "bridal mysticism" to be personally in love with Christ, indeed in union with Him, as the church is the Bride of Christ. Both permeate all his writings. Richard Rolle writes two independent commentaries, first a Latin version, then later a more mature, richer, vernacular commentary of the psalter; this is the first of its kind in the Middle Ages. In the Prologue he begins:

---

25. Margaret Deanesly, *The Lollard Bible and other Medieval Biblical Versions* (Cambridge: Cambridge University Press, 1920, rep. 1966), 120.

26. Ames, *op. cit.*, 73.

## THE REFORMING AGENCY OF A PSALM

A great fullness of spiritual comfort and joy in God comes into the hearts of those who recite or devoutly intone the psalms as an act of praise to Jesus Christ. They drop sweetness in men's souls and pour delight into their thoughts and kindle their wills with the fire of love, making them hot and burning within, and beautiful and lovely in Christ's eyes. And those who persevere in their devotion he raises up to the life of meditation and on many occasions, he exalts them to the melody and celebrations of heaven. The song of the psalms chases away devils, stirs up the angels to help us; it drives out and destroys discontent and resentment in the soul and makes a peace between body and soul; it brings desire of heaven and contempt of earthly things. Indeed, this radiant book is a choice song in God's presence...[27]

Likewise, the three prologues written for the Wyclifitte Psalter, are not academic but a practical call for social action, identifying David's ten-stringed harp with the ten commandments, as Peter Lombard had done. Later, Joachim of Fiora, as an apocalyptic mystic, uses symbolism extensively, and one of his favorites in his *Liber Figurae* is the harp. This he identifies with the Psalter, its meaning being "that of the disciplined soul which has curbed its passions and achieved harmony by being attuned to God and transformed by love."[28] The theme is the same—that David had been a notorious sinner—now he is the archetypal moralist, as the primary prophet of God.

William Langland (c.1330–c.1400), in his radical reform poem, *Piers Plowman,* uses Rolle's commentary. He refers five times over to the central question of Psalm 15: 1, "Lord, who may dwell in your sanctuary? Who may live on your holy hill?" For the psalms command a pre-eminent place in Langland's moral and literary imagination. Indeed he may have been an official "psalmist" in

---

27. Richard Rolle, *The English Writings,* trans. and ed. Rosamund S. Allen (New York: Paulist Press, 1988), 66-67.
28. Quoted by Bernard McGinn, *The Calabrian Abbot, Joachim of Fiore in the History of Western Thought* (New York: Macmillan Publishing Company, 1985), 109.

the local church, whose task was to read the psalms in the church services.[29] At least 107 times over, he quotes the psalms in his poem. Covetousness and the abuse of usury are key indictments of the need of social reform, as voiced by Langland's biographical *persona,* Will the Dreamer. The triumphal moment of the poem is in Passus XVIII, when the reconciliation of Mercy and Peace, with Justice and Truth occurs. In the universe of *Piers Plowman,* psalms and psalm verses do not merely have the force of ideas, but the palpability of directives, words becoming commands. Psalm phrases can not only be sung, but they must be acted upon *with moral intent.* "Charity" becomes a Davidic figure, whose honest labor is the antitype of the negligence of priests, in the same way that Will's incessant questioning is the converse of their blithe disregard for the faithful.

Langland's most radical use of the Psalms occurs when he makes his key psalmic figure not a priest, but a humble plowman, Piers himself, who lives out the moral portraiture of Psalm 15.[30] Chaucer also uses the Plowman as the idealized Christian, an occupation of critical importance after the Black Death for the revival of the agricultural economy, and yet one which had been so socially despised previously.[31] His poverty is now a sign of humility and Christlikeness, and indeed of the anonymous Christian "whose life is hid in Christ with God." So he is the chief antitype of pride, the true inheritor of the legacy of Christ and his apostles, and the last best hope of the Church. He, too, fits idealistically into the portraiture of "the righteous one" of Psalm 15. But more broadly within this

---

29. E. T. Donaldson, *Piers Plowman: The C Text and Its Poet* (Yale Studies in English; New Haven: Yale University Press, 1949), 205-206.

30. M. P. Kuczynski, Prophetic Song: The Psalms as Moral Discourse in Late Medieval England (Philadelphia: University of Pennsylvania Press, 1995), 209.

31. Joseph Horrell, "Chaucer's Symbolic Plowman," in *Chaucer Criticism: the Canterbury Tales,* ed. Richard Schoek and Jerome Taylor (Notre Dame: University of Notre Dame Press, 1960), 84-97.

period, it is the psalmist David who is depicted as the wise prophet. A flyleaf of a fifteenth-century copy of Rolle's English *Psalter* quotes: *Inter sapientes sapientior est qui humilior est*. For it is in the meekness of David and of Christ, that wisdom is truly gained from humility.[32]

Langland and the Lollard writers attempt to break the commercial hold which the concept of "Meed" or "Reward" had developed over society at large in the fourteenth century. Thus those who are "Covetous," and exhibit a life of moral "Sloth" are severely condemned. In the anti-clericalism of the times, the priests too, are exposed and judged. Bluntly, they are told that they need to leave off misdirected worldly activity, to re-dedicate themselves to learning and living out the Psalter. For this is only done, both devotionally as well as intelligently, if they are to communicate its moral precepts to the faithful. For there are two kinds of rewards, observes the poet: that truly given by God, and that selfishly and carnally sought by the ungodly.[33] When the grace of the Holy Spirit distributes his gifts, we are told Piers the Plowman, his reeve, will receive payments. But meanwhile Piers has to fulfill the role as the purveyor of Grace, tilling the Truth with a team of four oxen, the four Evangelists. The ground is harrowed by horses, which are the four Doctors of the Church, and the two harrows used are the Old and New Testaments; the Barn to hold the harvest, is of course the Church. In paying one's debts, primarily one must forgive others their trespasses against one, in the light of needing a far greater forgiveness, in echoing the petition of the Lord's Prayer. Then when Conscience for all this moral challenge of life, to conquer pride, the dreamer awakes! The allegory is finished. For demanding reform of the society and the church, concludes with the need to reform one's self.

---

32. Kuczynski, *op. cit.*,215.
33. See Nicolette Zeeman, *Piers Plowman and the Medieval Discourse of Desire* (Cambridge: Cambridge University Press, 2006).

For Langland, as for the other reformers of the period, theology and morality are one. The Psalter is the moral manual of Christian living. The action of Jesus in overturning the money-changers and his condemnation of them as "hypocrites," is the same for this medieval period, as it still should be today. All commentators on Psalm 15 during the last two thousand years might rise up and ask us the same question: why do we always need more money for "Christian ministry"? Is not *being a Torah person*, the primary need?

8

# Becoming the People's Book
## *A Brief History of the Bible in China*

GLEN G. SCORGIE

The Third World is rising in the geo-political order of our time, and its most ascendant member is Mainland China.[1] It is a nation of over 1.3 billion people, with at least one hundred cities of over a million persons spreading out across its landscape. The country is developing at a spectacular rate. Futurists agree that the next one hundred years will almost certainly be China's century.

In *The Next Christendom: The Coming of Global Christianity*, historian Philip Jenkins has shown that the center of Christianity is also shifting from the West to the Third World. And David Aikman, among others, has recently sketched the remarkable growth of

---

1. This article is written in honor of Carl Armerding, principal of Regent College during my sojourn there as a student from 1979-81. My wife Kate and I will always be grateful for the way Carl (and Betsy) welcomed us into the stimulating Regent community. He has inspired us by his unusual gift for relationships, his love and respect for the biblical text, and his life-long devotion to its international dissemination. I am grateful for the editorial assistance of Regent College alum Alex Chow in the preparation of this article.

## THE BIBLE IN WORLD CHRISTIAN PERSPECTIVE

Christianity in China, despite official opposition, just as that nation is poised for global ascendancy.[2]

In God's providence, the dominant nations in recent centuries—Great Britain in the nineteenth, and the United States in the twentieth, have been known for their robust Christian faith. So inevitably the question comes up: Will the same pattern of providence extend into this new century? Will China's rising geo-political influence be matched by a vibrant Christian formation of its national soul?

To a large extent the answer will hinge on whether the Bible will ever become more than a suspicious foreign artifact, or a mere literary curiosity, in this officially-atheist nation. The answer will depend on whether the Bible becomes truly "the people's book" of the People's Republic of China. The struggle to make it such has been a long one, and it continues to this day.

**Obscure First Contacts**

No one knows how long ago the Bible was first introduced to Chinese civilization. Some argue that many biblical concepts, especially ones from Genesis 1-11, are already mysteriously present in the characters of Chinese writing.[3] Admittedly, certain of these characters do seemingly resonate—sometimes startlingly so—with biblical themes. Such parallels are intriguing, and from a pragmatic evangelistic perspective may serve well as discussion-starters with Chinese seekers today. But from a historical perspective most are problematic, since the ideograms of Chinese writing had already coalesced long before the Bible was written. Moreover, a lot of these interpretations of Chinese characters are highly contrived. None-

---

2. Philip Jenkins, *The Next Christendom* (Oxford/ New York: Oxford University Press, 2002); David Aikman, *Jesus in Beijing: How Christianity is Transforming China and Changing the Global Balance of Power* (Washington: Regnery, 2003).

3. For example, see C. H. Kang and Ethel Nelson, *The Discovery of Genesis: How the Truths of Genesis Were Found Hidden in the Chinese Language* (St. Louis: Concordia, 1979).

theless it is at least possible that some characters reflect a shared cultural memory of ancient Near Eastern stories, and, if original Chinese ideograms continued to evolve through more recent redactions, it is possible that some witness to early Christian influence as well.

There are intriguing suggestions that Christianity may have reached China as early as the end of the first century. There is an Indian tradition, for example, that the intrepid Apostle Thomas ventured as far as China.[4] Supplementary evidence, recently reported in the *Chinese People's Daily*, consists of tombstone carvings dated around 86 AD that depict Bible stories and Christian designs.[5] But of this stage of Sino-Christian contact we have very little conclusive evidence.

We do have firm data, however, from the eighth-century Nestorian Monument (or Tablet) discovered in the neighborhood of Xian.[6] In 635 AD Nestorian Christian Bishop Alopen, following the Silk Route of the traders, was welcomed by Chinese emperor Tai Zong to his Tang dynasty capital of Xian, now world-famous for its Terracotta soldiers. The mission-minded Bishop Alopen and his followers were loyal to the tradition of Nestorius, one-time patriarch of Constantinople, who was deposed at the Council of Ephesus for his defective understanding (or at least tragically clumsy articulation) of the relationship between the two natures of Christ.

Historian John Foster has commented suggestively that "when Christianity arrived in China, it was greeted as a 'scriptural

---

4. Kenneth Scott Latourette, *A History of Christian Missions in China* (New York: Macmillan, 1929), 46-51; for more recent assessments of the pre-Protestant years, see Ian Gillman and Hans-Joachim Klimkeit, *Christians in Asia Before 1500* (Ann Arbor: University of Michigan Press, 1999), 265-305, and Samuel Hugh Moffett, *A History of Christianity in Asia*, vol. 1. (Maryknoll, NY: Orbis, 1998), 287-323, 442-69.
5. Ted Olson, "Under the Sun," *Christianity Today* (7 Oct. 2002): 13.
6. Whenever possible, the modern names of the historic sites referenced are used.

religion.'"[7] It would be worth exploring further the basis for this assessment. How earnestly the Nestorians promoted the Bible is not known, but manuscripts from their time in China, as well as the aforementioned Nestorian Monument, reflect a Bible-based theology.[8] Under later persecution, however, the Nestorians greatly declined in number and influence. The remnant that survived after 845 AD consisted mainly of foreigners.[9]

## Catholic Beginnings

The first documented encounter of orthodox Christianity with China occurred during the Yuan (Mongol) dynasty. Around 1271 Venetian trader and adventurer Marco Polo returned from the Mongol court near Beijing with an invitation from occupying ruler Khubilai Khan for one hundred Christian teachers of science and religion. The opportunity was not seized by the European Christian leadership with any special alacrity or vision, and ended up being essentially squandered.

An intriguing artifact from this period is the Laurentian Bible, a badly-worn thirteenth-century Latin Vulgate version now preserved in a Venetian library. It was deposited there in the seventeenth century by Philippe Couplet, a Belgian Jesuit missionary to China, who claimed to have collected it from a Chinese home in the province of Jiangsu. This Bible, still wrapped in Chinese silk, had been, according to Couplet, a gift to a Chinese family from Marco Polo himself. This claim is improbable; a more likely explanation is

---

7. Quoted by R. S. Sugirtharajah, *The Bible and the Third World* (Cambridge: Cambridge University Press, 2001), 22.

8. P. Y. Saeki, *The Nestorian Documents and Relics of China* (Tokyo: Academy of Oriental Culture, 1937); John Foster, *The Church of the T'ang Dynasty* (London: SPCK, 1939), 43.

9. Latourette, 65.

that it was taken to China by the first Franciscans in the thirteenth or fourteenth century.[10]

The Franciscans' most prominent figure, John of Montecorvino, appears from 1294 onwards. Evidently he had some success in his missionary endeavors. Of special interest to us are extant reports from Montecorvino back to the Vatican, indicating that he had translated the New Testament and the Psalms into the court language of the Mongol rulers. By the end of the Mongol dynasty in 1368 there may have been up to one hundred thousand Christian converts. But what happened to this infant church during the subsequent Ming dynasty of nationalistic Han rulers is unknown. Once again, as with the Nestorians, the Christian faith and its sacred book failed to gain a permanent niche in Chinese culture and society.[11]

It was like starting all over from scratch in the post-Reformation era with a Jesuit initiative spearheaded by Francis Xavier. He died off-shore in 1552, but three decades later his successor Matteo Ricci managed to enter China, via Portuguese Macao, and by 1601 had reached the Middle Kingdom's command center of Beijing. His strategy was to appeal to the elite by consciously imitating the ways of Buddhist monks and Confucian scholars. But the Jesuits were shortly followed by Dominicans and Franciscans, and these orders were deeply suspicious of the contextualizing methods of Ricci and the Jesuits. In 1634, for example, Franciscan friars marched through the port city of Fuzhou, "holding crucifixes in the air, shouting that 'the idols and sects of China are false, and deceits by which the devil leads them to hell forever.'"[12] Conversions occurred, despite this internal row among the Roman Catholic missionaries them-

---

10. Boleslaw Szczesniak, "The Laurentian Bible of Marco Polo," *Journal of the American Oriental Society* 75, no. 3 (July-Sept. 1955): 173-79.
11. Latourette, 63-77.
12. Henry Chadwick and G. R. Evans, eds., *Atlas of the Christian Church* (Oxford: Equinox, 1987), 122.

selves, and by the start of the 1700s there may have been up to two hundred thousand Chinese Christians.

However, for the third consecutive time things ended in tragedy. The contextualizing approach espoused by the Jesuits was bluntly condemned by the Vatican, and the alternative—now empowered by Rome's endorsement—became a growing affront to the Chinese themselves. In 1724, the Qin (Manchu) emperor banned the Christian faith altogether as insulting to the Chinese, and the indigenous church was obliged to go more or less underground.

By this time there had been an active and continuous Roman Catholic presence in China for well over a century. During this span of time Ricci himself had not engaged in Bible translation, and it was not a high priority for his successors either. The sporadic attempts that were made were based, of course, on Jerome's Latin Vulgate, rather than on the original languages of the Bible. It was true that "selections, elegantly illustrated, were published,"[13] but the translation work was partial at best, and even more serious, kept virtually hidden from the general public and ordinary believers. It was a deliberate strategy of the Roman Catholic effort in China to keep the translated text of the Bible out of the public eye, lest it be misinterpreted by the uninformed. Yet the partial results of certain Roman Catholic translation efforts later came to the attention of Protestant Bible translation pioneers, and provided them with a valuable foundation for, and jump start on, their own work.

**Protestant Passion and Partisanship**

For all this it is remarkable how recent China's *substantive* exposure to the Bible has been.[14] And it is equally remarkable that

---

13. Marshall Broomhall, *The Bible in China* (London/ Philadelphia: China Inland Mission, 1934), 41.

14. For a general overview of this period, see Daniel Bays, ed., *Christianity in China: From the Eighteenth Century to the Present* (Stanford: Stanford University Press, 1996).

after millennia of Chinese inaccessibility to the Bible, *two* independent (and inevitably competing) versions should finally emerge within a single year of each other. The 1800s were the great century of Protestant missions, and the departure for India of English Baptist shoemaker William Carey in 1792 is often regarded as its launch. Protestants have always been characterized by confidence in the power of the unleashed Word of God, and their nineteenth-century missionaries could count on support from the great Bible societies of Britain, America and Scotland.¹⁵ Carey's prodigious language-learning, dictionary-writing, and international Bible publication operation in Serampore, near Calcutta, embodied this Protestant prioritization of the Scriptures. Joshua Marshman, one of Carey's first companions in the field, with the help of a Macao-born Armenian assistant by the name of John Lassar, took on the challenge of a Chinese Bible translation. It ended up taking sixteen years—all outside of China—but they finished in 1822.

Meanwhile, in 1807, a younger Englishman, Robert Morrison (1782-1834) of the London Missionary Society (LMS), became the first Protestant missionary to stand on China's soil.¹⁶ For years he shuttled seasonally between Guangzhou (formerly known as Canton) on the mainland and nearby Portuguese Macao, devoting himself, amid considerable opposition in both places, to language-learning and Bible translation. His Bible, completed in collaboration with William Milne, his friend and fellow LMS missionary in Malacca, was published by the British and Foreign Bible Society (BFBS) in 1823, just one year after Marshman's version came off the mission press at Serampore. The work of Morrison and Milne was recognized as superior, but there was one ticklish discrepancy between the two that would loom large for years to come. Marshman, who, like

---

15. See, for example, John Hykes, *The American Bible Society in China* (Shanghai: Commercial Press, 1915).
16. J. Barton Starr, "The Legacy of Robert Morrison." *International Bulletin of Missionary Research* (April 1998): 73-6.

Carey, was a Baptist, had chosen for "baptize" (*baptizo*) a Chinese phrase that suggested immersion explicitly (*jinxili*). Morrison, on the other hand, representing Presbyterians and Congregationalists, had predictably opted for the more non-committal term (*xili*). Thus the seeds of Protestant partisanship were sown early on.

Another translation issue that bedeviled Chinese reception of the Bible was establishing consensus on the best word for "God." This had already been controversial among Roman Catholics in the 17th and early 18th centuries,[17] and the Vatican's unwillingness to opt for the term most commonly used by the Chinese to designate deity led eventually to the banning of the foreign missionaries. The problem resurfaced again with the second generation of Protestant Bible translations, and most notably with the Delegates' Version of the New Testament, which was pushed through by British missionary Walter Medhurst, and published by the BFBS in 1852. Unlike Morrison before him, Medhurst preferred *Shangdi* to designate "God" (*elohim* or *theos*), which flew in the face of the more conservative Protestants' preference for the less value-laden, but also more generic, term *Shen*. At root the debate was over whether the existing Chinese conception of the supreme God, and the Chinese name for him, could be validated by Christians as the Triune God imperfectly understood. This so-called "Term Question" was never definitively resolved.[18] Bibles to this day are published using one term or the other.

---

17. The Chinese emperor, and the Jesuits who followed Ricci's contextualizing approach, favored the traditional Chinese designations of *Tian* (Heaven) and *Shangdi* (Supreme God) for the Christian God. But the Pope, like more conservative Catholic missionaries, was suspicious that these were links to unworthy conceptions of the divine. He ruled accordingly by insisting on a relative neologism: *Tian-zhu* (Lord of Heaven).

18. Irene Eber, "The Interminable Term Question," in *Bible in Modern China: The Literary and Intellectual Impact*, ed. Irene Eber and others (Sankt Augustin: Institut Monumenta Serica, 1999), 135-61.

## Discovering China's *Lingua Franca*

The Roman Catholic Bible translation efforts of the 17th and 18th centuries, and those of the earliest Protestant translators, like Marshman and Morrison, were all undertaken in the classical Chinese (high Wenli) or lower classical (easy Wenli) styles. These were the styles used in Chinese classics and favored by society's elite. Even the elegant *Delegates' Version*, an outstanding rendition for its time, and a product of what would now be called a "dynamic equivalence" approach to translation, was still published in the classical style.

To be fair to the translators, the classical styles (high and easy Wenli) were for a time the only styles they knew to exist. But Mandarin's scope and potential eventually dawned on them as they moved northward and then inland. By mid-century they understood that the nation's chief living tongue was something other than Wenli. Mandarin was the dialect of the expansive north, and its corresponding written characters were intelligible throughout most of the south as well. It was a relatively coarser vernacular distained by the more educated upper classes as mere *baihua* (plain speech), but the Protestant missionaries recognized it as the living language of the vast majority of Chinese. Today around 800 million Chinese speak Mandarin; it may be the most spoken language in the world.[19]

One of the remarkable features of Mandarin is that its written characters remain consistent even where different dialects of Chinese are spoken. Orally, for example, the Cantonese, Fukien, and Amoy dialects spoken by millions in southern China are virtually separate languages. Yet for the most part they share a common Chinese written script. As Bob Whyte explains, "For Chinese culture,

---

19. This is not to underestimate the significance of Bible translations for other minority language groups within the geographic boundaries of the People's Republic of China (for example, Tibetans, Mongolians, Manchurians, and numerous smaller tribes). For profiles of these groups, see Paul Hattaway, *Operation China: Introducing All the Peoples of China* (Pasadena: William Carey Library, 2000).

throughout its four-thousand-year-old history, the written language has provided a focus of unity through the use of ideograms in which phonetic elements are incidental. The same written character is used for all Chinese spoken dialects, with the result that people from the North and from the South can write to each other but may not be able to converse!"[20]

Evangelicals have always had a disposition that favored the populace over the elites, and probably in the back of their minds was the fact that the New Testament itself was written in *koine*, not classical, Greek. And so the first Mandarin translation of the full Bible, the *Nanking Version*, was finally published in 1856, a half-century after Morrison's arrival—during the infamous Opium Wars, and on the very eve of the Christian advance up China's great rivers and inland for the first time in centuries. Since the 1920s classical Chinese has been waning in significance. Only Mandarin Bible translations have received continuous attention and updates. It is definitely the language of the people and of the future.

**The Union Bible of 1919**

It was a source of embarrassment to Christian missionaries that throughout China many competing versions of the Bible were circulating, and sometimes colliding, to the detriment of the overall credibility of the faith.[21] In 1890 delegates to a national missionary summit in Shanghai agreed to unite behind a single new translation of the Bible. Creating consensus among highly-autonomous missionary types can be akin to herding cats, so the agreement reached was regarded as something of an ecumenical triumph. The resultant Mandarin-style *Union Version* (NT, 1905; full Bible, 1919) proved

---

20. Bob Whyte, *Unfinished Encounter: China and Christianity* (Glasgow: Collins, 1988), 97.

21. For a careful listing of these, see the excellent appendices to Jost Oliver Zetzsche, *The Bible in China: The History of the* Union Version (Sankt Augustin: Institut Monumenta Serica, 1999), 405-25.

enormously successful, and acquired a stature, both within China and among the worldwide Chinese Diaspora, similar to that enjoyed until recently by the King James Version in the English-speaking world. With characteristic prescience, Robert Morrison wrote back in 1819: "The duty of a translator of any book is two-fold; first, to comprehend accurately the sense, and to feel the spirit of the original work; and secondly, to express in his version faithfully, perspicuously, and idiomatically (and, if he can attain it, elegantly), the sense and spirit of the original."[22] To some extent the *Union Version* captured Morrison's ideals, even that of literary elegance. That continues to be something valued in Chinese culture, despite the Philistine impact of modern communications technology.

Parallel to the ongoing life of the *Union Version* have been other smaller-scale translation initiatives.[23] These include efforts to replicate the translation philosophies of a number of popular English versions and paraphrases.[24] It remains to be seen whether any of these will obtain a significant market share in China itself. The illegality of imported Bibles remains a huge obstacle. So far the *Union Version* retains a position from which it will be difficult to dislodge it.

One such initiative warrants brief mention. The *Union Version* translators had retreated from the bold dynamic (or, functional) equivalence philosophy of the *Delegates' Bible* to a more conservative formal equivalence approach.[25] Some observers, including linguist Eugene Nida of the American Bible Society, were concerned

---

22. Quoted by Broomhall, 12.
23. For example, the New Chinese Version (also known as the *Shengjing xinyiben*) of 1992 was produced by a committee of more than 30 Chinese translators from Hong Kong and elsewhere outside of China.
24. For example, *The Bible in Modern Chinese* (1956) follows *The NT in English* by J.B. Phillips; *The Contemporary Bible* (1979-93) follows the *Living Bible*; and the *Chinese New International Version* (ca 2000) follows the *NIV*.
25. For an explanation of these and related categories, see Glen Scorgie, Mark Strauss, and Steven Voth, eds., *The Challenge of Bible Translation* (Grand Rapids: Zondervan, 2003).

that this philosophy had diminished reader access to, and comprehension of, the meaning of the biblical text. Consequently Nida got involved in the production of a Chinese equivalent to the *Today's English Version* (1976). The resultant work, actually produced in New York, was called the *Today's Chinese Version* (1980). It was not accepted, as its creators hoped it would be, as a replacement for the *Union Version*. Instead, off-shore discussions, with United Bible Society involvement, began in Hong Kong, Taiwan and Singapore in 1983 about a very modest revision of the old *Union Version*. These led to a series of editorial updates of the text from 1986 onwards.[26]

Since 1919, the greatest challenge has not been translation but circulation. The distribution efforts of Christian organizations and churches have been considerable through the years. The American Bible Society claimed that in 1914 alone it had distributed almost two million Bibles or Bible portions distributed, and estimated that the total distribution in China (of all the Bible Societies) for that year was over six million.[27] Much of the practical impact of the Bible on China has been through the efforts of courageous, and often heroic, colporteurs who have worked their way along hostile paths and door-slamming streets and alley ways.

**Under Communism since 1949**

Since 1949, most aspects of Christian faith and practice, including Bible distribution and reading, have been squeezed by the officially-atheist and xenophobic Communist regime. The nature and intensity of this opposition has varied regionally and chronologically in "the new China," so that it has been difficult for outsiders to obtain an accurate picture of conditions at ground level. But no one doubts that the most difficult period was the terrible years of the Cultural

---

26. Zetzsche, 348-56.
27. Hykes, 2, 14.

Revolution (1966-76), when Red Guards confiscated Bibles and punished readers.

For awhile the critical need for replacement Bibles was addressed by Bible smugglers.[28] Eventually a measure of calm returned to China. Around 1987 the Amity Printing Press was established in Nanjing as an independent commercial operation with ties to the Three Self Patriotic Movement (TSPM). In cooperation with the United Bible Societies (UBS) it resumed printing of the old 1919 edition of the *Union Version*. A total of 46 million copies of Bibles and New Testaments have been printed by Amity Press since. In 2005, for example, 5.2 million Bibles and New Testaments were produced—3 million for Mainland China and 2.2 million for export.[29] It is still illegal to import Bibles into China, but David Neff, editor of *Christianity Today* recently claimed that "legal Bibles are not in short supply" in China today.[30]

Not all China observers agree.[31] The capacity of this one small press to serve the needs of the entire nation is questionable. And there are enormous distribution challenges. The Bible cannot be purchased in local bookstores or ordered on-line. Availability, and for the poorer classes affordability, remain serious obstacles.[32] The text of the *Union Version* is also becoming problematic. In 1980 the TSPM of the Protestant churches in China, along with the China Christian Council, was able to resume printing of the original 1919 edition of the *Union Version*, but still with the old non-simplified

---

28. In a daring provocation in 1981, the Open Doors organization attempted to smuggle a million Bibles into China (Whyte, 376-77).
29. "The Bible by Numbers: Change, Church and China" [doc. on-line]; available from http://www.biblesociety.org/wr_399/399_17.htm; accessed 27 Dec. 2006.
30. David Neff, "Chinese Puzzle," *Christianity Today* (March 2003): 9.
31. For example, Nora Lam, *The Battle for the Chinese Bible* (San Jose: China Today Books, 1997).
32. To address this latter problem, the United Bible Society helps to subsidize the cost of Bibles for Amity Press; see http:www.ubscp.org/index.php?option=com_content&task=view&id=12&Itemid=48; accessed 8 Jan 2007.

characters. It was not until 1989 that the full Bible was finally available in newer simplified characters and arranged in horizontal lines—in other words, that it finally adapted to the modern public's established reading expectations.[33]

In 1979 Ding Guangxun, the chairman of TSPM and president of Nanjing Union Theological Seminary (the flagship school of the registered church) initiated a committee process for an indigenous Chinese update of the 1919 *Union Version*. The progress of the committee was followed with interest, and it was clear that its work would be contextually-nuanced and independent of the work of the off-shore UBS translators. To the dismay of everyone anticipating this revision, it was inexplicably cancelled at the very end. One should not be considered paranoid if they suspect that this failure to publish may have a political explanation.[34] The bottom line is that while Mandarin continues to morph in a context of brisk social change, the *Union Version* has not received a complete revision in more than seventy-five years.

**Becoming the People's Bible**

Somewhat penitently Marshall Broomhall of the China Inland Mission dedicated his history of *The Bible in China* to the memory of "the goodly company of unknown Chinese scholars (who labored with the missionary-translators) and to the noble army of colporteurs whose names are in the Book of Life."[35] Back in 1934 he was aware of how easily the devout missionaries had overlooked the role of the Chinese themselves in the work of bringing the Bible to their own people.[36] Even in photographs from that time the Chinese workers often remained unnamed and unknown.

---

33. Zetzsche, 356-57.
34. Ibid., 357-61.
35. Broomhall, v.
36. Zetzsche, 137.

This slowly changed over time. Gradually the Chinese themselves gained more of a voice. But such unintentional prejudice at the individual level was matched by a widespread ideological disposition of suspicion toward the larger culture, and linguistic designations for God, of the Chinese people as a whole. This greatly complicated, and may continue to impede, the effective translation of the Bible and the contextualization of the Gospel for the Middle Kingdom.[37]

On the positive side, the nineteenth-century Protestant Bible translators' discovery of Mandarin, and their pioneering decision to use this "coarser" vernacular for their purposes, put Christianity at the forefront of all China's progressive trends toward education, literacy and a more egalitarian society. By a fortunate coincidence, 1919, the very year the Mandarin Union Version was published, was also the year the Chinese government announced a new literary epoch in which Mandarin should henceforth be used as a modern literary language.[38]

Even so, Harold Rattenbury, a Wesleyan Methodist missionary, noted on the occasion of the publication of the Mandarin *Union Version* that it was probably "the last and the greatest translation of the Scriptures where the burden of the work ultimately rests on foreigners." He went on to predict that "the final Chinese version will never come until we have Chinese scholars, deeply versed in the original tongues, masters also of Mandarin, translating into their own native tongue." That day may no longer be far off, but the work will need to be done by Chinese who are not under any government-imposed restrictions, or artificial pressures, in their deliberations.[39]

The world powers of the last two centuries have been recognizably Christian in their religious orientation. It remains to be seen whether

---

37. On the general principles involved, see Lamin Sanneh, *Translating the Message: The Missionary Impact on Culture* (Maryknoll, NY: Orbis, 1989).
38. Zetzsche, 332.
39. Carol Lee Hamrin, "A New Framework for Promoting Religious Freedom in China," *Brandywine Review of Faith & International Affairs* 3, no. 1 (Spring 2005): 3-10.

China's growing international clout will be matched by a broadening Christian influence on its national ethos and conduct. Another way to phrase this question is to ask: Will the Bible become truly the "people's book" of China? For it to become this will require sustained efforts in contextually-sensitive translation, creative (and courageous) initiatives in Bible distribution, and formational education in the truths and values of the Christian Scriptures. How China will use its broadening powers, for good or for evil, depends on whether China will be baptized into a biblical way of seeing and living life.[40] The world may anticipate great blessing when the God-breathed text of Scripture is seen through China's eyes, grasped by its imagination, and obeyed with all its fervent resolve.

---

40. Already the impact has been considerable; see Eber and others, eds., *Bible in Modern China: the Literary and Intellectual Impact*.

9

# What Evangelicals can Learn from the Benedictines

## LAUREL GASQUE & W. WARD GASQUE

What can Evangelical Christians learn from the vision and mission of the monks of the Order of Saint Benedict?
When we were students at a leading Evangelical seminary in the early sixties, the answer to this question would have been a quick "Not much, if anything!" The focus was rather on what we as Evangelical Protestants might have to teach them, namely, the pure gospel of God's free grace and justification by faith alone.
The fact was, however, scarcely anyone at a Protestant seminary in the 1960s knew anything about the Benedictines, or any of the other Catholic orders, for that matter. Actually, we knew next to nothing about the Roman Catholic Church, its practices, and teachings. What we thought we knew was centuries out of date, and even this was probably a caricature of mainstream Catholic doctrine and practice in an earlier age.
Our ignorance of Catholic teaching and practice was vividly brought home to us through our friendship with a brilliant young theologian we met at Basel University in academic year of 1966–67. Fred was a graduate of the Gregorian University and was pursuing

a second doctorate at Basel. He was by far the most impressive graduate student in the Faculty of Theology at the time. During the course of the year, Professor Heinrich Ott's *Englisches Kolloquium* tended to be dominated by a discussion of the ideas that our friend had brought with him from Rome, ideas that we subsequently learned were traceable to the Canadian theologian, Bernard Lonergan (1904–1984), whose works had not yet been translated from Latin so that Protestants could read them, rather than by the agenda of the professor.

As we discussed spiritual and theological matters with our friend and his wife (who, incidentally, had been on the staff of Young Life), it became clear that we agreed with them concerning the nature of the Christian faith and life in almost every detail. They talked like Evangelical Protestants, but the husband was a devout Roman Catholic.

One day as we were discussing matters such as conversion, regeneration, justification by faith, and the like, Ward commented: "This sounds awfully much like Evangelical Protestant doctrine to me! Are you sure that what you are saying really represents Catholic doctrine? This is very different from what I thought Catholics believed."

Fred responded by asking what I had read of Catholic theology. It dawned on me for the first time that almost everything I knew about Roman Catholic theology I had learned second hand, from Protestants—and rather reactionary Protestants at that. True, I had read a fair amount of classic theological texts written prior to the Reformation, and had even read excerpts from the canons of the Council of Trent (as interpreted by my Protestant mentors), but I had read next to nothing of modern Catholic theology. My contact with 20th century Catholic scholarship had been limited to reading the important commentaries and the burgeoning literature of Catholic biblical scholarship, most of which, I found, to my surprise, much more to my liking than the more liberal Protestant works.

So in Basel we began to read the work of contemporary Roman Catholic theologians, as well as the Bible scholars, including the documents coming out of the Second Vatican Council and the theological reference works influenced by Vatican II. And, sure enough, we found there a very different type of theology from what we had been led to expect, a theology surprisingly akin to the Evangelical theology that we had been taught.

That seems like ages ago. But it was the beginning of a change of attitude on our part concerning Catholics and Catholic theology. Since then, we have both read widely and fellowshipped broadly and have grown to see so much that is good about the Catholic tradition as well as contemporary Catholic Christians. As members of the (very) "Open" Brethren, we were taught that we should not separate ourselves from any of the good things that any of our brothers and sisters in Christ have to teach us, even if we disagree with them theologically concerning this or that doctrine. We gradually came to see that the oneness in Christ that we celebrated in our weekly meetings for worship included not only Protestants but also many who were convinced Roman Catholics. And so our faith and lives have been enriched enormously in more recent years as we have sat at the feet, so to speak, of Catholic as well as Protestant teachers, principally through their writings.

Today, much of the best of the Christian scholarship in biblical studies, moral theology, Christianity and culture, spiritual theology, and philosophy is being done by Roman Catholics. In fact, only in the area of Biblical studies have contemporary Evangelical scholars come close to matching the depth and breadth of Catholic scholarship. All of us have been the richer for what has been and is being done by our brothers and sisters in the Catholic Church.

However, this is not the area of our primary focus in this paper. Rather, we are looking at what we as Evangelicals can learn from the ideals and experiences of an important Catholic order, namely, the Order of Saint Benedict.

As one looks closely at the Catholic Church, it is obvious, at least to an outsider, that the most dynamic forces within the Church are its religious orders. The hierarchy may set certain parameters for doctrine and practice and sometimes act like they think they are *the* Church, but the orders provide the creativity and the energy for the Catholic mission. Even when you find laity who are outspoken in their faith and seek to live out the implications of their baptism and confirmation, you often find that they have a special relationship with one or other Catholic order.

We have come to the conclusion that the religious orders of the Catholic Church perform a similar function within Catholicism to that performed by the parachurch and mission societies within Evangelical Protestantism. Whatever church bureaucrats and some local clergy may think, the Evangelical parachurch movements are not only integral to the church but the source of much, if not most, of the creativity and energy within Evangelical Protestantism. Rather than saying that what the parachurch groups are doing should be done within "the church," Evangelical church leaders should seek to follow the example of the Catholic hierarchy and find ways of including and encouraging the vision and activities of the parachurch movements within the on-going life of both the congregations and the varied denominations. Those who seek to exclude them, do so to their own loss and to the detriment of their people.

Some years ago, Ward had occasion to reflect on what Evangelical Christians can learn from the Jesuits.[1] Here we have a very different, but also a very important, religious order. The Jesuits are a much more recent order than the Benedictines. They came on the scene a thousand years after the Order of Benedict, as a result of what came to be known as the Counter or Catholic Reformation.

---

1. "What We Can Learn About Higher Education from the Jesuits," in *Should God Get Tenure?*, ed. David W. Gill (Grand Rapids: Eerdmans, 1997), 179-194.

## WHAT EVANGELICALS CAN LEARN FROM THE BENEDICTINES

The Jesuits have been the longest lived, continuously active missionary society in Christendom. A careful study of the Jesuits has much to teach Protestants, especially those who are concerned with the Christian world mission and higher education.

Our reflections of what we can learn from the Benedictines arise out of our shared experience at the Institute for Ecumenical and Cultural Research (IECR) on the campus of Saint John's University in Collegeville, Minnesota, where we spent five months in 1995.

Saint John's University is a small Catholic university, owned and operated by a community of Benedictine monks. Today, they number just over 200. They also own and operate a theological seminary, a prep school, and a major publication company (Liturgical Press) which is the source of much good literature related to the renewal of both biblical studies and the liturgy in the American Catholic Church.

The Institute for Ecumenical and Cultural Research was founded in 1967 by Father Kilian McDonnell, a Benedictine monk who had been sent by the abbot to Germany to do a doctorate in Protestant theology. Father McDonnell is well-known as an authority on Evangelical and Pentecostal Protestantism and as a leader in the Catholic charismatic movement. The idea of the Institute (whose name was recently changed to The Collegeville Institute for Ecumenical and Cultural Research) is to bring a small number of Christian scholars together in the interest of sharing common concerns and commitments.

The program is very simple: each of the ten scholars brings a writing project. During the course of the year or semester, each participant presents seminar paper for feedback from colleagues and also a public lecture related to the research topic. Resident scholars and their families are warmly welcomed into the community, in keeping with the Benedictine ideal of receiving every person as one who receives Christ, and are encouraged to talk with one another as the occasion arises. As friendships develop, one might be invited to give a lecture in a class at Saint John's University, Saint John's

Seminary, or at its sister institution, the College of Saint Benedict; and the ten guests generally become friends.

In addition to the provision of attractive and comfortably furnished apartments in a beautiful setting overlooking a small lake, which were, along with the Abbey Church and the Alcuin Library, designed by Marcel Breuer the distinguished Bauhaus architect who also designed the Princeton Institute for Advanced Study, scholars are provided with a spacious study in the bowels of the Alcuin Library and faculty status, including free access to the Internet and Interlibrary Loan services. One pays a very modest rent for housing.

Our major projects for the time we were in Collegeville were, for Ward, research on the religious roots of American philanthropy, and, for Laurel, on the Christian stake in the arts and an essay on the work of Canadian artist, Terry Black. All in all, it was a very enriching experience for us both. Along the way, we became very appreciative of the vision and practice of the Benedictine monks, whose guests we were

**Common Elements Shared by Evangelicals and Benedictines**

To begin with, we might ask: What are some of the common elements shared by Evangelical Christians and Benedictine Monks? First and fundamental is *a common desire to know God*. The whole purpose of becoming a monk is to give oneself unreservedly to the contemplation of God, to turn one's back on sin and the world, and to live a life of prayer and worship. One's whole life is focused on knowing and loving God, thus preparing for eternal blessedness. Evangelical Christians have been ushered by conversion into fellowship with the Triune God and have sensed a dual call "to know him and to make him known." Through prayer and Bible study, they seek to be changed into the likeness of the One whose glory they contemplate (2 Cor. 3:18).

## WHAT EVANGELICALS CAN LEARN FROM THE BENEDICTINES

Both Evangelicals and Benedictines seek to give the Scriptures a central place in their lives, though the way the Scriptures are mediated to them is quite different. Evangelicals read and study the Bible individually and in small groups, and they value its proclamation and teaching from their pulpits. Benedictines listen to the reading of Scripture in their celebration of the divine office, nowadays four times each day, and they read the Bible meditatively in their personal devotions. Both are "people of the Book," though Evangelicals tend to think of the Bible as a textbook and the Benedictines, as a hymn and prayer book.

Both groups place a strong emphasis upon shared religious experience. Although Evangelicals have often gone in for mass meetings, it is the small, intimate group that has always been at the heart of Evangelical piety—whether house churches, *collegia pietatis et biblica*, class meetings, prayer and Bible study groups, or other meetings for fellowship. Occasionally, small groups of Evangelicals have chosen to live in community, but this has not been the common pattern. Benedictines, however, have chosen to live and worship together as a community, to literally share "all things in common."

Both Benedictines and Evangelicals have professed to turn their backs on the world in order to follow Christ. They have consciously rejected the world's values and attractions that lead one away from, rather than toward, the vision of God. Although at various times in their history, both have been influenced by the world more than they have realized, the fundamental focus of each is otherworldly.

Finally, both Evangelicals and Benedictines have been in the forefront of the church's mission to the world. Evangelicals are by definition concerned to share the "Good News" to the world, though this has not always been as central as it should be. The mission of the Order of Saint Benedict has been to create communities of those whose greatest desire is to love and know God, but in the process these little communities of monks (and their corresponding communities of nuns) have been the means of transforming peoples and cultures all around the world by the message of "Good News."

Indeed, at various historical periods, the Benedictines have almost single-handedly kept the Christian world mission alive.

**Differences**

Thus it is clear that there are many things that Evangelicals and Benedictines share in common. There are obvious differences, however, most of them related to the call to monastic life. Benedictine monks take vows of stability, fidelity to monastic life, and obedience. They commit themselves to live in a particular place according to the guidelines of the *Rule of Saint Benedict*. When they join the community, the monks turn their backs on the accumulation of individual wealth and on normal family life. Evangelical Protestants live out their lay and clerical vocations within the context of general society. While they are sometimes poor, they do not feel themselves called to this state. Sometimes they have interpreted financial success as a sign of God's blessing; rarely have they considered it as a snare. And they tend to think in terms of married life as the norm for all, including those who are called to a life of service in, or on behalf of, the church.

The Benedictine monks have been for a millennium and a half a major force in preserving the great traditions of Western culture, its literature and its learning. This has not been their primary aim, but simply a by-product of their vocation to love and worship God. Although St. Benedict of Nursia (c. AD 480 – c. AD 550) founded no order, the humane Rule drawn up in about AD 540 became the generally accepted directive for spiritual and administrative life of Western monasticism. It remains to this day one of the most remarkable working documents in the whole history of Western civilization, still informing living communities of men and women, monks and nuns, and lay men and women around the world.

St. Benedict's Rule and its serviceable monasticism went hand in hand with St. Boniface's great missionary endeavor to evangelize Germany in the eighth century. And though many reforms and orders, such as Cluny, the Cistericians and Carthusians, followed in later centuries and evolved from the Benedictine model, the Rule long was the single link between many autonomous abbeys in the West. The Reformation, and later the French Revolution, powerfully suppressed Benedictine life, but did not eradicate it. Since the early nineteenth century there has been a remarkable resurgence of Benedictine foundations, especially in Europe and North America.

The impact of Evangelicals on culture has been primarily in philanthropic and social institutions in the countries of the Protestant Reformation and in North America, especially the USA. For a time, many major academic institutions in the USA were Evangelical, but this lasted for but a short period and traces of their Evangelical heritage have almost entirely disappeared. Evangelicalism never made great, lasting impact on mainstream Western culture, nor any significant contribution to the preservation of culture. Rather, it has tended to be molded by the varied trends of contemporary, secular culture.

Perhaps the biggest ideological difference between Evangelicals and Benedictines lies in attitudes toward community. With very few exceptions, Evangelicals are radical individualists. Whether considering salvation or ethics, church or society, education or politics, it is the individual that counts. Salvation is a simply personal matter between you and your God. The church is a place to go to be blessed, and perhaps to serve, but if something happens to displease you, you quickly move to the church down the street or across town. Christian community and the sacraments have all too often been dispensable to Evangelical Christians. Today, there is an ever-growing number of people who describe themselves as Evangelical or "born again" Christians but who rarely attend any church and have no communal involvement with other believers.[2] Even those who attend church

---

2. George Barna's *Revolution* (Wheaton: Tyndale House Publishers, 2005) has celebrated this spiritually self-sufficient individualism as a mark of strength and pathway of the future shape of Christianity.

regularly and are involved in a small group rarely have a deep and long-term commitment to either. Nothing could differ more from the Benedictine vision.

But what are some of the lessons that the Benedictine vision and experience have to teach us as Evangelicals? How can we learn from their collective wisdom?

**Lessons to be Learned**

Outstanding among the lessons that we hyperactive and frequently pragmatic Evangelicals need to learn from the Benedictines is *the importance of worship*. At the heart of the biblical faith is the call to worship God.

"Hear, O Israel: The LORD our God is one LORD; and you shall love the LORD your God with all your heart, and with all your soul, and with all your might" (Deut 6:4–5).

Throughout the Bible, God calls his people first to worship him and then to serve him in the world. God is our Creator and therefore deserving of our adoration; but he is also our Saviour and thus deserving of our gratitude. Paul's prayer for the churches is that all may "know the love of Christ which surpasses knowledge" and that they "may be filled with all the fullness of God" (Eph 3:19). Therefore, the life of faith must be a life dedicated to worship.

The motto of the Benedictines is *ora et labora*, "pray and work", in that order. The life of a Benedictine monk is anything but idle, since there is work to be done for the kingdom of God, and there is work to be done that is necessitated by the needs of the community. But it is the primacy of worship that gives a sense of rhythm to a monk's life.

Some years ago, an Anglican friend observed that he did not get nearly as much work done within the context of an American theological school as he did in other institutions where he had worked where daily prayers were an integral part of community life. He missed the regular times of communal worship, which tended to give order and discipline to his life.

Even though taking time out of one's work schedule to worship strikes the modern Protestant as inefficient (as the peripheral place that worship plays in the life of nearly all Evangelical educational institutions known to us bears all too eloquent witness) the facts actually tend to point in the opposite direction. As Patrick Henry, the former executive director of the IECR (himself a Protestant) once remarked, the disciplines of the *opus dei*—the daily scheduled times of prayers, praise, listening to the Word of God, and sharing in the liturgy —provide a pattern for one's work that seems to help you get more done than otherwise might be the case. Times of prayer give sanctity to one's everyday life, with prayer and work going together like hand and glove. The massive scholarship and creative work coming out of Catholic communities, in contrast to the intellectual and academic paucity of Evangelical educational institutions, seem to demonstrate this.

Truth in a Benedictine abbey is not just intellectualized and historicized. It is painfully and joyously lived. Whether monks feel like it or not, whether they are emotionally up or down, happy with each other or not, they come together several times a day to pray, literally facing one another. As pilgrims they read and sing through the Psalms together monthly, and they share most of the rest of the Scripture together annually. The weaving together worship and work is a matter for all days and for all seasons. Worshipping together several times a day doesn't interrupt their day. It isn't impractical. It gives the wisdom and strength for long-term commitments.

A second value that we Evangelicals need to learn from the Benedictines is *the value of listening. The Rule of Saint Benedict* begins with the words: "Listen carefully, my son, to the master's instructions, and attend to them with the ear of your heart. This is advice from a father who loves you; welcome it, and faithfully put it into practice" (Prologue 1). A few paragraphs on, the Prologue to the Rule reads: "What, dear brothers, is more delightful than this voice of the Lord calling to us? See how the Lord in his love shows us the way of life. Clothed then with faith and the performance of good works, let us set out on this way, with the Gospel for our guide, that we may deserve to see him who has called us to his kingdom" (Prologue 19-21).

As Jean Leclercq pointed out, the content of monastic culture is both symbolized and synthesized by two words: grammar and spirituality. "On the one hand, learning is necessary if one is to approach God and to express what is perceived of Him; on the other hand, literature must be continually transcended and elevated in the striving to attain eternal life."[3]

During most of their history, Benedictine monks have been extremely literate individuals. They have learned their grammar well. They have immersed themselves in the Scripture, the writings of the Fathers, and in the classical literature of Greece and Rome. Indeed, they have preserved these three great literary traditions that represent the mainstays of Western civilization.

However, the study of grammar, the reading and copying of ancient texts, the preservation of literary forms and conventions were by no means ends in themselves. Rather, they were means of grace, instruments used in the pursuit of God. To participate meaningfully in the liturgy, one needed to be literate. In order to understand God's word, one needed to be able to read it. In order to learn to interpret the Bible properly, one needed to be familiar with the expositions of those who have listened to its teaching most carefully. In order to pass on the faith to the next generation, one needs to master the arts of writing and speaking well. Hence, reading is fundamental to the spiritual life, and it is this that monks have spent most of their lives doing, to our great benefit.

---

3. Jean Leclercq, *The Love of Learning and the Desire for God* (ET, New York: Fordham University Press, 1962), 57.

But the monastic tradition of reading is not the modern experience of reading. The technological changes in the West subsequent to the Gutenberg revolution have been a decidedly mixed blessing. We have access to so much more literature—more than 276,000 new books published last year in North America alone.[4] We read faster, and silently, but we remember very little of what we read. The accent is on quantity rather than quality. The art of meditation, which has been the precious possession of humankind almost from the beginning, has been all but lost in our culture. And with the coming of the Internet, hailed by some as the most important breakthrough in the history of human culture but put in its place by one of its most celebrated engineers as "silicon snake oil,"[5] matters get much worse. The art of writing, already suffering greatly from the effects of television, risks extinction by the culture of techno-babble.

Without attempting to persuade you to log-off the Internet, may we at least remind you of the monastic practice of *lectio*?[6] While the emphasis in the scholastic tradition was upon the study of texts for their own sake, the focus here is on the benefits that the reader derives personally from reading. That is to say, the accent is upon "listening" to the text being read, to "hear" what wisdom the writer has to offer, in short, to make progress along the pathway toward perfection.

In the scholastic tradition, *lectio* is linked to the *quaestio* (searching inquiry) and *disputatio* (debate, discussion), while in the

---

4. Jim Milliot, "On-Demand Titles Drive Jump in Book Output," *Publishers Weekly*, on-line (5/28/2008). When on-demand and short run books are added, the figure jumps to 411,000+ new titles and editions! It is not clear whether this includes titles that are only published as e-books.

5. Clifford Stoll, *Silicon Snake Oil: Second Thoughts on the Information Highway* (New York: Anchor/Doubleday, 1996); and *High Tech Heretic* (New York: Anchor/Doubleday, 2000).

6. *Lectio* is Latin for "reading" in the sense of reading the Scriptures and other uplifting Christian literature in a prayerful, thoughtful manner that is intended to lead one into a deeper fellowship with God.

monastic tradition it is oriented toward the *meditatio* (pondering thoughtfully) and the *oratio* (prayer). The goal of the first is "science and knowledge; of the second, wisdom and appreciation."[7]

As has been frequently pointed out, all reading prior to the invention of the printing press was reading aloud. In antiquity, one read with the ear as well as with the eye. The effect is a much better memory of what has been read than is currently the case in our contemporary culture. Memorization was then a natural feature of everyday life.

Thus reading (*lectio*) in the monastic tradition leads naturally to meditation (*meditatio*), the repeated mastication of texts as a means of spiritual nourishment. To read and to mediate on biblical and patristic texts is to ruminate, to assimilate the full meaning into one's heart and mind, to chew upon its thought until it releases its full flavor into one's soul. Thus, reading becomes something like a prayer and "engages the whole person in whom the Scripture takes root, later on to bear fruit."[8]

When we read the medieval monastic expositions, it strikes us as amazing that the authors are able to quote text after text of Scripture and other writings, extensively and accurately, quite apart from access to modern technologies such as the printed and electronic concordances that we depend upon in our day. And without offering detailed proof at the moment, let us say that the power of the interpretative imagination, the grasp of the contours of the theology of the Old and New Testaments, and the insight into God's self-revelation that these medieval monks demonstrate has much to teach the modern Protestant, whether Evangelical or Liberal. What we learned in seminary was, in this regard, far off the mark.

C.S. Lewis has been frequently quoted as proposing that one should read two old books for every one new book, as a way of

---

7. Leclercq, *op cit.*, 78.
8. *Ibid.*, 79.

coping with the ever-increasing flow of books from the printing press.[9] Perhaps we should adapt this to the new era by suggesting that one should meditate for an hour on a text that has already been proved to be wisdom before we spend an hour sorting through our E-mail!

The Benedictine habit of listening has another side to it. It is not simply a question of listening to the wisdom of the past—whether from Scripture itself, the fathers who have expounded the Holy Scriptures, the Roman and Greek authors who provide one with models of clear thinking and good expression, the liturgy, and the instruction of one's superiors—it also includes a willingness to listen to each member of the community.

A Benedictine monastery is set up as a school for those who desire to follow Christ in community with others. Structured like an old-fashioned family, in which the abbot as the *pater familias* has the authority to command absolute obedience, the Benedictine monastery is actually a very democratic community. The monks of Saint John's as a community, for example, own the university, and the prep school, and the publishing company, and the varied educational enterprises arising from their common life together. The Board of the university is an advisory board, appointed by the monks and reporting to the monks, concerned with giving guidance to the operation of the university and, above all, with fund raising. However, all major decisions are made by the plenary body of the monks. The abbot is elected by the monks, and it is an open secret

---

9. In his introduction to the new translation of Athanasius' essay *On the Incarnation* by 'A Religious of C. S. M. V.' [The Community of St Mary the Virgin in Wantage, England], [=Sister Penelope Lawson] (London: Centenary Press, 1944; New York: Macmillan, 1946). Published in a 2nd ed. by Mowbray (London, 1953); and as *St. Athanasius, On the Incarnation* (Crestwood: St. Vladimir's Orthodox Theological Seminary, 1982). What C. S. Lewis actually wrote was: "It is a good rule, after reading a new book, never to allow yourself another new one till you have read an old one in between. If that is too much for you, you should at least read one old one to every three new ones." (St. Vladimir's edition, 4.)

that they never elect anyone to be abbot who is thought to desire the job.

*The Rule of Saint Benedict* has this to say:

> As often as anything important is to be done in the monastery, the abbot shall call the whole community together and himself explain what the business is; and after hearing the advice of the brothers, let him ponder it and follow what he judges the wiser course. The reason why we have said all should be called for counsel is that the Lord often reveals what is better to the younger. (*RSB* 3:1-3).

It goes on to say:

> If less important business of the monastery is to be transacted, [the abbot] shall take counsel with the seniors only (3:12).

It is important, then, to listen to everyone in the community, young and old, inexperienced and experienced. Each brings gifts to the table, and each has positive wisdom to contribute. Therefore, each member of the community must be taken seriously.

It is perhaps significant to note that as the monks process into the Abbey Church they first bow individually to the altar and then to one another. First, they honor God; and then they honor one another. "This, then," writes Benedict, "is the good zeal which monks must foster with fervent love: they should each try to be the first to show respect to the other (Rom 12:10), supporting with the greatest patience one another's weaknesses of body or behavior, and earnestly competing in obedience to one another. No one is to pursue what he judges better for himself, but, instead, what he judges better for someone else. To their fellow monks they show the pure love of brothers; to God, loving fear; to their abbot, unfeigned and humble love" (72:3-10).

A third important cultural value of the Benedictines is *hospitality*. Each visitor to a monastery is to be received as one would receive Christ, who will himself say on the Day of Judgment: "I was a stranger and you welcomed me" [Matt 25:35] (53:1). Rather than delegate the reception of guests to underlings, the abbot or other superior leads the way in welcoming the visitor "with all the courtesy of love" (53:3). There are well-furnished guest quarters in every monastery (53:21-22). The guests join the abbot at his table, and the abbot is free to break a fast in order to entertain the visitors (53:10). The Rule legislates: "Great care and concern are to be shown in receiving poor people and pilgrims, because in them more particularly Christ is received" (53:15a). It is assumed that the rich will be held in respect in any event (53:15b).

In terms of our experience, we have been as warmly received by the monks of Saint John's and the sisters of the nearby College of Saint Benedict as anywhere we have ever been. They went out of their way to make us feel at home, extending a welcome to Laurel's mother who joined us for the duration of our sojourn and led her first Bible study at the age of 77. We were welcomed on campus at every turn, offered the right hand of fellowship at the various times of worship, invited to dinner with the abbot on two occasions, encouraged to eat regularly with the theological students and faculty, bidden to two special receptions in our honor, and offered every service available on campus. On each occasion, the reception, dinner, or event was done with style. The monks are not rich in this world's goods, nor are Saint John's and Saint Ben's especially well endowed colleges; but both the monks and the sisters are extremely generous and lavish in the care with which they seek to honor their guests.

We have also been warmly welcomed in Evangelical communities as well, but we have noticed a trend in recent years, at least in North America, of moving away from the valuing of hospitality. Tea and coffee in a Styrofoam cup, store-bought cookies or a sticky bun on a paper plate are all too often the rule of the day. Students on work-study are sent to the airport to pick up visitors; alternatively, guests have to make their own way to campus the best way they can. Frequently, the president or the dean is too busy with more important things than to take time to welcome guests. If you ask people not to go to any special trouble, that's just what they do. What a contrast to the Benedictine tradition! We seem to remember a time when hospitality was a more valuable currency in the Evangelical community. We need to reclaim this lost heritage.

Benedictines seem to *revel in human diversity and* allow full scope to *the unique gifts of each member of the community.* In contrast to some of the early and later monastic rules, the Rule of Saint Benedict is a very practical document that contains a lot of down-to-earth wisdom for living in community. It is not a strenuous rule at all. Benedict calls it "a little rule for beginners" (73:8). He realizes that people often fail to live up to their ideals; indeed, he exhorts the abbot to "distrust his own frailty" (64:13). He is concerned to help the weak and therefore urges the abbot to "so regulate and arrange all matters that souls may be saved and the brothers may go about their activities without justifiable grumbling."

In electing the abbot, the community should look for one of their number who is set apart by his "goodness of life and wisdom in teaching..., even if he is the last in community rank" (64:2). "Once in office, the abbot must keep constantly in mind the nature of the burden he has received and remember to whom he will have to give an account of his stewardship [Luke 16:2] (64:7). "His goal must be profit for the monks, not preeminence for himself" (64:8). The abbot needs to be "learned in the divine law" (64:9a), but he must also be "chaste, temperate and merciful" (64:9b). "He must hate faults but love the brothers" (64:10). And when he must mete out punishment, "he should use prudence and avoid extremes; otherwise, by rubbing too hard to remove the rust, he may break the vessel" (64:12). The abbot should "strive to be loved rather than feared" (64:15). Above all, his leadership of the community should be characterized by "discretion, the mother of virtues" (64:19a). His goal is to "so arrange everything [so] that the strong have something to yearn for and the weak nothing to run from" (64:19b).

## WHAT EVANGELICALS CAN LEARN FROM THE BENEDICTINES

A Benedictine monastery is "a school for the Lord's service" (Prologue 45). Thus the Rule contains "nothing harsh, nothing burdensome" (Prologue 46). If there are aspects of the commitment to a Benedictine community and its discipline that seem a little strict to the natural man, we should recognize that "the road that leads to salvation" is only "bound to be narrow at the outset. But as we progress in this way of life and in faith, we shall run on the path of God's commandments, our hearts overflowing with the inexpressible delight of love" (Prologue 47-49).

There is a place within the Benedictine community for everyone called to follow Christ in this way: young and old, rich and poor, educated and uneducated, clerics and laity (37, 58-62). And there is work for all: manual labor and teaching, farming and artistry, domestic work and administration. We have observed this at Saint John's and Saint Ben's: in contrast to the very pragmatic and economically stripped-down curricula and extra-curricular activities of many Evangelical colleges, the arts are celebrated on both campuses. There are sculptures, paintings and prints, studios, pottery kilns, three radio stations (National Public Radio began at Saint John's as a result of the vision of a monk), aesthetically pleasing buildings designed to last for centuries rather than decades. There was a novelist in residence when we were there, along with poets and other writers and representatives of the musical and dramatic arts. Music is as important a part of the liturgy as the spoken word, and Saint John's Abbey has been a center of the liturgical renewal in the Catholic Church since the early days of Vatican II. The monks of SJU must face the financial realities of other independent educational institutions; nevertheless, they seem to have avoided the blandness of many Evangelical institutions.

A comment that he have heard more than once is this: Once the monks have committed themselves to the demands of their vocation, namely, a life of celibacy and obedience (poverty is not explicitly mentioned as a commitment), and a rather unusual dress code, they seem to become the freest people in the world. The men that we have met are real characters. There seems to be no attempt to force them into some type of conformity. They are united in their pursuit of God and in commitment to a particular place and the demands of their vocation. Otherwise, they seem the freest of the Lord's free agents. The same can be said of the sisters that we met.

Kathleen Norris, the American Protestant poet and Benedictine oblate, has this to say in her bestselling book, *Dakota: A Spiritual Geography*: "Monasteries are full of people who feel free to be themselves, often to the point of eccentricity. (An abbot once said to me, 'If there is any such thing as a 'typical' monk, we sure don't have any here.') A monastery is cohesive; it is not a schismatic society that survives by expelling those who don't fit into a mold. The differences might be summed up in two versions of heaven I once heard from a Benedictine nun: in one, heaven is full of people you love, and in the other, heaven is where you love everyone who is there."[10] Monks are preparing themselves for heaven, so they attempt to establish a community that is made up of the varied types of people who will be there.

The life-style of the Benedictine monks is marked by *the beauty of simplicity*. They have left all to follow Christ, but what they have given up has freed them to devote themselves to their true calling. They don't have to spend time paying bills, washing cars, commuting to work, thinning out their wardrobes, finding room in their closets for their shoes, cleaning out the garage, pleasing a spouse, raising kids, filling out income tax forms, going to the dry cleaners, cooking (unless that is their job in the monastery), keeping an eye on the stock market, worrying about falling real estate values, and the like. Like the members of the Jerusalem church, they possess "all things in common" (Acts 2:44) "so that no one presumes to call anything his own" ([Acts 4:32], Rule 33:6).

---

10. (Boston: Houghton Mifflin/Mariner Books, 1993), 115.

Rather, their life is given over to a combination of *worship and work*. Their communal day begins with morning prayers at 7:00 am. Then, there is a mid-day prayer service at noon, followed by mass at 5:00 pm and vespers at 7:00 pm. In between these services they do their work. If they are called to scholarship and teaching, that is what they do. But some are called to carpentry work—they make much of their own, beautifully designed furniture for the campus; others, to the management of the various enterprises, including their own food services, buildings and grounds operations, printing press and publishing company, and fire department. They used to raise their own food, but that is no longer cost effective. In theory, each monk is doing what he seems best suited to do. As far as we can tell, the system works.

A sixth characteristic of the life of the Benedictine monks is their *sense of place*. They have not only responded to the Lord's call to seek his face as a life's goal, but they have also committed themselves to a place. They have joined a monastery, in a specific location; in the case of the monks of Saint John's, it is Collegeville, Minnesota, miles away from nowhere (especially when they first arrived there in 1858!). But this sense of rootedness gives the monks stability in their lives, similar to the framework provided by the *opus dei*.

Kathleen Norris observes many aspects of Benedictine life that contrast eccentrically with current cultural values and yet seem to contain the seed of health and healing that contemporary society needs. "Benedictines represent continuity...." [11]

A final quality of Benedictine life that we have come to appreciate is *the value of tradition*. The Benedictines are conscious of being heirs to a long tradition. When the Great Schism took place between the Eastern and Western Churches in 1054, the Benedictines were 500 years old. When Martin Luther nailed his 95 theses on the

---

11.   *Op. cit.*, 8

door of the *Schlosskirche* at Wittenberg in 1517, the Benedictine movement was nearly a thousand years old.

By contrast, Evangelicalism is a relatively new movement. Whether you trace its origins to the Protestant Reformation in the 16th century or to the Wesleyan revivalism of the 18th century or to the Evangelical wing within the Anglican Church or to American revivalism of 19th century, it does not have a very long history. Furthermore, most Evangelicals are ignorant of the history of their own tradition (with the exception of a broadening group of historical specialists). The old timers tend to think of the hymns of Fanny Crosby as "the old hymns of the faith," and the younger members of the movement give the same place of honor to Graham Kendrick.

Jaroslav Pelikan defines "tradition" as "the living faith of the dead" and "traditionalism" as "the dead faith of the living."[12] Evangelicals actually have a glorious tradition, as our good friend Ian S. Rennie never tires of reminding us. But we are generally too active, or, perhaps, too pragmatically oriented, to stop to celebrate it.

However, the Benedictines celebrate their long tradition daily. First, there is the wonderful Rule that so clearly and helpfully articulates the spiritual and cultural values of their community. There is simply nothing quite like this in the Evangelical tradition. Then, there are the liturgies of the set periods of daily worship. The reading and singing of the Psalms pushes back their roots another thousand years, the Gospel and Epistle link them with the Christian community of the first century, the daily mass connects them with the second century, the creeds and hymns with the church down through the subsequent centuries right up to the present day.

When we have been with the Benedictine monks, we have had a similar feeling to what we felt when we attended the Bar Mitzvah of the son of a messianic Jewish friend of ours. What a wonderful

---

12. Jaroslav Pelikan, *Vindication of Tradition* (New Haven: Yale University Press, 1984), 65.

heritage! Many of the churches we have attended over the years seem to have little interest in their historical roots. Evangelicals tend to miss the difference between tradition and traditionalism. And "having no root," Evangelical movements have a tendency to spring up quickly but also to quickly "wither away" (Mark 4:6).

Whether we admit it or not, we Evangelicals need the Benedictines a lot more than they need us. They provide us with an object lesson in tradition and community, an example of spiritual salt that both preserves and provides flavor. The Benedictines teach us that we don't have to be tyrannized by the immediate or by short-term goals and agenda that are pressed upon us. Benedictines take the long view. They are thinking not in terms of AD 2000 but rather AD 3000. They have had bad days and good days. Their monasteries have been destroyed by invasions, revolutions, and alleged reforms; but they have endured. And they are in for the long haul. They may soon die and be buried among the hundreds of uniform tombstones of their colleagues, but their places will be taken by others, who will continue to seek the face of God daily and, in the process, perhaps change the world.

Two particular projects at Saint John's Abbey that reflect this type of judgment are the Collegeville Institute and The Hill Monastic Manuscript Library. Neither one of these endeavors has a short-term return, to use the terminology of economics. They both, however, have long-term kingdom value.

The CIECR, in which we have participated, is more than a forum to share nice little ideas about the church. Rather, it is a community where Christian scholars from different traditions live together and meet regularly, in similar fashion to the monks. Resident scholars actually get to know each other, not just each other's theological positions and opinions, although they do come to know these as well. A by-product of our experience is the incremental advancement of Christian unity.

Even more integral to Benedictine tradition is The Hill Monastic Manuscript Library, the most important library for the study of medieval manuscripts in the world. Monks are not sitting around and copying these manuscripts today, but they are out scouting for them. So far more than 90,000 medieval manuscripts have been photographed. And they are contributing to the future of illuminated manuscripts by commissioning the production of the magnificent *Saint John's Bible*, described as 'A Bible for Our Time'.

Both scholars and ordinary folk from near and far can and do come to investigate these resources. War and natural disaster have destroyed many of the originals recorded years ago by The Hill Monastic Manuscript Library. Yet evidence of their existence and content are preserved here and copied so that foundations that have lost their originals can still have a record of them and some kind of access to them, and so that scholars can study them. In this way, the monks of Saint John's continue their work in the preservation of the heritage of Western civilization in keeping with their great tradition.

These, then, are a few of the lessons that we learned during our brief sojourn among the Benedictines, lessons we believe can prove very helpful for contemporary Evangelical Christians.[13]

---

13. For further study of the topic, the following books are recommended: *Monk Habits for Everyday People: Benedictine Spirituality for Protestants* by Dennis Okholm (Grand Rapids: Brazos, 2007) offers a brief introduction to the subject in a similar spirit to our essay. *Wisdom Distilled from the Daily: Living the Rule of St. Benedict* by Joan Chittister, OSB (San Francisco: HarperCollins, 1990) is the classic introduction by an insider. Anglican Esther deWaal's *Seeking God: The Way of St. Benedict* (2nd ed; Collegeville: Liturgical Press, 2001) is an equally attractive introduction for the interested layperson. Kathleen Norris' books, *Dakota: A Spiritual Geography* (Boston: Houghton Mifflin/Mariner Books, 1993) and *The Cloister Walk* (New York: Riverhead/Penguin, 1996) offer a fascinating entrée from the perspective of a Presbyterian lay preacher and prize-winning poet. David Robinson, another Presbyterian, adapts the Rule to family life in *The Family Cloister: Benedictine Wisdom for the Home* (New York: Crossroad, 2000). Benet Tvedten, OSB, explains *How to be a Monastic and Not Leave Your Day Job* (Brewster: Paraclete, 2006); the sub-title is "An Invitation to the Oblate Life." Linda Kulzer and Roberta Bondi gather together the witness of a variety of Benedictine oblates in their edited work, *Benedict in the World* (Collegeville: Liturgical Press, 2002). *The*

We conclude with a quotation from the next to last chapter of the Rule (72:11-12):

> Prefer nothing whatever to Christ,
> and may he bring us all to everlasting life.

---

*Benedictine Handbook* (Collegeville: Liturgical Press, 2003) offers a translation and brief introduction to the Rule. Timothy Fry, OSB, ed, *RB1980: The Rule of St Benedict in Latin and English with Notes* (Collegeville: Liturgical Press, 1980) is a much more academic and extensive work than the handbook mentioned above. Those who wish to follow the *Ordo* (the liturgical calendar of the Church for any given year) are encouraged to go to the website *www.osb.org/ordo/* for a daily listing of the 'feasts' of a multitude of saints to be celebrated with their liturgical rank and color, together with the liturgical rubrics to be observed in the recitation of the Divine Office (including appropriate Scriptures). Following the biblical readings through the calendar year will bury the prejudice that assumes that only Protestants read the Bible.

10

# Apologetics Today
*Learning from a Master*

MICHAEL GREEN

I am honored to take part in this *Festschrift* for Dr. Carl Armerding, a talented and courageous friend. He turned his back on the normal route of academic progress to help launch the tiny acorn of Regent College, Vancouver, and did not leave it until it had become a mighty oak tree, the largest and best tertiary theological institution in Canada. He showed himself to be a delightful colleague, a brilliant lecturer, a gifted Old Testament scholar and a wise and enterprising Principal. But among the many gifts I admired was his courage and initiative. He left Regent to pioneer the leadership of another fledgling enterprise, Schloss Mittersill in Austria, which in turn became a powerful training institution for those in Eastern Europe wishing to go further in their faith and their academic studies. So what I offer him now is not a contribution to the biblical studies in which he excels, but an encouragement in the evangelism and apologetics which is a real but perhaps less well known part of his expertise.

A generation ago we had many apologists of great stature. One has only to think of names like Tolkien, C. S. Lewis, Solzhenistsyn,

G. K. Chesterton, Stephen Neill. Today we are much worse off, but the need is as great as ever. Apologetics is currently in low water. There are at least three reasons for this.

First, the climate of opinion has turned decisively against Christianity in both popular and academic circles in the West. To many it seems no longer a plausible worldview.

Second, modern Christians have developed considerable distaste for apologetics. Perhaps they fear defeat in argument. Perhaps they feel, rightly, that you can never argue anybody into the kingdom of God. But it does deeper than this. The average church member simply does not feel equipped, despite many years in church, to talk to friends about the deepest things in life. Postmodernism maintains that truth claims are power games and as such unacceptable. In any case, political correctness forbids the invasion of another's private space!

Yet apologetics is vitally important. To be sure, people will not be won to Christianity by argument alone. But neither should they be expected to believe without good reason. The gospel transcends what reason could have dared to hope for, but it is not unreasonable, and its presentation must not be anti-rational. New Testament Christianity is both credible and profoundly relevant to men and women today, so often lost in subjectivism, relativism and short-term goals.

But of course apologetics alone is barren. It needs to be accompanied by an attractive Christian lifestyle in individual and church alike if it is to carry weight. It also needs to have a clear evangelistic objective. It is not intended for intellectual victory. It is the handmaid of sensitive evangelism, and as such often requires a destructive as well as a constructive role. The delusions under which so many suffer need first to be removed by thoughtful and loving confrontation if our friends are going to become open to the possibility of Christian truth. The head, the heart and the will combine to make that quality of impact. Apologetics, then, has a real but subsidiary part in advancing the Christian cause.

## APOLOGETICS TODAY

Probably the greatest apologist in the latter part of the twentieth century was Bishop Lesslie Newbigin. He spent most of his ministry as a missionary and later as a missionary bishop in India, where, among his other labors, he was constantly engaged in high level apologetics with leading Hindus. When he returned to England, supposedly for retirement, he found the biggest job of his life awaiting him. He recognized the massive de-Christianization of England, and determined to face up to the deconstructionism and postmodernism of the day. He was a man who, somewhat like Irenaeus, straddled East and West as a missionary theologian. I propose to examine his work in three areas, by taking a typical book from each area. Of course he cannot be contained in so limited a compass. His literary output was brilliant and copious. But perhaps we can gain the main thrust of his contribution to Christian apologetics by looking at three books. First, *The Finality of Christ*,[1] directed particularly towards the debate between Christianity and Hinduism. Second, *The Gospel in a Pluralist Society*,[2] a major apologetic against the "religion" of secularism which he found to be choking the West. Finally we will examine his last book. He gave me one of the first copies. It is called *Proper Confidence*.[3] As we look at these three books we will see certain themes re-appearing (his writing was discursive and rather repetitive) and others being eclipsed by even more pressing issues.

*The Finality of Christ*, though only actually written in 1960, belongs to the early part of his missionary career. It emerges from encounter over many years with holy men of different faiths with whom he consorted in India. Nourished in a rather orthodox tradition, a sensitive man like Newbigin was constantly wrestling

---

1. Lesslie Newbigin, *The Finality of Christ* (Richmond: John Knox Press, 1969).
2. Lesslie Newbigin, *The Gospel in a Pluralist Society* (Grand Rapids: Eerdmans/ Geneva: WCC Publications, 1989).
3. Lesslie Newbigin, *Proper Confidence: Faith, Doubt, and Certainty in Christian Discipleship* (Grand Rapids: Eerdmans, 1995).

with the issue of how finality could be ascribed to Christ when so many millions of good men and women went to Christless graves. He has no difficulty in showing that other religions are not beginnings which are completed in the gospel. They face in very different directions and ask fundamentally different questions. In any case, the situation has changed. No longer is it an internal debate between Christianity and other faiths. The "value of the religious concepts of non-Christian religions" is no longer the central question. Worldwide secularization has forced the debate into other channels. Many of the changes in Asian countries which Christians had striven for in previous decades are now being brought about efficiently by secular agencies. There is a strong feeling among Asian Christians that God is at work in all this. Consequently the finality of Christ is now posed not so much with respect to his relation to other faiths as to his meaning for the secular history of mankind.

Newbigin therefore sets out to show that the teaching of Jesus about the kingdom of God concerns the whole of life, not some religious aspect of it. It is not about timeless truths, but about God's action in the secular world which looks to the climax of all human history. Newbigin observes how strange this seems to the Hindu.

> I have never forgotten the astonishment with which a devout and learned teacher of the Ramakrishna Mission regarded me when he discovered that I was prepared to rest my whole faith as a Christian upon the substantial historical truth of the record concerning Jesus in the New Testament. To him it seemed axiomatic that such vital matters of religious truth could not be allowed to depend on the accidents of history.

Of course this is the position of much German theology stemming from Lessing, and indeed of its disjunction of *Historie* and *Geschichte*. But the bishop will have nothing to do with the popular divide between the inner world of personal experience and the outer world of historical event. This is to be found both in the Hindu distinction of the real world of the self from the realm of *maya,* and the Western existentialist's assumption that the only meaning of external events is that given them by the individual. This division was there in antiquity, too, originating with Plato, between the sensible world and the intelligible world. And it was precisely this dichotomy which Christianity was so concerned to overcome. The Absolute had broken into the world of time and space. So the gospel does not allow us to withdraw into a private spiritual world. It is the interpretation not only of personal spiritual life but also of world history. In a similar way, salvation is not primarily about personal survival after death, but about participating (in foretaste now, and in fullness at the end) in the final victory of Christ.

So Newbigin's basic position is clear. He will not start with generalities about the religious feelings of mankind or the commonalities between Christianity and other faiths. Everything depends on your starting point. And his is unambiguously Jesus Christ. He recognizes this as a vulnerable position, but you have to take a starting point somewhere, and where is there a better one than Jesus? Of course, we will only be able to demonstrate its correctness at the end of the road, the culmination of human history. So to speak of the finality of Christ is to maintain that he is the clue to universal history.

He has a particularly helpful picture to explain the yawning difference between the gospel and the Hinduism in which he was immersed for so long. It is the wheel and the road. It demonstrates the great divide among religions. The Hindu sees history as a wheel—with its unending cycle of birth, growth, decay, death, always in movement and always returning on itself. You can only find a way to escape from this endless and meaningless movement by taking one of the spokes, (i.e. religions—it does not matter which) leading to the centre where all is still. The Christian, however, sees history as a journey. The movement we are involved in is not meaningless. It leads to the goal which we believe in but do not yet see. The ultimate resting place will only be at the end of the road.

## THE BIBLE IN WORLD CHRISTIAN PERSPECTIVE

Newbigin is not claiming finality for Christianity, but for Christ. However that claim is meaningless unless it is lived out in the life of a community which lives by the apostolic message. That means that in some sense there is a decisive role for the church in world history: it must be engaged, fruitful, creative, constructive. We do not know all the answers. We cannot yet experience the goal. Yet we claim that at the end of the story it will be seen that commitment to Christ was indeed the proper way to go. It will sometimes mean suffering, failure and defeat. But it will also mean resurrection. Defeat will finally be turned into victory. To claim finality for Christ is not to assert that one day the majority of men will become Christians, or to assert that all others will be damned. It is to claim that commitment to him is the way in which men can be truly aligned to that ultimate end for which all things were made.

*The Gospel in a Pluralist Society* is a very wide-ranging treatment of the interface between the gospel and a pluralist society. It represents his most acute analysis of the weaknesses of the liberal secularist worldview, which is the commonly accepted plausibility structure in our society. There is much discussion on mission, the gospel and world religions, the gospel and cultures, and his beloved and entirely proper theme of the Christian congregation as the hermeneutic of the gospel. This is a point of utmost importance. Few other apologists even mention it. But Newbigin insists that the best apologetic we can offer is to recount the gospel message which has captured us, and so live it out in our personal and corporate lives that the lifestyle of the church interprets and commends the gospel. The book ends with a couple of pages on confidence in the gospel, a theme he will develop further in the third of his books.

But curiously enough his most powerful chapter in terms of apologetics is the first one in the book, on dogma and doubt in a pluralist culture. He acknowledges that dogma is in great disrepute in a society where there is no one approved pattern of belief or behaviour, where a culture of skepticism about all universals is the order of the day. But with characteristic confidence he sets out to defend dogma. Not of course in the sense of a viewpoint forcibly imposed on others, as it sometimes was by the mediaeval church. Nor in the sense of blind acceptance, as is sometimes to be found in Roman Catholic or fundamentalist churches. But the word derives from the Greek *dokein*, to seem or to appear. Newbigin points out acutely that every thought process has to start somewhere, and that the One who has split history into two is no bad place to start. In the gospel something radically new has been offered to mankind. It is quite different from religious experience as found in the great religions. It cannot be derived from rational reflection. It is a new fact, to be received by faith, as a gift of grace. As such it is either the rock which is the foundation for all knowing, or else the stone on which one stumbles to disaster. But it is certainly not something for private opinion. Those who have experienced this grace must not water it down or try to explain it in terms of something else, but proclaim it with confidence, realising it can and will be opposed. There is no space here to examine his assault on the rationalist camp, but he. pertinently asks of those who want to criticise the gospel on the grounds of some supposed superior insight, how they know that their perspective is right. What privileged access to reality do they have, which enables them to relativize all other claims but their own? It is sheer arrogance, and we should not be embarrassed by such accusations. We must not, like the liberals, domesticate the Christian message within the plausibility structure acceptable to secular society. We must not make the mistake of supposing that revelation and reason are two parallel paths to truth, or that revelation must be tested at the bar of reason. Reason is simply the power of the human mind to grasp meaningful patterns, and is involved in knowledge of any kind. Reason is not an independent source of information about life. It is one aspect of the human activity by which we seek to understand the world and ourselves. Believers and unbelievers alike exercise reason. They simply interpret the data differently, data which are potentially available to all.

He takes the empty tomb as an example. Liberals explain it away as the result of pre-existent faith among the disciples, in precise reversal of the biblical record. Here is a classic example of the domestication of the gospel into the reigning plausibility structure. But it is obvious that the story of the resurrection cannot be fitted into any existing worldview—except the one of which it is the starting point. It is analogous to what happened on the day the cosmos came into being. Once accept that claim in faith, and you will find it a wholly new way of understanding our human experience and destiny, a way which makes much more sense than the existential despair embodied in the contemporary sceptical worldview. You do not defend the new worldview by trying to demonstrate its compatibility with the old. You challenge the old with the dogma, how it "appears" to the believer.

Newbigin insists that the dogma, the thing offered for our acceptance in faith, is not a timeless set of propositions, but a story. A story as yet unfinished. A story in which we are involved personally. We do not yet see the end of the story, so we rely on a faith commitment based on the resurrection. But this is not unreasonable. No human life is possible without some idea, explicit or implicit, about what the story means. The Christian faith is historical in two senses. It is based on what actually happened in history, and it is an interpretation of universal history, where all human life is headed. So its defence, he concludes, will be as much concerned with how we act as what we say.

Newbigin laments that most ordinary people and many sociologists and economists still operate with the myth of value-free facts and a mechanical universe, where everything is to be explained in terms of its causes. This is manifestly inadequate. You only begin to understand something when you discern its purpose. A computer, for example is inexplicable without some understanding of the purpose for which its hard drive and software came together. Powerfully Newbigin contends for the inclusion of purpose in our understanding of the world. With biting scorn he writes:

To see the cosmos as a machine which creates itself and exists for no purpose is something which in most periods of human history would have been thought to exceed the imagination of even the most credulous. Yet it is still widely diffused and given credence by respected scientists. It is this concept of a cosmos without purpose which provides the validation for the division of our world into two—a world of facts without value and a world of values which have no basis in facts.

Finally he shows that the quest for certainty through universal doubt, so characteristic of our culture, is a blind alley. All doubt is based on some prior-held belief. Faith is logically prior to doubt, though both are needed if we are to gain a proper assessment of any situation.

What Newbigin has done in this powerful book is to expose the false epistemological foundations of liberal secularism. He has shown that even scientific enquiry holds ultimate commitments based on faith, just as the Christian faith does.

But his main purpose has been to show that the Enlightenment attempt to found truths on a basis from which faith is eliminated is not only nonsense but highly dangerous. Without faith and values science and technology bid fair to destroy all life. Any scientific explanation which excludes purpose is inadequate, and the critical principle of universal skepticism is folly. He wants to lead us to a post-critical period in which we know we have to find a new basis for confidence for the whole human enterprise. And he maintains that it is not only tenable but the best of all explanations to adopt the story of which Christ is the centre. For it proposes a meaning and a goal for the whole of human history. It is therefore not a matter of private opinion but of public truth. We must proclaim it fearlessly and live it attractively. And so "when the church is faithful to the Lord then the powers of the Kingdom are present and people begin to ask the questions to which the gospel is the answer."

We now come to consider a third book of Newbigin's, *Proper Confidence*, which he wrote in his late eighties. As Geoffrey Wainwright of Duke University observed, "Seeing both liberal and fundamentalist Christians imprisoned in the epistemological presuppositions of the Enlightenment, Lesslie Newbigin offers them liberation by pointing to the fiduciary character of all human knowledge." Both Liberals and Conservatives have tended to operate within the Enlightenment disjunction of facts and values. The Conservatives have espoused Scripture as indubitable fact, while the Liberals have assigned higher value to their own opinions. Newbigin is keen to transcend this most unfortunate quarrel and turn it into constructive dialogue. As a result he was not entirely trusted in either the liberal or the conservative camp!

He begins by showing that what distinguishes Europe from the rest of the Asian landmass is the confluence of two streams, the humanist classical culture on the one hand and the Hebrew-Christian faith on the other. For Greek rationality, the biblical story could not be the place where ultimate truth was found. But the first Christians took an entirely new starting point, a factum or fact—God had acted. The Word had become flesh. If the Ultimate had indeed come into the world of the relative, then the dualism of Greek humanist thought separating the material from the spiritual was overcome. Ultimate reality was no longer unknowable. Final truth is available to us in the person of Jesus. And that biblical story has shaped Europe for more than 1500 years. But if Christ is the author of the story, so to speak, who has silenced our endless questions by entering the room, then personal knowledge is indispensable. It cannot begin without an act of trust—and trust always involves risk. So the certainty we have is not without risk, but it rests on the faithfulness of the One whose story it is. We walk by faith, since the story is still unfinished.

Newbigin returns to Descartes, who was commissioned by a Catholic cardinal to defeat skepticism and to silence atheism, actually two incompatible aims. Descartes built his new structure of indubitable knowledge on the foundation of skepticism, until he arrived at the famous cogito, which he could not doubt. The critical principle of relentless skepticism was the only secure way to knowledge. But of course this approach strongly reinforced the dualism of mind and matter which had been so debilitating in the classical world. It polarised subjectivity and objectivity, and it enhanced the dichotomy between theory and practice. Though Descartes was himself a believer in God, it did not take his followers long to remove God from certain knowledge by means of this critical principle. And it was left to Nietzsche in the late nineteenth century ruthlessly to expose the inevitable conclusion of Descartes's method. The critical principle must necessarily destroy itself. For if the critical principle is to have the supreme place in knowing, then the possibility of knowing anything at all is destroyed. All values, all distinctions between right and wrong are now words without meaning. They are simply expressions of the will, where might is right. Violence is the fundamental element of human life and history. The quest for absolute certainty had proved a stepping stone to nihilism. That is what Nietzsche foresaw, mad though he became. And that is the way our society seems to be heading.

Is there an alternative? Newbigin is sure there is. It does not lie in indubitable propositions but in a story, the story recorded in the Bible and supremely in the Word made flesh. You cannot be sure of the truth of that story by rational reflection alone. As Martin Buber recognised in his epoch-making book *I and Thou*,[4] the I-It knowledge we have of ideas and propositions is very different from the I-Thou knowledge we have of a person. Therefore Augustine and Athanasius were right. *Credo ut intelligam*. I have to believe, to trust, if I am to understand. I can have no assured knowledge of Christ without commitment to him. And once that happens the biblical story becomes my story too. I am part of its action, caught up in its direction towards the consummation of all history. The

---

4. Martin Buber, *I and Thou* (Trans. R. G. Smith; Edinburgh: T. &. T. Clark, 1937 and subsequent editions).

corollary, of course, is that my faith must lead to obedience. My commitment to Christ must lead to commitment to his people, for the church is the hermeneutic of the gospel. If so, I may have proper confidence, deep assurance. But it is not that death-dealing certainty to which Descartes' method led, and for which some Christians lust. It is that assurance which relies completely on the trustworthiness of the person we have begun to know Jesus Christ himself. Such is the proper confidence Christians may possess. And so he concludes by asserting that the proper form of apologetics is to grasp this new arche, this fundamental principle which the gospel provides, not to attempt to answer questions arising out of other ways of looking at the world. The gospel itself is the alternative structure we need to commend by our lives, our Christian communities and our words.

If we attempt a form of apologetics which tries to show that the gospel is reasonable, we contradict and betray the gospel. For it means we are looking for the *logos*, the rationale of all things, elsewhere than in Jesus. We are witnesses to the One who has shown himself utterly reliable. What further assurance do we need?

I find it very fresh and helpful that Newbigin rejects the traditional role assigned to apologetics since the Enlightenment of trying to show the reasonableness of the Christian faith in a manner acceptable to secular culture. Instead he argues for apologetics to take on the role of interpreting the culture from a new perspective, the gospel, and he shows, quite brilliantly, how this can be done. That is what Paul did at Athens when he grasped a new starting point for enquiry by insisting on the resurrection. That is what Augustine did when the pagan hordes were pouring into Rome. He sat down and wrote *The City of God*, an entirely new starting point from that adopted by the classical culture in which he had been nurtured. It became one of the most influential books in the world for the next thousand years. And now Lesslie Newbigin has done it afresh, in a day when the barbarian hordes are no longer at the gates but have long been inhabiting our parliaments, media and university departments and advocating a disastrous secularist world view, which has been swallowed whole by society at large. Newbigin has taken an entirely new starting point, the coming, dying and rising of the Son of God, itself, and in its light has devastatingly criticised the prevailing worldview of secular liberalism, and has pointed the way to humble but confident Christian assurance. Bishop Newbigin set out to paint the big picture which, if we have the courage to adopt it, may yet rescue our society from destruction.

11

# Old Testament Narrative and Christian Ethics

JONATHAN R. WILSON

In this essay I will argue that "narrative" is fundamental and indispensable to reading the Old Testament in faithfulness, wherever that reading takes place—in a scholarly commentary, a neighborhood Bible study, or elsewhere. This claim requires considerable explication because of the cacophony of voices laying claim to "narrative" and story. However, my approach to clarification will not be by way of dialectical engagement with other positions but by way of analysis of the gospel itself. I am not concerned with defeating other positions but with faithfully submitting to the good news of Jesus of Nazareth as Israel's messiah and Savior of the world. This does not mean that my position is unassailable; indeed, it becomes more vulnerable because I recognize that at best I can point toward the good news. I am witness not owner.

"Narrative" is fundamental and indispensable to reading the OT in faithfulness.[1] This is so because narrative names more than (but not less than) a literary genre, the unity of self, the structure of

---

1. I will typically use "narrative" rather than "story" because I judge narrative to be more open to multiple meanings than is "story." At this point I will also drop the scare quotes.

morality, and the Christian faith. *Narrative identifies the fundamental actuality of God's life and thus of life itself. In doing so, narrative also identifies the work of God in creation and redemption.* Once this is established, we may more fully understand the significance of genre, self, morality and Christian faith. Briefly put (to be more expansively described below), when properly rooted in God's life and work, narrative may be properly seen as a necessary rather than an accidental feature of our work. Such an understanding has far reaching implications for Christian scholarship.

Since God is eternally Father, Son, and Holy Spirit, God lives eternally in actuality. That is, God is eternally act. If we understand ourselves to be saying "Father, Son, and Holy Spirit," when we say God (as we must if we belong to the church), then we are already identifying God by the narrative of God's life. There is no other way to say "God" in faithfulness to Scripture and the wisdom of the church's theological reflection. Father, Son, and Holy Spirit identifies the act of each person of the Trinity giving identity to each other. For example, the Father gives identity to the Son by acting as Father to the Son and in so doing also gives identity to himself as Father. This act of giving and identifying is characteristic of each person of the Trinity and constitutes God's life as Triune. So, to say "Father, Son, and Spirit," to say "God" as a Christian is to bear witness to an actuality of life that requires a narrative to be understood.

The way that I have exposited this claim is crucial to its faithfulness. It is not that narrative is a useful or memorable way of communicating sound teaching about God. It is that God's very life is actual—it is always activity. This is true of God's life eternally. God's actuality does not begin with creation. "In the beginning" identifies the beginning of God's activity of creation but it does not identify the beginning of God's activity. Narrative is not the best means among many possibilities by which we identify God. Rather, since God is eternally actuality, narrative bows before God in faithful witness to God's living. In this way, God's own actuality creates narrative; it is not narrative that gives us a means to understand God. Rather because we are saved by God who is eternally actuality, and who saves us by act, narrative necessarily identifies that salvation.[2]

In the OT, this is what we learn when God names Godself "I AM" in the context of God's saving act toward nascent Israel in Egypt. When we understand YHWH epexegeted by *"eyeh asher eyeh,"* then we know God to be "the living ONE." This livingness is the declaration that God is life, God has life in Godself. When we receive the Word made flesh and come to know that God is triune, we have come to live more fully in relationship to the living one. Triunity is the form of the life of the I AM. But even that is not quite right. Bending our language toward the actuality who is God, we must say that what we specify by "Trinity" is the life of "I AM."

*At this po*int we may acknowledge that there is to narrative a necessary metaphysical dimension. But it is only at this point that we are free to acknowledge this dimension, because this metaphysical necessity flows from God's life, it is not imposed upon God from above or without. By metaphysics here I mean an implicit or explicit understanding of the nature of reality. If our statements have meaning, they do so as part of an understanding of reality. For those who seek faithfulness to the gospel, narrative requires a metaphysics of personal agency—this is what it means to say "Father, Son, and Holy Spirit."[3]

---

2. For all of his insights, N.T. Wright leads us away from this actuality when he recurs to the language of "worldview." See, for example, N.T. Wright, *Christian Origins and the Question of God. Volume Two. Jesus and the Victory of God* (Minneapolis: Fortress, 1996), 200-201. Jesus came not to teach a new worldview or even a variant on Israel's worldview. He came to enact the kingdom of God, which is actuality. The "story" of the kingdom is not a vehicle for a worldview; rather, the "story" of the kingdom is witness to the actuality of the kingdom and invitation to enter into its life, its actuality. It is not an invitation to change one's worldview.

3. For a complementary account, see Robert W. Jenson, *Systematic Theology, Volume 1: The Triune God* (New York: Oxford University Press, 1997).

Such a metaphysics may be implicit and still be faithful. There are many people who cannot articulate a metaphysics and may not even know the term, who can nevertheless make statements that are still metaphysically appropriate to the actuality of God's life. But to maintain this faithfulness and guard it, the church also needs some who are skilled in explicit metaphysical reflection. Someone must be able to say why the metaphysics implicit in an unreflective statement is faithful to God. Some must also be able to identify and correct statements that are unfaithful to the metaphysical demands of actuality. And they must be able to teach others to pass on the witness that they have received.

This does not mean that only one vocabulary or conceptual scheme serves the purposes of faithfulness. In different times and places, different vocabularies have been set free from other conceptual schemes and taken captive to God's actuality. This is entirely appropriate because it is not the metaphysical scheme that gives us access to God. It is God's self-giving that creates the capacity of the language of metaphysics to bear faithfully upon God.

So although the OT does not display the explicit metaphysical discourse of Greek or modern conceptualities, it does provide us with a witness to God's actuality that is metaphysically rich. Because it does so in other literary genres does not make it less metaphysical; we have committed a significant error in thinking that metaphysical conviction is absent from the OT because we do not recognize its mode of expression.

These metaphysical convictions must follow logically from the gospel of Israel as God's people and Jesus as Israel's Messiah and the world's Savior. Thus, as our language about these acts of God, metaphysics is subservient to the gospel, the good news of God's salvation. Logically, then, metaphysics must be re-placed, moved from a primary and determinative position to a secondary position. We do not first establish a set of metaphysical convictions and language apart from the gospel and then conform the gospel and our witness to those convictions and language. Rather, our participation in God's actuality generates the metaphysical convictions and shapes the language that we use.

Analytically, however, the metaphysical resonances and convictions reflected in our language must be continuously identified and consciously criticized. None of our language is innocent of metaphysics, whether that metaphysics is implicit or explicit. Because Christian faith knows that God is acting in Israel's messiah for the salvation of the world, we must continually examine our language for its metaphysical presumptions. Does our language reflect the mistaken belief that ideas rather than acts are at the metaphysical center of the world? Does our language presume that the acts of human beings are constitutive of reality, so that reality has no meaning apart from the meaning that we give it? Does our language presume that no meaning can be given, so that talk of reality and even life is illusory and nonsensical? As we analyze our teaching and our living, we must bring our metaphysics under the discipline of the good news that God is acting in Christ for our salvation. Such a metaphysics will necessarily answer to narrative as the way by which we know God to act for us. The presence of metaphysical presumptions must be examined in all of our teaching and living so that we can be faithful to the actuality of the gospel. This metaphysical work must be logically secondary to the gospel, but it must be analytically present at the beginning of our theological work so that we can identify and correct the betrayals of the actuality of God and God's work throughout our teaching and living.

We can learn this kind of examination and criticism from the OT through the priests who are charged to teach the covenant to the people by their practices, the prophets who are called to criticize and correct the mistaken narrative that underwrites Israel's idolatry, immorality, and injustice, and through the sages who guide Israel's participation in God's actuality. A proper reading of the OT for the people of God makes these resources available to us today so that we may also enter into God's actuality by grace.

In addition to its impact on metaphysics, this understanding of the necessity of narrative to actuality also has an impact on "history." There is a long and lively argument about the use of "history" as a description of the intentions of the writers of the OT. Here the argument is not about literary genre (to which we will turn next), but about the kind of claim that is being made in the OT. Do its writers intend to claim that they are describing historical events? Or is it more appropriate to describe their intention as "mythical"? In this case they lay claim to truth, but their claims rest not on "historical events" but on the power of perspective. The issues here are complex; for the purposes of this essay I will presume a familiarity with the debates.

For those of us who believe that the OT bears witness to God whose very life is actual and whose truth is the work of creating and redeeming, the link of narrative to that actuality guides us through the question of the intentions of the writers of the OT. For the OT, God's life and work is the actuality of creating and redeeming such that the only way to give an account in witness to that actuality, to keep Israel within that actuality and to invite others in, is to provide a narrative in keeping with that actuality. Such a narrative is not history in our usual sense, when history carries with it metaphysical convictions that preclude history being the history of God's actuality. History in this usual sense excludes God as agent, except in those rare instances when we might admit that the history is sufficiently puzzling to not yet foreclose the possibility of God's agency. But here the evidence and argument are so weak that we must jettison most of the biblical claims about God's actuality. We end with a severely attenuated possibility of God.

When this understanding of history forecloses the possibility of God as agent, biblical scholarship and theology has often turned to "salvation history" or biblical perspective or story. These strategies have generated their own well-known controversies. But what has not been present in any significant way to my knowledge is the argument that the actuality of God and God's work requires a narrative that identifies God as the agent.

To put it in Julian Hartt's language, this understanding of actuality leads us to "story as the art of historical truth."[4] In this case, we are asking how best to be faithful in witness and participation in the actuality of God's life. That actuality is what creates, sustains, and redeems the world. That actuality is at work in this world and in Israel as the people chosen to bear the knowledge of God and be participants in and witnesses to God's work. So this actuality is historical—Israel names a people who can be identified in time and space. And the convictions that we have about that historical work are ones for which we claim truth. But the nature of that work and our convictions is such that we cannot display their historical truth as "history." We would betray the good news of Israel's messiah if we sought to give an account of this actuality apart from God's agency, apart from grace (understood as gratuitous, inexplicable interruption and transformation of the way things are), and apart from a teleology that gives it all meaning. So "history" will not do unless we devote enormous energy to undoing its control of what may be admitted to the status of history.

In place of history, we have other candidates. Hans Frei proposes "history-like narrative." Others use the bare "narrative." Still others cast their lot with "story." It really matters little which we endorse if we do not ground our endorsement and our use in the convictions that I have sketched here. At times the adoption of one or another of these terms has seemed like special pleading: "We don't have good history in these texts and if we accept the rules of history for the contest, we will lose. So we'll find another description for what we have in these OT texts." But this strategy is seldom rooted in clear reasoning about the actuality of God and God's work. Indeed there

---

4. This is the title of chapter 8 in Julian N. Hartt, *Theological Method and Imagination* (New York: Seabury, 1977).

too often seems to be an absence of belief in the actuality of God and a consequent strategy of making do with some defective texts. But if we believe the witness of the texts and live in that actuality today, then the narrative of Scripture is precisely what is necessary to that actuality. The story, the history-like narrative, the saga, is precisely suited to the actuality of God's agency, the work of that agency in the world, and the teleology of that agency. "Recourse to" narrative, then, is not an apologetic fallback position, but a perfectly fitting witness to the creating and redeeming work of God. And thus it is not "recourse to" but recognition of the actuality of God.

At this point we may move from metaphysics and history to the topic that has continually threatened to make a premature entrance into our consideration; the topic of literary genre. Here is the most immediate question that arises when one hears "narrative." It has been necessary to postpone this discussion until now in order to lay the proper foundation for exploring the literary genre of the OT. At times, unreflective critics have rejected and even mocked the significance of "narrative" or "story" because so much of the OT is written in a genre other than narrative—laws, wisdom sayings, prophetic messages, and even genealogies are given in evidence against the importance of narrative.

But the argument that I am advancing here is that "narrative" signifies far more than genre. Narrative identifies and enters into the actuality of God. If we have this conviction and life, then we can properly place the genres of the Bible. All of the OT depends for its significance upon its participation in the actuality of God. But once it has that place, it can take many different literary forms. The laws of Torah, the poetry of the psalmists, the sayings of the wise, the proclamations of the prophets, and everything else in the OT makes sense as they participate in and enable their hearers to participate in the actuality of God's work. So it is a mistake to pit genre against genre. Instead we must relate them all to participation in the actuality of God's work.

But once we have oriented the relationships properly, narrative becomes the means by which we know the actuality of God and participate in it. Then other genres can be properly placed in relation to the narrative. Narrative is not accidental or dispensable; it is not a temporary container for principles, commands, or concepts; it is not something to be discarded once we get the message or the moral of the story. Rather, narrative is the indispensable witness to God's actuality, to the living One whose creating and redeeming work is our salvation. Other genres arise from and echo the narrative that witnesses to that actuality.

All of the OT is responsive to and participant in the work of I AM. Since this actuality of God is prior to any narrative, the question of "metanarrative" is actually misleading. What followers of the Messiah have is not a metanarrative but the actuality of God that has taken hold of them and swept them up into God's redeeming work. This work is identified in many narratives and genres that all have in common the one actuality of God's creating and redeeming actuality. This actuality, and not a metanarrative, is what apprehends followers of the Messiah. To argue on the basis of having or not having a metanarrative is to once again misplace the argument by denying the primacy of the actuality of God.

Finally, we come to the question of OT narrative and ethics. The preceding analysis has been necessary in order to make the inescapable claim that the "ethical" import of OT narratives is the blessing and command to participate in the actuality of God's creating and redeeming work in the world. In this way, ethics becomes completely reoriented so that it may even be better not to speak of ethics. On the basis of my analysis, ethics is not something that follows from belief in God; rather, those concerns that we assign to ethics, however varied ethics may be, are about our participation in the life that God has given to creation. Therefore, when ethics is understood as our participation in God's actuality, we must recognize that what is necessary about narrative is not that it is the most clever rhetorical device, or the most persuasive rhetorical form, or the most memorable way of communication, or the most entertaining. It may be any or all of these, but none makes narrative necessary. What makes narrative necessary is that it is the only way to bear witness to God's creating and redeeming.

Our "ethics" then simply is the form, the actuality of our life in God, and narrative makes the form and actuality of that life conscious to us. That is, the actuality of God in the work of creating and redeeming requires narrative by virtue of its actuality. And its actuality is known to us by its narratability. These twin truths may be summed up in the acknowledgment of "narrative" as the essential practice of theological ethics that directs the work of ethics. Most importantly narrative safeguards the call to participation in God's life which is initiated and empowered by God. In other words, it is by grace that we live. Ethics is not a means to grace but the life of grace in the reality of God's work through the Messiah.[5] Narrative that is rooted in the actuality of God also identifies the hope that creates *shalom* for a world that is always coming apart. And as we are called to a life of grace that finds its coherence not in our ability to narrate its unity but in the actuality of God that holds all things together and redeems our unfaithfulness, we become the people who live as God calls us to live, who, when all is said and done in the faithfulness of God, quite simply . . . live . . . forever.

---

5. This concern is developed with insight and intensity in Dietrich Bonhoeffer, *Ethics* (Dietrich Bonhoeffer Works 6; R. Krauss et al., trans.; Minneapolis: Fortress, 2005), esp. 47-75.

12

# Turning a Blind Eye
## *Emmanuel Levinas, John 9 and the Blindness of Responsibility*

JEFF KEUSS

**Abstract:**
According to Levinas, ethics, not ontology, constitutes first philosophy. Rather than investigating the being of the self as the origin and ground of identity, Levinas focuses in *Totality and Infinity* (1961) on the encounter with the face of the other as antecedent to being and the subject; in *Otherwise Than Being* (1974) he maintains that the infinite responsibility for the other precedes origin and essence. This responsibility is not assumed or willed by a self already constituted; instead, it finds itself and its meaning in proximity to the other, in putting oneself in the place of the other, in an open-ended saying rather than what is finalized and said. The pre-original responsibility for the other escapes and proceeds being, definition, and identity. Although ethics concentrates on individual responsibility, in Levinas' thought ethics does not fall mute and powerless in the realm of politics. Indeed, ethics can both inform and critique political practice and reason, as Levinas' interviews on contemporary events indicate.

THE BIBLE IN WORLD CHRISTIAN PERSPECTIVE

## Introduction

Sin, fault, or error—the fall also means that blindness *violates* what can here be called Nature. It is an accident that interrupts the regular course of things or transgresses natural laws. It sometimes leads one to think that the affliction affects both Nature and a nature of the will, the will to know [*savior*] as the will to see [*voir*]. A bad will—an unwillingness—would have driven man to close his eyes. The blind do not want to know, or rather, would like not to know: that is to say, not to see. *Idein, eidos, idea:* the whole history, the whole semantics of the European idea, in its Greek genealogy, as we know—as we see—relates seeing to knowing[1]

As Derrida reminds us in this opening reflection on the role of seeing and blindness in Western cultural history, to truly see is to know—and to be "blind" is related to ignorance and denial of truth that is before us. This basic assertion remains intact—and thoroughly supported—in the Gospel of John, but that which constitutes "blindness" and "sight" is radically reinterpreted around the notion of signs [*sēmeion*] either beheld in wonder or turned away from in fear. John's Gospel is ultimately a testament of "signs" and what it means to "see signs." As Jesus finishes feeding the multitude in John 6:26, Jesus underscores the importance of "seeing signs" when he rebukes the gathered masses: "You are looking for me, *not because you saw signs* [*sēmeion*] but because you ate your fill of the loaves." In short, to follow Christ is more than mere existential needs being met, but a new way of seeing. As Robert Kysar puts it in his book *John: The Maverick Gospel*:

> Hence [in John's Gospel], in order for signs to provoke faith they must be experienced from a perspective that already presupposes faith—at least to a minimal degree. "Seeing signs"

---

1. Jacques Derrida, *Memoirs of the Blind: The Self Portrait and Other Ruins* (Chicago: University of Chicago Press, 1993), 12.

then, in the profound sense, is experiencing the acts of Jesus and understanding them correctly. It is seeing through them, as it were, to the true identity of the actor. Insofar as we may call an openness to the possibility of God's reality and activity "faith," the signs require faith as well as *provoke* faith.[2]

The role that semiotics—the seeing of signs—has played in the hermeneutic history of John's Gospel is exemplified in the legacy of Rudolf Bultmann, whose great work is not *Jesus Christ and Mythology*, which he wrote trying to explain his "demythologizing" theology to the laity, but his magisterial study of *The Gospel of John* which Bultmann produced while holding John's Gospel side by side with Kierkegaard's *Philosophical Fragments*. Kierkegaard maintained that the life and ministry of Jesus can be determined, at best, only with approximate historical certainty. Moreover, such historical certainty is not necessary for faith in Jesus as the Messiah, the Christ. This follows, regardless of the historical records of the gospel writers, because the believer must make a "leap of faith" by accepting the gospel tradition as true. Kierkegaard expressed this thought in the statement, "Truth is subjectivity." According to Kierkegaard in *Concluding Unscientific Postscript to Philosophical Fragments* (1846),[3] faith is a subjective, personal, passionate interestedness in attaining eternal happiness, as found through appropriation. Faith is a category of decision-making in which an individual confronts an "either-or" situation, either accepting or rejecting subjectivity. Kierkegaard argues that the falsehood of objectivity may be revealed by a lack of need for personal commitment, and by a lack of need for decision-making, while the truth of subjectivity may be revealed by a need for personal commitment, and by a

---

2. Robert Kysar, *John: The Maverick Gospel* (rev. ed.; Louisville: Westminster John Knox Press, 1993), 84.
3. See Søren Kierkegaard, *Concluding Unscientific Postscript to "Philosophical Fragments"* (International Kierkegaard Commentary, Volume 12; ed. Robert Perkins; Macon: Mercer University Press, 1997).

need for decision-making. The speculative thinker attempts to stand apart from his or her own existence, and attempts to view existence objectively. In contrast, the subjective thinker realizes that he or she cannot stand apart from existence, and that the truth of his or her own existence is found in his or her own subjectivity. This means truth can be determined only by the believer. That Jesus is actually the Christ, the Son of God, is not an objective historical truth apart from faith. Bultmann accepted Kierkegaard's concept of subjectivity, but differed from him in that he perceived little if any possibility of establishing the historical objectivity of Jesus in the gospels. That "truth is subjectivity" became radicalized by Bultmann in relation to Bultmann's appreciation of Martin Heidegger's notion of authenticity. Heidegger, who was colleague with Bultmann at Marburg University, affirmed that the human race resides in a state of fallenness in a world of death and nothingness, and therefore lives an inauthentic existence. At the same time a person possesses the possibility of recognizing one's own fallen state, accepting the world for what it is, and resolving to live authentically. The decision to live in authenticity is present to anyone by the voice of conscience. Bultmann agreed with Heidegger's idea of resolution or decision, but differed from him in that the opportunity of authenticity is made possible to a person only by God's act of grace in Christ.

How does the human subject move from a state of false objectivity toward a repose of authentic subjectivity in relation to the signs [*sēmeion*] that before us as Jesus the Christ? As will be discussed throughout the remainder of this paper, the move called for by John the Evangelist is a deep blindness that allows for and provokes the seeing of signs that, as Derrida says, puts us face to face with the *mysterium tremendums*, that which always makes us tremble to our very core. It is, in fact, an existential trembling, a terror in one's being, a fear of eradication.

TURNING A BLIND EYE

## From "ought" to "who"

Similar to Bultmann's reading of John's Gospel alongside Kierkegaard's aphorism that "truth is subjectivity," French philosopher and literary theorist Emmanuel Levinas holds that ethics is, first and foremost, born on the concrete level of person to person contact. Put more directly, the central question is not "ought" but "whom." He does not find the moral "ought" inscribed within the laws of the cosmos, in reason, or in any universal desire for pleasure. Instead, each particular instance of moral conflict produces the moral "ought" itself in and through relationships.

As a point of clarification, I will dialogue with Levinas' use of the ethical "ought" in relation to John's Gospel through the primary understanding of ethics as that which can only occur in and through community as the context for relational abiding with other people. This is integral not only to reading Levinas, but the Gospel accounts as testimonies of the eschatological Kingdom. In summary, it can be argued that the basis of Levinas' ethical project is as follows: to establish the source of contact between persons or the source of interpersonal meaning, and in finding this meaning, Levinas finds the ethical.

Core to Levinas' understanding of persons as moral agents is the freedom given to all people by God and the propensity to strip that freedom through a process of what Levinas terms "totalization." Anytime I take the person in my idea to be the real person, I have closed off contact with the real person; I have cut off the connection with the other that is necessary if ethics is to refer to real other people. This is a central violence to the other that denies the other his/her own autonomy. Levinas calls this violence "totalization" and it occurs whenever I limit the other to a set of rational categories, be they racial, sexual, or otherwise. Indeed, it occurs whenever I already know what the other is about before the other has spoken. Totalization is a denial of the other's difference, the denial of the otherness of the other. That is, it is the inscription of the other in the same. If ethics presupposes the real other person, then such totalization will, in itself, be unethical.

If reducing the other to my sphere of ideas cuts off contact with the other, then we are presupposing that contact with the other has already been established. And if contact with the other cannot be established through ideas, then we must look elsewhere. Thus, Levinas looks not to reason, but to sensibility, to find the real essence of the Other.

Sensibility, for Levinas, goes back to a point before thought originates, before the ordering of a world into a system or totality. Sensibility is a profound waiting, not an active seeking after as thought is, and it finds its contextual grounding in joy. Life as it is lived, (rather than understood), is lived as the satisfaction of being "filled" with sensations, the satisfaction of feeding on the environment.

Levinas at this point seeks to deepen Heidegger's project in relation to Heidegger's notion of "tool Reading the earlier Heidegger in *Being and Time*, we find Heidegger maintaining that inauthentic *existenz* contextualises itself in the world of things by relating to things (including other people) as mere tools—devices to be used for a particular purpose. Furthering this argument, Levinas maintains that we live from these things or people as nourishments—we do not merely seek to stand apart from them, but digest them into ourself in an act of totalization. I eat my bread; in the activity of eating it becomes a part of my body. I digest the language and meaning of George Eliot's *Middlemarch* and I bathe in the music of Miles Davis's "Kind of Blue In the act of reading and listening to art, I do not stall for a hermeneutic repose prior to understanding— I am engaged as I engage as one descending into a pool, not with a distanced objectivity providing passive reflection on the event. I "digest" the art. It becomes me. This "living from" is a matter of consumption, a matter of taking what is other and making it become a part of me. Levinas writes:

Nourishment, as a means of invigoration, is the transmutation of the other into the same, which is the essence of enjoyment; an energy that is other, recognized as other, recognized ... as sustaining the very act that is directed upon it becomes, in enjoyment, my own energy, my strength, me.[4]

In a way, Levinas resonates with Jean Baurillard's correction of Marxist critique. Where Marx argued that power is seen in the modes of production, Baudrillard argues that power is seen and manifested in our role as consumers. This taking on of what nourishes me conveys a separation between me and what has yet to nourish me. "Enjoyment is made," writes Levinas, "of the memory of its thirst; it is a quenching."[5] Enjoyment then includes the memory of once not having been satisfied with what now satisfies me. Thus, enjoyment also involves stepping back from my environment; "living from ... delineates independence itself, the independence of enjoyment and happiness ..."[6] Before enjoyment, there is me and the other thing that has yet to nourish me, even if the otherness of what will nourish me becomes apparent only in enjoyment, in the "memory" of its thirst. I can represent the bread, but this will not feed me. I must eat it. But then in eating bread, the memory of hunger, demonstrates a separation between the bread and me. Thus, in enjoyment, the self emerges already as the subject of its need.

If Levinas is correct, then, the human being starts first as one motivated toward joy. This enjoyment—being summoned by joy as independence—is the initial formation of the I. It is at this point that the Enlightenment seems to stall with the echo of Polonius' words to Laertes in Hamlet Act 1, Scene III "This above all: to thine ownself be true." But, this self, the self of enjoyment, constitutes an egoism. It is happy, but selfish. The self of enjoyment journeys into the world to make everything other part of itself, and it succeeds very well at this task. Richard Cohen summarizes Levinas on this point:

---

4. Levinas, *Totality and Infinity: An Essay on Exteriority*, Alphonso Lingis, trans. (Pittsburgh: Duquesne University Press, 1969), 111.
5. Levinas, *Totality and Infinity*, 113.
6. Levinas, *Totality and Infinity*, 110.

[Sensation] is called "happiness" because at this level of sensibility the subject is entirely self-satisfied, self-complacement [sic], content, sufficient. Instead of [rational] synthesis, there are vibrations; instead of unifications, there are excitations; rather than an ecstatic self, there are margins of intensities, scattered stupidities, involutions without centers—egoism and solitude without substantial unity; a sensational happiness ... This event does not happen *to* subjectivity, this eventfulness, this flux, *is* subjectivity.[7]

Thus, Levinas finds on the level of sensibility a subjectivity that is more primordial than rational subjectivity.[8] It is not limited by the sphere of one's own ideas, but by the egoist self that goes out to enjoy the world. What is important here is that, unlike the sphere of ideas, sensibility reaches further out into the domain of the extra-mental.[9]

Establishing subjectivity on the level of sensibility provides Levinas with a place "where" the other can be met, not in the cabinet of consciousness, but on the street, in the classroom, or in the workplace, where the egoism of enjoyment has the possibility of becoming "filled" with sensations. Furthermore, establishing subjectivity on the level of sensibility leads Levinas to a point where he can establish that the human subject is, first and foremost, passive. Sensations come to me from the outside (unlike the Augustinian tradition of *Noli foras ire, in teipsum redi; in interiore homine habitat veritas* "Do not go outward; return within yourself. In the

---

7. Richard Cohen, "Emmanuel Levinas Happiness is a Sensational Time," *Philosophy Today* 25 (1981): 201.

8. There are at least three different types of subjectivity in Levinas: 1) rational subjectivity—the self of representation that occurs in the "I think"; 2) subjectivity of being—the self of enjoyment and need; and 3) ethical subjectivity—the social self that arises from transcendent interpersonal contact.

9. Levinas, *Totality and Infinity*, 109. "If cognition in the form of the objectifying act does not seem to us to be at the level of the metaphysical relation, this is not because the exteriority contemplated as an object, the theme, would withdraw from the subject as fast as the abstractions proceed; on the contrary, it does not withdraw far enough."

inward man dwells truth"[10]) only to be swallowed up on the inside. "But, unlike the contents of ideas, sensations are discovered, given. They are not invented." The ethical moment, the moment in which the moral "ought" shows itself, is found, for Levinas, on the level of sensibility when the egoist self comes across something that it wants to enjoy, something that it wants to make a part of itself, but cannot. Thus, for Levinas, the other has some power over me. Indeed, the other is a transcendence that comes from beyond the categories of my thought, from beyond the world, from the other side of Being. Because of the other-worldliness of the epiphany of the other in the face-to-face, the (other) face speaks thus: "I am not yours to be enjoyed: I am absolutely other," or to put the claim in Levinas' terms, "thou shalt not kill."

**Astonishment as Initial Approach**

John Burke holds that the initial approach of the other person as described in Levinas' writings can be seen in terms of astonishment or surprise. In so doing, he also notes the essential element of radical passivity that arises from contact with the other person. He writes, "My astonishment seems less an activity of mine, a willful projection of a function of my interests, than the deepest mode of passivity."[11] Vulnerability arises from such a surprise, a being caught off guard by the epiphany of the other person. My solitude is invaded by the other person who seemingly comes from nowhere.[12]

---

10. Saint Augustine, *De vera Religione*, XXXIX, 72.
11. John Patrick Burke, "The Ethical Significance of the Face," *ACPA Proceedings* 56 (1982): 198.
12. See Burke, "The Ethical Significance of the Face," 198. The reason that the other "comes from nowhere" is seen in the fact that the "world" for Levinas is constituted by my reason and exists "for me." The Other comes from beyond the world, hence, from a domain that is not able to be located by me.

This element of "catching off-guard" is important in our reading of John 9 in light of Levinas' project because it indicates more about the presence of the other than the mere perception of the other. This catching off-guard makes me aware of the presence of the other as an "other" who is due my concern, not because I choose to give it to the other, but because it is demanded of me. In short, I want to consume the other, but cannot.[13] Two steps involved in elucidating this moment are *proximity* and *substitution*. These two notions will lead us to an understanding of ethical responsibility in Levinas, though it must be understood that responsibility is not derived from these steps; it is, rather, bound up with them.

**Astonishment in John 9:1-5:**

Turning to John 9, we see (both literally and figuratively) that the story begins with an encounter between Jesus and a man blind from birth. That the journey faith begins in blindness is akin to noting that language (or in the Johannine ethos—the Word) begins in silence. Although the dialogue regarding the man's status is between Jesus and the disciples, John does not say that the blind man does not hear the exchange, and it seems likely to me that the man does. The dialogue concerns the disciples' assumption that the man's blindness is the result of sin (his own, or that of his parents: cf. Gen 19:11; Jer 32:18). Jesus refutes this assumption, saying that the man was born blind "that the works of God may be made manifest in him. We must work the works of him who sent me, while it is day; night comes, and no one can work. As long as I am in the world, I am the light of the world" (vv. 3-6). Jesus has related not only his "works" but also those of his disciples to the creative power of God, using the same word (*erqa*) that we find in Gen 2:2,

---

13. Levinas makes a distinction between desire and need. Need differs from desire to the extent that a need can be satisfied while a desire cannot. Thus, desire has a metaphysical significance. Put concretely, I desire the other person, but since the other cannot be reduced to the domain of the same, my desire for the other can never be fulfilled.

Exod 34:10, and in the Psalms.[14] No doubt John intends this to refer to the "disciples" who constitute the Johannine community as well; they must realize that their works in Christ partake of divine power, and they must continue to do God's will in the present time despite their tribulations.[15]

Jesus has also identified himself as the light of the world. It is interesting to note, however, that this is not a typical "I am" saying; the "I" is not emphasized, and "light" has no definite article.[16] As the blind man hears this dialogue; given John's intention to show the development of the man's faith as one who "sees" yet is still "blind", a definitive pronouncement of identity from Jesus would be inappropriate at this time because the man is not ready for it. Jesus does say that he and his disciples (John refers here to his contemporaries as well) have a special relationship with God and a calling to bring light to the world, which he then demonstrates in action. So the initial revelation comes from Jesus himself, through the spoken word. By hearing this word, the blind man (as well as the reader) allows Jesus to open his eyes and begin, not fulfill, the development of faith (cf. John 5:24).

## John 9: 8–12: Proximity and the Face

Perplexed and skeptical after Jesus' healing of the man at Siloam[17], the people wonder whether they have truly seen a miraculous cure.

---

14. John J. Huckle and Paul Visokay, *The Gospel According to St. John*, Vol. 1 (New York: Crossroad, 1981), 128.
15. Rudolph Schnackenburg, *The Gospel According to John*, Vol. 2 (New York: Seabury, 1980), 241.
16. J. N. Sanders and B. A. Mastin, *A Commentary on the Gospel According to St. John* (London: Black, 1968), 238.
17. "Siloam" means "sent," just as Jesus (the source of "living water"—cf. John 4:10; Jer 2:17; 17:13) is sent by God to do God's work—as are the Christians to whom John writes. In Isaiah 8:6ff, the waters of Siloam signify God's loving-kindness (*hesed*), which Israel rejected. That rejection brought judgment upon Israel, as does the rejection of Jesus, and later of his followers, by the Jews (see John 9:39).

The formerly blind man testifies that he has indeed been cured, and the people inquire after Jesus. But the man, who is at the first stage of faith, does not know where Jesus is. Trusting in Jesus, he has gained the power to see yet is still blind—his faith is bound up with the "sign" of the healing. For him, the bringer of light remains "the *man* called Jesus" (v. 11) as an objective signifier rather than a subjective embrace. In this regard he does not know where Jesus has gone since he is not "looking" for him but reveling in "sight" that ultimately (given that he does not know where Jesus—the source of sight and light of the world) is blindness. Similarly, those people in John's world whose faith was based on miraculous signs were to understand that the living Christ would not truly be present to them until their faith matured beyond dependence on signs. This section represents a climax in the revelation of the identity of Jesus. The cured man does not yet understand fully what has happened, but he knows it is Jesus who has given him the gift of sight.

This movement of Jesus close enough to the man to bring sight without invitation is akin to Levinas' notion of the face of the other, that element of the other that is the ground of interpersonal contact, indicates immediacy with the other person that Levinas calls "proximity."[18] Proximity is felt as immediate contact. Levinas describes proximity in this way:

> ... the proximity of the Other is not simply close to me in space, or close like a parent, but he approaches me essentially insofar as I feel myself—insofar as I am—responsible for him. It is a structure that in nowise resembles the intentional relation which in knowledge attaches us to the object—to no matter what object, be it a human object. Proximity does not revert to this

---

18. See Andrew Tallon, "Intentionality, Intersubjectivity, and the Between: Buber and Levinas on Affectivity and the Dialogical Principle," *Thought* 53 (1978): 304. "The radical passivity of Levinas's self ... emerges only with the advent of the other, with the face of the other drawing near me; This nearness (*proximité*) is, of course, not an intentionality by me or him alone, not a mental "state" or activity, but meaning between us."

intentionality; in particular it does not revert to the fact that the other is known to me.[19]

**The proximity of the other demands a response**

In this way, Levinas claims that proximity is responsibility, or the ability to respond.[20] Proximity must then be thought of as a weight upon me that comes from the outside. But unlike Sartre who finds an antagonism in this entry of the other from the outside, Levinas finds the possibility of ethics, or the ground upon which ethics first shows itself. Not only does the possibility of ethics show itself here, the self now takes on a different characteristic. A new subjectivity is born that indicates that my self, as a subject, is a primary projection towards the other as a move of responsibility to the other. The very meaning of being a social subject is to be for-the-other.

This responsiveness is seen in John 9: 35—38. The man has now been cut off from family, religion, and society, yet his faith has not only not wavered, but has continued to deepen and mature. It is at this point that Jesus reappears and reveals himself fully. Jesus now shows himself as the Son of Man, the heavenly, pre-existent eschatological agent of God. (We see the realized or presentist eschatology of John; in the Synoptics, Jesus usually speaks of the Son of Man in the future tense, but, in verse 37, John has Jesus say to the man, "You have seen him, and it is he who speaks to you now.") Immediately the man believes and bows down in worship before Jesus (v. 38—the verb used here for worship is used elsewhere by John to refer to "the worship due to God"—cf. John 4:20-24). [22]

---

19. Emmanuel Levinas, *Ethics and Infinity: Conversations with Phillipe Nemo* (Richard Cohen, trans.; Pittsburgh: Duquesne University Press, 1985), 97. This elegant little book goes a long way in making Levinas' thought approachable to the uninitiated.

20. See Emmanuel Levinas, *Otherwise than Being or Beyond Essence* (Alphonso Lingis, trans.; Boston: Martinus Nijhoff Publishers, 1981), 139: "Proximity, difference which is non-indifference, is responsibility."

For Levinas, the fact remains—"Subjectivity is being a hostage."[21] That is to say, subjectivity arises from confrontation with the other where the other is dominant, never reducible to the domain of the same. Subjectivity means, in this context, subjection to the other. The self is a *sub-jectum*: it is under the weight of the universe ... the unity of the universe is not what my gaze embraces in its unity of apperception, but what is incumbent upon me from all sides, regards me, is my affair.[22]

The self is *subjected* to the other who comes from on high to intrude upon my solitude and interrupt my egoist enjoyment. The self, feeling the exterior in the guise of the other passes through its world, is already obligated to respond to the transcendent other who holds the self hostage. In turn, this means that "the latent birth of the subject occurs in obligation where no commitment was made."[23] I do not agree to live ethically with the other at first, I am ordered to do so. The meaning of my being a self is found in opposition to the other, as an essential ability to respond to the other. I am, above all things, a social self indentured *a priori*, made to stand in the place of the other.

**Substitution and Standing in the Place of the Other**

This standing in the place of the other provides Levinas with one of his most powerful concepts, "substitution." Substitution arises directly from the self as held hostage by the other. It is the means by which my being responds to the other before I know that it does. Indeed, substitution is a sign of how other-directed the human being actually is. In comporting myself towards the other person in substitution, my identity becomes concrete. "In substitution my being

---

21. Levinas, *Otherwise than Being*, 127.
22. Levinas, *Otherwise than Being*, 127.
23. Levinas, *Otherwise than Being*, 140.

that belongs to me and not to another is undone, and it is through substitution that I am not "another," but me."[24]

What Levinas proposes at this stage is that the depth-giving meaning of being a social subject is primarily to be for the other person. Again, substitution is indicative of a sacrifice of self—it cannot be merely the idea of being in the place of the other person, for ideas have yet to come on the scene. Alphonso Lingis in the introduction to *Otherwise than Being* puts it this way:
One is held to bear the burden of others: the substitution is a passive effect, which one does not succeed in converting into an active initiative or into one's own virtue.[25]

While it is true that Levinas is vague on the essence of substitution, the suggestion seems to be that in being persecuted by an other person, I am made to consider the person as an other. However, since such consideration cannot be made on the conceptual level, this consideration becomes manifest in a comportment of the self to the other person. Consideration for the other means being-considerate-for-the-other. Substitution then is recognizing myself in the place of the other, not with the force of a conceptual recognition, but in the sense of finding myself in the place of the other as a hostage for the other. Substitution is the conversion of my being as a subjection *by* the other into a subjection *for* the other.

In substitution Levinas is also arguing for the ethical summons as that which is a primary connection between moral agents that is not in need of mediation. This is the difference between watching an act of violence on television and seeing an act of violence in person. In which case do you feel the greater summons to respond - the encounter that is mediated or the personal encounter? When the summons is brought forward, Levinas says that at this moment, the

---

24. Levinas, *Otherwise than Being*, 127.
25. Alphonso Lingis in the translator's introduction to *Otherwise than Being*, xxxi. This introduction consists of a concise exposition of Levinas' thought in this work.

ethical command has been waged. You are obligated to respond. If the desire to respond does not, at first, present itself as a command, and you respond because you want to respond, then you have just been witness to the depth that substitution has taken in your own being. The desire to respond is already a responsiveness to the command of the other.

This brings us, at last, to Levinas' notion of ethical "responsibility." This notion of responsibility, much in line with our concept of responsiveness, means that in being a subject I am already in the grip of the Other. It also entails that all thought enters on the scene after the epiphany of the other in the face-to-face. This is to say that the other person precedes my ethical subjectivity, and that ethics precedes any conceptual science. Inasmuch as responsibility is foundational for all interpersonal relationships, it is in responsibility that we are going to find a means to pass from an encounter with the real other person into ethics. Levinas writes:

> In [*Otherwise than Being*] I speak of responsibility as the essential, primary and fundamental mode of subjectivity. For I describe subjectivity in ethical terms. Ethics, here, does not supplement a preceding existential base [as Heidegger would have it]; the very node of the subjective is knotted in ethics understood as responsibility.[26]

Furthermore, "the tie with the Other is knotted only as responsibility"[27] as well. Thus, responsibility *is* the link between the subject and the other person, or, in more general terms, the source of the moral "ought" and the appearance of the other person *as person and not as thing* are one and the same—"other as person and not thing"—anticipate this in the first reference to "other person." To say that responsibility is foundational for ethics and interpersonal relations is to say then not only that responsibility is what relates

---

26. Levinas, *Ethics and Infinity*, 95.
27. Levinas, *Ethics and Infinity*, 97.

one subject to another, but it is to go on to say that the meaning of the otherness of the other person is given in responsibility, and not in my interpretation of the other person. The very meaning of being an other person is "the one to whom I am responsible." Thus, the contact with the real other person that I spoke of at the beginning as something presupposed by the very meaning of ethics turns out to be, in Levinas' account, the source of the moral "ought."

**The Responsible Self—Seeing Blindly**

As seen in the movement of the man born blind who gropes though walking with eyes wide open toward an understanding of the "why" of his sightedness, the subject moves toward the radical other (in this case Jesus Christ) through responsibility. Since the subjective condition of the individual precedes and undoes consciousness, the I finds itself excluded from the field where knowledge and judgment are possible. The Other who summons the subject therefore radically transcends language and knowing—sight as we have been accustomed to it is akin to blindness. The responsible self and the other cannot be coordinated within a common horizon, and terms other than those derived from knowledge and being are called for—we look through a glass darkly. This is a haunting and dangerous place for faith to find a center point, but an authentic place nonetheless. For it is this liminal space—a thoroughly kenotic place of self-emptying and freed from the ability to totalise the Other—that Levinas summons those seeking community. This is a place that recalls Heidegger's idea of *lichtung*—a clearing that is unfettered and illuminated where the potential of *aletheia* may indeed arise under the ever-deconstructing temples of our own construction. It is here that Levinas enters a mystical rhetoric: this liminal space is ultimately figured by a *Good Beyond Being*. Insofar as responsibility describes the genesis of the subject prior to its being, responsibility must be described in terms of a Good beyond Being. Levinas writes, "If ethical terms arise in our discourse..., it is because... the subject finds himself committed to the Good in the very passivity of supporting."[28] This commitment to the Good, according to Levinas, is the very genesis or birth of the subject in responsibility. "The Good chooses me first before I can be in a position to choose, that is, welcome its choice... The Good is before being."[29] In this way, the Good summons me before I am, before I have being, and it is in response to that summons that I am born as a responsible self. "The way I appear is as a summons."[30] The relation between the Good and the self whose origin it marks is here described in terms of a summons, or call, which cannot be reduced to the relation between cause and effect or to any relation between two beings since the summons precedes and determines the eventual being of the other. The drama played out in responsibility is not acted by two beings, each seeking to pursue their own ends and to persevere in their own being, but in terms of goodness where I give up all that I could call my own in obedient response to the command of the hidden Good. Levinas writes, "the self is goodness, or under the demand for an abandon of all having... Goodness invests me in my obedience to the hidden Good."[31] Like the created soul who is what it is in terms of the good it has received, the responsible self exists only on account of its having received an investment of goodness which demands the dispossession of its own being in the proximity of the other.

---

28. Ibid., 122.
29. Ibid.
30. Ibid., 139.
31. Ibid., 118.

13

# Mission as the Integrating Center of Theological Education

JEFFREY P. GREENMAN

In presenting this approach, I hope to stimulate renewed conversation among theological educators and church leaders, in North America and beyond, about how theological schools should understand their purpose and frame their programmatic offerings and academic curricula, in light of the missionary nature of the church as presented in Scripture. My argument claims little originality, since a number of thinkers have pointed in this direction, especially since the early 1990's. Nevertheless, the sort of missional paradigm presented in this essay appears to remain counter-cultural, or perhaps even radical, in the face of the firmly established and widely held assumptions and patterns of Bible colleges, divinity schools and theological seminaries.

I have come to believe that every theological school—whether offering undergraduate or graduate-level studies; whether providing formal, non-formal or informal training; whether denominationally based or intentionally multi-denominational; whether operating with traditional or non-traditional delivery systems; whether located in urban or suburban or rural settings; whether in the affluent West or in the Majority World—is guided in critical ways by a dominant image of the local congregation. In other words, every theological school gears its programs of academic instruction and pastoral formation (therefore, also its faculty hiring practices and reward systems) around an operative ecclesiology, that is, a particular vision of the nature and mission of the church. Sometimes these images of the church are formally adopted, explicitly stated and are intentionally championed by the faculty. In other cases, the dominant image has no official status, operates more implicitly, and is rarely the subject of self-conscious discussion among faculty. Probably in most cases, there is a well-defined official ecclesiology, but a quite different operative ecclesiology. In any case, there is an ecclesial vision that orients the school's courses and programs.

The most deeply rooted pattern of theological education in North America (so readily exported around the globe) reflects what has been called a "professional paradigm" of ministry.[1] The operative ecclesiology revolves around seeing the church as a membership organization. Organized around the image of the "minister as professional," seminary programs have concentrated on training for the "designated tasks or activities which occur (or should occur) in the parish or in some specialized ministry."[2] According to this approach, ministry is assumed to be the activities of an ordained pastor performed in an institutionalized setting. These activities include leading worship, preaching, providing pastoral care, organizing Christian education, and supplying efficient administrative oversight of a congregation. This pattern is what might be called the "clerical-professional-functionalist" paradigm because it focuses on what full-time clergy are expected to do and how they should perform their professional duties. It is "functionalist" in gearing the various facets of theological education toward training students to perform certain important tasks or ministry functions.

---

1. Cf. Edward Farley, *Theologia: The Fragmentation and Unity of Theological Education* (Philadelphia: Fortress Press, 1983).

2. Farley, 11.

## MISSION AS THE INTEGRATING CENTER

Even a quick glance at seminary catalogues would show that the typical list of courses required for the Master of Divinity degree emphasizes the school's role in developing a student's skills in these specific areas. Farley notes that what provides the coherence or unifying thread of a theological education is that the "disparate fields and courses are connected by their capacity to prepare the student for future clergy responsibilities."[3] Courses in "academic" or "theoretical" subjects such as biblical studies, systematic theology or church history are expected to yield "usable" knowledge that serves the needs of future pastors in performing these functions. Often a great deal of effort is given to the attempt to "translate" or "apply" what is learned from Bible scholars, theologians or historians into the "real life" situations of parish life and work. In reality, the operative question of application standardly becomes: "How can I preach this in my church?"

According to this paradigm, the value of those "abstract" areas of study is largely determined by their capacity to inform "practical" concerns of congregational functioning, usually by means of the cultivation of the cognitive skills associated with "theological reflection." Commonly, what is offered to the student is a series of introductions to a range of theological sub-fields. Notice how academic catalogues are usually filled with course titles such as "Introduction to Apologetics" or "Introduction to Ethics" or "Introduction to Old Testament." Farley has observed that these sub-disciplines, "each with its own method, bibliography, scope, current issues, and so forth," are "introduced" as largely independent or self-constituted disciplines. The professors who teach these courses operate largely in intellectual isolation from each other, having adopted the prevailing norms of specialization and sub-specialization that drive the Western academy, including the theological guild. The unfortunate result is that theological education "has the character of a mélange

---

3.  Ibid., 98, note 38.

of introductions" (in Farley's delightful phrase) without a cohesive framework or unifying vision. This is a major factor in what he has labeled the "fragmentation" of theological education.

For my purposes, it is important to notice that the rationale and unity of the theological curriculum within this approach is provided by the requirements of a very specific understanding of the church and the role of the pastoral leader. In this traditional paradigm, what is emphasized is that the pastor's ministry primarily involves "taking care of his own." That is, the clergy's responsibilities are focused on the internal functions of the church, especially its Sunday activities, supplemented by mid-week programs or visitation. The pastor is expected to address the spiritual needs of an already-existing group of people. In somewhat crass terms, one might say that this paradigm is geared toward producing institutional caretakers. In the words of Newbigin: "Ministerial training as currently conceived is still far too much training for the pastoral care of existing congregations, and far too little oriented toward the missionary calling to claim the whole of public life for Christ and his Kingdom."[4] For Newbigin, Bosch and others, the inward-focus of the church reflects the power of the "Christendom" situation of the West, according to which the role of the church in an already-Christianized social context was aimed primarily at gathering in nominal Christians, deepening their spiritual commitment to Christianity, and caring for their personal needs.

Of course it would be foolish to deny that every congregation needs high quality leadership in preaching, worship, education and pastoral care. No one can doubt the spiritual power of biblical preaching, Christ-focused worship, and compassionate pastoral care. The problem with this paradigm is not that those ministries are unimportant, but that those tasks are framed within a rather imbal-

---

4. Lesslie Newbigin, *The Gospel in a Pluralistic Society* (Grand Rapids: Eerdmans, 1989), 231.

anced and minimalist ecclesiology. In particular, my concern is that the dominant paradigm typically assumes that the church as organization naturally is turned inward upon itself. On this approach, "ministry" is typically defined (either implicitly or explicitly) as what pastors do in rendering expert professional services on Sundays or throughout the week. The unfortunate effect of this mindset is that pastoral leadership is defined largely in managerial terms. Another regrettable consequence is that the laity's ministry is defined as "helping out" with lower level organizational functions within the institutionalized church settings (e.g., teaching Sunday School or being an usher or fundraising) since "having a ministry" is construed as performing a function inside the church building or helping to run church-based programs.

This traditional paradigm operates with the assumption that the church is, in Bosch's words, "a place where something is done, not a living organism doing something."[5] For Bosch, an underlying theological mistake is an ecclesiology that is static, rather than dynamic. What is emphasized is that the congregation is the place where certain things happen inside the walls of the church—primarily, the gospel in preached and the sacraments are administered. Under the contemporary North American (and increasingly global?) cultural conditions of consumer capitalism, privatized individualism and an increasingly therapeutic worldview, the "place where" account of the church has shifted: we often see the church as a "vendor of religious goods and services."[6]

Kraemer, Bosch, Newbigin, and various contemporary thinkers associated with the Gospel and Our Culture Network in recent years, drawing on a variety of sources in contemporary and classical

---

5. David Bosch, *Transforming Mission: Paradigm Shifts in Theology of Mission* (Maryknoll: Orbis, 1991), 249.
6. George R. Hunsberger, "Sizing up the Shape of the Church," in *The Church Between Gospel and Culture: The Emerging Mission in North America*, eds. George R. Hunsberger and Craig van Gelder (Grand Rapids: Eerdmans, 1996), 337-8.

theology, have attempted to articulate a biblical theology of the church's nature and mission that provides an important corrective to the operative ecclesiology of the traditional paradigm.[7] Missional ecclesiology offers a dynamic, outward-looking and doctrinally orthodox alternative to the static, inward-looking "place where" concept of the church that has long dominated Protestant theology and theological education. An apt slogan for missional ecclesiology would be: the church is not a place where people go, but a people who go places. For instance, Bosch typically refers to the church as "a body of people sent on a mission." The people of God are a missionary people, called into communion with God as a gathered people, brought together in order to be commissioned, empowered by the Holy Spirit and sent out to represent the reign of God in every aspect of life and in every corner of the world.[8] The result is that "mission is not just a program of the church" but rather constitutes the nature of the church itself. Often quoted in this theological conversation is Emil Brunner's dictum: "The Church exists by mission as fire exists by burning."[9] This entails that "the essential nature of the local congregation is, in and of itself, mission, or else the congregation is not really the Church."[10]

This view of the church has its strongest theological roots in an understanding of the biblical doctrine of God. In short, missional

---

7. For the most sophisticated statement of missional ecclesiology, see Darrel Guder, ed., *Missional Church: A Vision for the Sending of the Church in North America* (Grand Rapids: Eerdmans, 1998). For a succinct summary of a missional paradigm, see Darrel Guder, "The Church as Missional Community," in The Community of the Word" *Toward an Evangelical Ecclesiology,* ed. Mark Husbands and Daniel J. Treier (Downers Grove: InterVarsity Press, 2005), 114-28.

8.   Some Protestant readers might not be aware that this sort of missional understanding is the dominant conception to be found in a key Vatican II document on the "Dogmatic Constitution of the Church," *Lumen Gentium.*

9.   Emil Brunner, *The Word and the World* (London: SCM Press, 1931), 108.

10.   Charles van Engen, *God's Missionary People: Rethinking the Purpose of the Local Church* (Grand Rapids: Baker, 1991), 70.

thinking starts from the deeply Trinitarian view that the true and living God is a missionary God, who sends his Son, Jesus Christ, into world in order to accomplish his purposes for his creation, and who sends his Spirit to indwell his people so that they can share in Christ's work in the world, and become representatives of his Kingdom. Our God is a sending God, and as God's people, our deepest identity is found in belonging to God as those who are sent on his behalf into a needy world. It holds that God's people are a royal priesthood and holy nation (1 Pet 2:9-10), set apart for faithful witness and sent forth as participants in God's own mission (*missio Dei*), engaged in a missionary encounter with the world's cultures, demonstrating in word and deed the reality of the gospel. A missional paradigm would highlight the Reformational emphasis on the ministering priesthood of all believers. In the words of Newbigin: "Men and women are not ordained to [the] ministerial priesthood in order to take priesthood away from the people, but in order to nourish and sustain the priesthood of the people."[11]

There is much more that could be said about this conception of God and God's church, with attention to its major proponents, various nuances and theological implications. But for our purposes, this sketch is sufficient to provide us with the theological resources needed to form an alternative to the "clerical-professional-functionalist" paradigm of theological education. From this standpoint, the church is the whole people of God, and ministry is the privilege of the whole body of Christ in using their Spirit-given gifts as God's representatives in the world. Missional ecclesiology at its best has a de-clericalized view of ministry, and sees the major ministry of ordained leaders as equipping the saints for their own work of ministry (Eph 4:11-12). According to Newbigin, "the business of leadership is precisely to enable, encourage, and sustain the activity

---

11. Newbigin, *Gospel*, 235.

of all the members."[12] Under the traditional paradigm, ministry is what the clergy do in performing their professional tasks of "taking care of one's own." But if the church is constituted missionally, the proper emphasis of pastoral leadership is forming and equipping a community of authentic disciples to participate in mission to their culture and to the wider world. The role of the laity is not reduced to supporting the pastor's ministry, but involves discovering the variety of callings in the world wherein their gifts can be used faithfully. Ministry happens in the world—in and through homes, offices, factories, businesses—wherever God's people are using their gifts, living lives pleasing to the Lord, and offering their lives to God in service to their neighbors.

The pastor's challenge becomes fostering an environment (indeed, doing so through preaching, worship and education) where men and women can grow together as a community toward mature Christian discipleship, always understood as "discipleship-in-movement-to-the-world."[13] In the words of Lesslie Newbigin: "The task of ministry is to lead the congregation as a whole in a mission to the community as a whole, to claim its whole public life, as well as the personal lives of all its people, for God's rule."[14]

In the missional congregation, there will be a natural rhythm of gathering (assembling, in Jesus' name, for edification and intercession) and sending (scattering, in the Spirit's power, for mission and service). In these ways, the congregation and its leaders are turned outward, yet mission is not reduced merely to another program or an isolated function of the church (e.g., the workings of a church "mission committee" that has little to do with the vast majority of the church's life). Authentically missional congregations do not forget to "take care of one's own" because God's people should be marked as those who love each other (John 15:12). Yet they do

---

12. Ibid., 235.
13. van Engen, 76.
14. Newbigin, *Gospel,* 238.

not neglect the public witness of the gospel and the public lives of Christ's disciples. There is no dichotomy between inward and outward dimensions of balanced, biblical Christianity.

Missional ecclesiology draws attention to the importance of recapturing a mission-centered conception of theology, and by extension, a mission-centered paradigm of theological education. Bosch cites the view of Martin Kaehler that "mission is the mother of the church" and that theology began as "an accompanying manifestation of the Christian mission."[15] As such, the purpose of theology involves glorifying God by equipping and mobilizing the church to fulfill its missional calling. This challenges the tendency of the Western theological guild to talk and write theology as if it were a free-standing discipline disconnected from the human calling to know and love God, and from God's missional purposes of the Church.

A missional view of theology challenges biblical and theological scholars in theological schools to orient their labors not primarily toward what gains them recognition in their professional guilds, but toward what equips the church's leaders and empowers God's people to engage their world faithfully. In many theological schools, the pursuit of "academic excellence" has contributed to an "academic" or even "scholastic paradigm" rather than a missional one. In such cases, "academic success" has become most readily associated with meeting the rigorous standards and expectations of professional guilds, and is measured by the student's capacity to learn sophisticated critical methodologies and write footnote-saturated research papers (using proper bibliographic conventions!). In missional terms, "academic excellence" should be redefined in terms of the Christian's pursuit of intellectual maturity, involving loving God with all our minds, as cultivated through the renewal of our minds by God's Spirit according to his word in Scripture,

---

15. Bosch, 16.

and as measured by a capacity to think biblically and live faithfully on behalf of God's mission to the world as representatives of his Kingdom.

An example of this notion of theology is provided by J. Andrew Kirk: "All true theology is, by definition, missionary theology, for it has as its object the study of the ways of a God who is by nature missionary and a foundation text by and for missionaries. Mission as a discipline is not, then, the roof of a building that completes the whole structure, already constructed by blocks that stand on their own, but both the foundation and the mortar in the joints, which cements together everything else. Theology should not be pursued as a set of isolated disciplines."[16] Needless to say, this alternative view lies at the margins of respectability in the Western theological academy. Theologians or institutions that pursue this vision run the risk of being marginalized within prestigious academic circles. Yet this mission-centered approach offers significant promise as the most likely way to overcome the fragmentation of theological knowledge that characterizes so much of traditional theological education.

Conceiving of theology as "the accompanying manifestation" of the missional church calls for a fundamental rethinking of the shape and focus of theological education. It puts front and center the Gospel's engagement with every dimension of life so that Christians in every culture are equipped to take a missionary perspective toward their own contexts. This means that every Christian leader, and certainly every congregational pastor, needs missiological skills, especially a capacity to "read" the surrounding culture, to discern God's intentions for his or her faith community in that situation, and to build teams of people committed to shared ministry. The key questions become, "What is God already doing in

---

16. J. Andrew Kirk, *The Mission of Theology and Theology as Mission* (Valley Forge: Trinity Press International, 1997), 50-1.

this community and how can we join it? And where is God sending us, in this community, as his witnesses in word and deed?" The process of forming men and women for ministry as biblically understood needs to be considered as equipping the saints for missional engagement with culture, so that they represent God's reign in word and deed, and so that they are able to equip others to participate in Christ's work in the world.

If this theological argument is right—namely, that our God is a missionary God, and therefore, God's people are a missionary people—then our paradigms of theological education should developed in light of these core convictions. My view is that the entire theological curriculum can achieve a considerable measure of unity and cohesion by operating out of an intentionally missional framework expressed throughout the various academic disciplines. Formation for mission can serve successfully as a unifying thread in a way that a disjointed series of "Introductions to..." can never do. If reframed missionally around knowing and serving our missionary God as God's sent people, then courses in biblical studies, theology, ethics, church history, leadership, spirituality, preaching, evangelism, and pastoral care each can contribute importantly toward the formation of missional leaders. These courses might well look quite different from what we usually associate with the "professional paradigm."

Despite the obvious perils of treading as a non-specialist on someone else's disciplinary turf, let me offer a brief suggestive sketch of how the overarching goal of "formation for mission" might reshape some of these traditional courses. Each of these disciplines offers rich resources for a "missional paradigm."

Biblical studies courses should not presume that students know the basic content and historical storyline of the Bible. Beyond that descriptive knowledge, courses in biblical studies should be concerned to develop a synthetic biblical theology and to hone the capacity to interpret the texts of Old and New Testaments in exegetically responsible ways. This requires a more deeply theological engagement with Scripture, as we ask questions about the nature and character of God, his purposes in raising up a distinct people as his witnesses, and the ways that those people interact with their surrounding contexts. Too often, traditional academic approaches tend to emphasize linguistic and historical backgrounds to the text at the expense of the text's theological message. As I. Howard Marshall has stated: "New Testament theology is essentially missionary theology."[17] Thinking in terms of the central and crucial role of Scripture in forming communities of faith would mean enabling students to develop a "missional hermeneutic" of Scripture that proceeds from the assumption that the whole Bible "renders to us the story of God's mission through God's people in their engagement with God's world for the sake of the whole of God's creation."[18] According to Wright, "the task of a missional reading is to see how a text often has its origin in some issue, need, controversy or threat, which the people of God needed to address in the context of their mission. The text itself is a product of mission in action."[19] The educational aim should be to cultivate a capacity to think biblically, i.e., think "with the grain of the Bible" about its message in missional terms, so that students would be able to move from exegesis to sermon to praxis as people who can discern the contours of the church's contemporary life and witness in its many contexts.[20]

---

17. I. Howard Marshall, *New Testament Theology* (Downers Grove: InterVarsity Press, 2004), 34.

18. See Christopher Wright, "Mission as a Matrix for Hermeneutics and Biblical Theology," in *Out of Egypt*, ed. Craig Bartholomew, Mary Healy, Karl Möller and Robin Parry (Grand Rapids: Zondervan, 2004), 103. See also Wright's full-scale attempt at a missional reading of Scripture in *The Mission of God: Unlocking the Bible's Grand Narrative* (Downers Grove: InterVarsity Press, 2006).

19. Ibid., 121.

20. The "Missional Bible Study Project" being undertaken by the Gospel and Our Culture Network is suggestive of a new direction in thinking missionally about Scripture, and allowing Scripture's missional orientation to reorient us. The basic question is: "How did this text equip and shape God's people for their missional witness then, and how does it shape us today?" This question is expanded into five sub-questions: "How does this

Theological studies should focus not only on grounding the student's understanding of classical Christian doctrine but would also seek to foster what Miroslav Volf calls the "habits that sustain a lifelong intellectual exploration of the love and knowledge of God in service of God's world."[21] A missional paradigm calls for a more seriously theological integration across the curriculum rather is normally experienced in traditional models. A missional approach to theology would require teaching and learning Christian doctrinal convictions in historically nuanced ways as theology (both Western and Eastern) was forged in the light of specific challenges faced by the church's mission. It would also necessitate a new organizing scheme to the often-disconnected topics in traditional renditions of "systematic" theology; most standard textbooks of Protestant systematic theology reflect the non-missional, Christendom assumptions of the Western academy. The educational aim should be to cultivate a capacity to think theologically, including a capacity to formulate a "local theology" that contextualizes the Gospel and the church's witness in a specific place and time.[22]

Ethics should become a study of the ways Christians in community live out the distinctive marks of Christian character and engage their culture in light of Christ's Lordship over both public and private spheres, thus over family, sexuality, politics, economics, work, and so on. For example, courses on marriage or sexual ethics

---

text evangelize us with Good News? Convert us in personal and corporate life? Read us and our world? Focus us on God's inbreaking reign? Send us and equip our witness?" On these questions, see the GOCN website, www.gocn.org/MissionalBibleStudy.htm. For a helpful example of how this framework helps us to understand 2 Corinthians, see Darrell L. Guder, *Unlikely Ambassadors: Clay Jar Christians in God's Service* (Louisville: Presbyterian Distribution Service, 2002).

21. Miroslav Volf, "Dancing for God: Challenges Facing Theological Education Today," in *The Bible and the Business of Life*, eds. Simon Carey Holt and Gordon Preece (Adelaide: ATF Press, 2004), 134.

22. Cf. Robert Schreiter, *Constructing Local Theologies* (Maryknoll: Orbis, 1985).

would operate with missional assumptions, rather than therapeutic ones, and therefore ask: "What does the family have to do with the Kingdom of God and the mission of the Church? What is the Good News for our community's families? How do our culture's views of family and aspirations for family life relate to the biblical teaching about the Kingdom?" Rethinking this discipline would mean that ethics would be approached more from the standpoint of contextualized biblical theology rather from the starting point of Western philosophical systems (deontology, utilitarianism, virtue theory, and so on) and their attendant "moral dilemmas."

Church history should be reframed as a reading of the engagement of Christians over the centuries and around the world with their diverse cultural contexts. Bosch has suggested that church history could be appropriately viewed as "the history of the sending of God."[23] Key questions become: How has the church proclaimed the Gospel, fostered authentic discipleship and engaged in public witness? What can we learn from the Church's major traditions of kerygmatic and diaconal ministry? How has the church discerned the shape of faithfulness rather than cultural compromise or faithless accommodation under the pressures of its surrounding cultures? The "professional paradigm" of theological education often has reduced church history to the story of a particular denominational or ideological triumph, or has overemphasized church history as the story of intra-church disputes rather than as the church's attempts at faithful embodiment of the reign of God.

Leadership in a missional model should move away from the dominant managerial paradigm of leadership taught in the "clerical-professional-functionalist" approach with its static ecclesiology. Rethinking leadership courses in missional categories means emphasizing the role of the community's leader as someone who models Christian faithfulness, who operates with a biblical

---

23. Bosch, *Transforming Mission*, 495.

theology of leadership, and whose concern is to foster the formation of authentic communities of disciples. This means that missional leadership is concerned more with multiplying leaders and with bringing about meaningful change, for the sake of strengthening a congregation's engagement with the world, rather than being focused on filling slots on committees or with the maintenance of existing structures or patterns. Because missional congregations will take risks, and will face opposition both from within and from without, missional leaders will benefit from a practical understanding of organizational dynamics, teamwork and team building, and conflict resolution. They will also need a coherent theology of suffering and struggle.[24]

Spirituality courses in a missional model should set high expectations for the student's spiritual formation through an emphasis on the cultivation of a way of life shaped continually by engagement with God through historic practices of spiritual disciplines. Biblical meditation and contemplative prayer are essentials for missional engagement with the world. There is much to celebrate in the Protestant and evangelical rediscovery of the spiritual disciplines in the past few decades. Within this recovery movement, the missional paradigm would also emphasize the corporate and outward-focused disciplines such as service to the poor, hospitality to strangers, and simplicity of lifestyle. It would seek to develop both a spirituality of justice, social action, daily work and public engagement and a spirituality of contemplation, retreat and silence, as being as fully interdependent as two wings of bird (to borrow an image from John Stott's analysis of the interconnection of evangelism and social action).

---

24. The work of Alan Roxburgh on missional leadership is particularly important: Alan Roxburgh and Fred Romanuk, *The Missional Leader: Equipping Your Church to Reach a Changing World* (San Francisco: Jossey-Bass, 2006); also, Alan J. Roxburgh, *The Missionary Congregation, Leadership and Liminality* (Harrisburg: Trinity Press International, 1997).

Preaching courses should move away from the traditional emphasis on practicing the techniques of sermon delivery toward a more deeply theological approach, with an emphasis on working from the biblical texts (whether in original languages or in translation) through responsible exegesis to the formation of a message suited for the student's ministry setting and its implications for prayer, worship, ethics and evangelism. An experimental approach worth attempting is the integration of preaching-related assignments into every course the student takes, so that a preaching component is built into courses on the Bible, theology, ethics, spirituality, leadership and the like.[25] This intentionally integrative pedagogy can be another source of cohesion within the theological curriculum.

Evangelism in a missional paradigm of theological education should be framed in richly theological and historical terms, so that students would come to understand for themselves the meaning of the Gospel as the Good News of God's Kingdom and the Church's diverse ways of proclaiming that message in its varied cultural settings. Rather than focusing on the pastor as solo evangelist whose preaching in the church building or through church programs offers men and women salvation, as in the dominant paradigm, the missional approach would go further and head in different directions. Thinking missionally would suggest an emphasis on the pastor as an evangelist who fosters in a congregation an atmosphere of confidence in the Gospel through consistent biblical teaching, who equips others for witness to the Gospel (in word and deed) using their diverse gifts, who mobilizes the congregation to engage

---

25. As I write, this experiment is being attempted in the "In-Ministry M.Div. Program" at Tyndale Seminary in Toronto. There is no "free-standing" preaching course required in the degree. Students encounter an integrative preaching component of each course, are required to preach to one another "real" sermons (ungraded) in the context of their weekly communal chapels, and receive personalized feedback from faculty about their sermons. In addition, they are expected to be preaching in their home congregations.

their workplaces and neighborhoods, and who invites their people to join with them as they cross boundaries of unbelief in order to befriend and engage those who have not yet given their allegiance to Christ and his Kingdom.

Pastoral care in a missional paradigm is a topic about which there is virtually no active conversation taking place. There is scant literature that takes a missional approach to pastoral work. Missionally-framed pastoral preparation should emphasize the congregational leader's role as a "skilled helper" who is able to provide appropriate short-term attention to spiritual or personal needs, and who is able to discern situations involving spiritual warfare or psychiatric distress, but whose chief role is to equip a team of people (perhaps staff and/or lay ministers) to use their spiritual and professional gifts in counseling contexts and to provide the longer term care that many people will need. The goal is to equip a congregation that presses beyond "taking care of one's own" to become a healing community that seeks to bring wholeness to the lives of people in the surrounding neighborhoods and throughout their town or city.

These are some suggestions about how various disciplines of the traditional curriculum could be revised or framed in more missional terms. If we aim to move in these directions, any missional paradigm of theological education will also involve a major rethinking of traditional delivery systems, will call for the discovery of new forms of communal learning (such as cohort programs) and will flourish with an "action-reflection" model of learning. It would require another essay (or several!) to explore these dimensions of a missional paradigm. Robert Banks' book, *Reenvisioning Theological Education,* has made a significant contribution in these areas.[26] My own experience at Tyndale Seminary in Toronto would suggest that Banks' insights about community and pedagogy in theologi-

---

26. Robert Banks, *Reenvisioning Theological Education: Exploring a Missional Alternative to Current Models* (Grand Rapids: Eerdmans, 1999).

cal education can be put into practice with considerable success in focused programs that are given institutional "space" to experiment with new approaches.

My purpose in this essay has been to describe what a missional paradigm of theological education might look like, and explore why this approach should be seen as a viable option for theological schools, both across North America and beyond. The fact that a number of theological schools are finding that their experiments with missional reframings of their programs are leading to educationally transformative outcomes in the lives of their students suggests that this sort of approach is workable, even in institutions that have used traditional models for decades, and even without substantial new infusions of funds.[27] But beyond being workable, my argument is that this way of rethinking theological education is necessary for deep-seated theological reasons. If our God is truly a "missionary God" who sends raises up, empowers and sends his people into the world as his representatives, then the content and structure of theological education needs to be shaped by missional theology. This shaping, or reshaping, which aims at equipping God's people for faithful witness to Christ in every culture and in every sphere of society, not only is both an urgent need for Christ's church in a post-Christendom context, but also represents an exciting opportunity for theological educators.[28]

---

27. Some of the Protestant schools that have been exploring this sort of approach during the past decade include Luther Seminary, Western Theological Seminary, Biblical Theological Seminary, and Tyndale Seminary.

28. I would like to thank Donald Goertz and Tom Sweeney for their suggestions about previous drafts of this essay. I am grateful to my former colleagues at Tyndale Seminary for their willingness to explore these ideas through extended conversation and practical experimentation.

14

# Reading the Bible in the Global Markeplace

R. PAUL STEVENS

"What do you teach at Regent College?" This seemingly innocent question was broached by the guestmaster of an Orthodox monastery. I had undertaken a four-day pilgrimage on Mount Athos, the monastic peninsula of the Eastern church. In the course of praying my way from monastery to monastery I struck up a soul friendship with one of the guestmasters. "Marketplace theology is what I teach." "What's that?"—his inquisitiveness now aroused by something foreign, he thought, to the spiritual life. "It is the integration of Christian faith with work in the world." "It's not possible," he retorted. "That's why I am a monk." I can understand how he came to that erroneous view. It has to do with how we read the Bible, how we regard the spiritual life and whether the God-coming of Jesus was really into the work-a-day world that we inhabit.

It is a joy to write a chapter in honour of Carl Armerding, not only because he has been a dear friend, supporter and guide in the multiple contexts where we have served together—church, college and global mission—but more particularly because as a Bible teacher and professor he has a lifetime of bringing the Word of God "home" to people where they are. Again it has to do with *how* we read the Bible. But not just how: *what* we read.

## The Marketplace in the Bible

*What* we read in the Bible should be enough to convince us that God is at work in our worldly enterprise. The Incarnation is a wonderful scandal—God going through a complete human experience from conception to resurrection. Jesus, God's Son, works in a carpenter's shop for twenty years when so many souls around him were lost. The Father speaks approval of him at his baptism even though he has never preached a sermon or worked a miracle. The Bible itself, in both testaments, is itself a scandalously common book. God speaks through the language of the street: Aramaic and Hebrew in the Old Testament and common street-Greek in the New. The great English Greek Scholar, James Hope Moulton, following up evidence gained through the discovery of the Oxyrhynchus papyrus fragments in Egypt, said, "The Holy Ghost spoke absolutely in the language of the people, as we might have expected He would."[1]

In his formidable series on biblical spirituality Eugene Peterson notes that even the word "daily bread" placed in the strategic centre of the Lord's Prayer—often interpreted by church people as spiritual bread, Eucharistic bread or heavenly bread—is, as we now know from the Oxyrhynchus fragments, to be the ordinary bread from the market, purchased along with chickpeas and straw.[2] Without having access to these recent discoveries Adolf Deissmann had speculated that *epiousion*[3] (daily) "had the appearance of a word that originated in the trade and traffic of the everyday life of the people."

---

1. James Hope Moulton, *A Grammar of New Testament Greek*, vol. 1 (3rd ed.; Edinburgh: T&T Clark, 1908), 5, quoted in Eugene H. Peterson, *Eat This Book: A Conversation in the Art of Spiritual Reading* (Grand Rapids: Eerdmans, 2006), 146.
2. Peterson, *Eat This Book*, 149.
3. Adolf Deissmann, *Light from the Ancient East* (Lionel Strachan, trans.; 4th ed. (New York: George H. Doran, 1927), 78, quoted in Peterson, *Eat This Book*, 149.

Add to that the fact that of Jesus' 132 public appearances in the New Testament, 122 were in the marketplace. Of 52 parables Jesus told, 45 had a workplace context. Of 40 divine interventions recorded in Acts, 39 were in the marketplace or the public square. Jesus called 12 normal working individuals, not clergy, to build his church and some of them had questionable professions.[4]

**The Marketplace as a Common Occupation of Bible Characters**

Walter Duckat in his book, *Beggar to King: All the Occupations of Biblical Times,* lists over two hundred different occupations found in biblical times, giving archeological and literary evidence for the history of that occupation. Many of these are found in Scripture. Some of the occupations are exotic, such as the snake charmer, the magician, the mirror-maker, pawn-broker, gambler, dream-interpreter, the prostitute, counterfeiter, and candy maker. But what is remarkable is the number of occupations that we find in the work world of the 21st century: accountant, actor, architect, banker, spy, barber, census taker, clothier, druggist, furniture designer, hair-dresser, housewife, jeweler, lawyer, merchant, money-changer, nurse, physician, realtor, ship-builder, soldier, spice-dealer, teacher, theatre-worker, treasurer, vintner, weights and measures inspector. On each of these Duckat states what they did, and where they are mentioned in the Bible, in Jewish literature (such as the Talmud), or in the evidence of ancient manuscripts. He has a section on commerce and trade: transportation for trade purposes, methods of transportation, products, markets, fairs, exports, imports, royal merchants, business regulations, money, income, wealth, attitudes to workers, female workers, guilds and strikes.[5] We can profitably look at a few.

---

4. I owe this summary to Al Bussard, Director of Integra, Bratislava, Slovakia.
5. Walter Duckat, *Beggar to King: All the Occupations of Biblical Times* (Garden City: Doubleday & Co., 1968).

In Genesis 24:52 Abraham's servant buys a wife for Isaac. Isaac becomes very wealthy through the blessing of God (26:12), so the Philistines envied his monopoly and stopped up his wells (26:14-15)—a hostile takeover. Jacob negotiates with Laban for a salaried position that would allow him to get what he needs for his family while giving Laban "nothing" (30:31) since Jacob knows that Laban does not really want to give him anything.[6] Dinah's brothers make an unscrupulous arrangement for the bride-price for Dinah with Shechem, never intending to fulfill the bargain. The result of this deceitful transaction is that they have to run (34:13-17).

Joseph is the first "futures" trader in the Bible—saving food during the seven years of plenty for the coming seven years of famine and, in the process, enslaving the whole nation to Pharaoh (Gen 37). Jethro visits Moses and counsels this almost burned out CEO how to delegate his work to "capable men from all the people" (Exod 18:21). Solomon makes a deal with Hiram to provide the materials for the temple in exchange for wheat and oil (1 Kgs 5). Job gives an elaborate description of the technology of mining in the context of affirming that wisdom cannot so easily be found and is gained through the fear of the Lord (Job 28).

The wisdom of Proverbs is especially fascinating, counseling the gradual creation of wealth rather than embracing a "get rich quick" scheme: "Dishonest money dwindles away, but he who gathers money little by little makes it grow" (13:11). "All hard work brings a profit, but mere talk only leads to poverty" (14:23). "Of what use is money in the hand of a fool, since he has no desire to get wisdom" (17:16). Proverbs 31 describes the entrepreneurial wife—she buys fields and sees that her trading is profitable: "Give her the reward she has earned and let her works bring her praise at the city gate."

---

6. See my *Down-to-Earth Spirituality: Encountering God in the Ordinary, Boring Stuff of Life* (Downers Grove: InterVarsity Press, 2003), 92-102.

In Ecclesiastes the Professor reflects on the futility of great enterprises "under the sun." "Whoever loves money never has enough; whoever loves wealth is never satisfied with his income. This too is meaningless" (5:10). "The abundance of the rich man permits him no sleep" (5:12). And yet good work and wealth are a gift of God. "When God gives any man wealth and possessions, and enables him to enjoy them, to accept his lot and be happy in his work—this is a gift of God" (5:19, see the opposite in 6:2).

In Ezekiel 27 the prophet laments for Tyre, a powerful hint that we should lament an unjust economic system. Tyre is under the judgment of God. Her extensive international trading described in 27:9-24 includes silver, iron, tin, lead, slaves, articles of bronze, work horses, war horses, mules, ivory tusks and ebony, turquoise, purple fabric, embroidered work, fine linen, coral, rubies, wheat, confections, honey, oil, balm, wine, wool, cassia, calamus, saddle blankets, lambs, rams, goats, spices, precious stones, beautiful garments, blue fabric, and multicolored rugs.

In the New Testament, Jesus, in the so-called "silent years," worked as a carpenter, or possibly an entrepreneur (since the word usually translated "carpenter" can also means one who designs and implements the building of a house or a boat). Paul worked with Aquila and Priscilla as a tentmaker and sold his products in the marketplace (Acts 18:1-4). He also exploited the marketplace location and the rhythm of economic life to provide an apologetic and evangelistic ministry in the workplace in the rented Hall of Tyrannus (Acts 19:9). More than describing people working in the marketplace, the Bible tells us how the marketplace relates to the purpose of God. A cartoon shows two men talking. One says to the other, "I have just discovered the meaning of life. Unfortunately it has no business application." Nothing could be more wrong.

**The Marketplace in the Purpose of God**

From the beginning of Genesis we learn that God created humankind to enjoy communion with God, to build community and to be co-creators with God (having dominion, expressing stewardship and taking care of the earth—Gen 1:28; 2:15). This involves everything from agriculture to agribusiness, from animal husbandry to domestic husbandry, from tool-making to city-making. Speaking to the purpose of God, Kenneth Kantzer says that business was apparently in God's mind from the very beginning:

> By creation, human beings are social beings, never intended to live alone. Because of our social nature, we are specialized (each person is in one sense unique), interdependent and, therefore, necessarily dependent on exchange. Exchange is built into our very nature. And this *is* business.[7]

One of the earliest references to the world beyond Eden denotes the land of Havilah where "the gold is good" (Gen 2:12). It is implicit in the Genesis account that God intended Adam and Eve (and their descendents) to "fill the earth." This involved extending the glorification of God in all of life through expanding the sanctuary garden into the world. The Garden (sanctuary), Eden (home) and the lands (the world) are like three concentric circles, expanding the mission globally. Ironically, their expulsion from the Garden was both judgment (for their sin) and fulfillment (for it forced them to fill the world). We see a sign in this direction in the descendents of Cain who engaged in commerce—living in tents and raising livestock, making and playing musical instruments and forging tools (Genesis 4:20-22). We are not to assume that because they were descendents of the murderer Cain that their activity was evil. This was the beginning of commerce, culture and crafts. Of necessity people were forced to engage in exchange and *this is business*.

The tower of Babel represents autonomous enterprise that was idolatrous: the city and the tower (Gen 11). Their expulsion, and the

---

7. Kenneth S. Kantzer, "God Intends His Precepts to Transform Society," in Richard C. Chewning, ed., *Biblical Principles & Business: The Foundations* (Colorado Springs: Navpress, 1989), vol. 1, 24.

diversification of languages, was, like that of Adam and Eve, both judgment and fulfillment. They were judged for their self-promoting arrogance and yet forced to go about "filling the earth" (read "global wholistic mission" that includes enterprise). But enterprise and exchange is to be undertaken in dependence on God. Deuteronomy 8:3 speaks to this. God says through Moses, "He humbled you ... and then [fed] you with manna...to teach you that man does not live on bread alone but on every word that comes from the mouth of God." The word from the mouth of God is not mere speech but the dynamic self-revelation that causes things to happen, in this case food. God reveals himself in provision. We see this also in the Garden in Eden, where God's first gift was food to be eaten with gratitude and in communion with God. Therein always lies the danger: "When you have eaten and are satisfied ... be careful that you do not forget the Lord" (8:10-18); it is the Lord that "gives you the ability to produce wealth" (8:18). In the last book of the Bible, Revelation 18:1-24, God will judge the corrupt marketplace. The merchants weep because Babylon has fallen. "All your riches and splendor have vanished, never to be recovered."

And yet, this final vision of the Lord's full reign, the full coming of the Kingdom and the new heaven and new earth, suggests that there will be economic and enterprising work in what is commonly called "heaven" but is in fact a totally renewed creation: "My chosen ones will long enjoy the works of their hands. They will not toil in vain..." (Isa 65:22-3). "The kings of the earth will bring their splendor into (the holy city) .... The glory and honor of the nations will be brought into it" (Rev 21:24-26[8]).[9] This has led two professor of marketing

---

8.     Additional Scriptures: Gen 13; Ps 8:6; Deut 28:1-68; Job 8:7, 22:21 (but also see 31:24-28).

9.     See Richard J. Mouw, *When the Kings Come Marching In: Isaiah and the New Jerusalem* (Grand Rapids: Eerdmans, 2002) and Paul Marshall, *Heaven Is Not My Home: Living in the Now of God's Creation* (Nashville: Word, 1998).

to argue that there will be marketing in heaven![10] Even if scarcity does not exist there, will be choices to make about the sequential ordering of activities that we choose to engage in. We will also need to process information and make decisions. Even though we will know more, we will not be omniscient. They argue:

> The ability to provide information and to innovate will be a spiritual gift that will in many ways benefit the body of Christ.... Marketing will be a process for loving one's neighbour as well as a process for loving God since, as Martin Luther proposed, we show our love for God by loving our neighbour and we show our love for our neighbour in our daily work.[11]

But, back to life in the here and now.

**The Revelation of God in the Marketplace**

Abraham had apparently the same attitude as many pastors and Christians toward the marketplace: it is a place bereft of God. In Genesis 20:1-18 Abraham passes off Sarah as his sister because he thinks, there is no "fear of God" in the secular marketplace of Abimelech's kingdom and some will kill him to gain his beautiful wife. But God speaks to Abimelech in a dream, confronts the believer with his duplicity, gives gifts to Abraham, and offers him to live wherever he wishes. God reveals himself to Jacob in the context of his work. Jacob is given a dream about his breeding project on Laban's farm (Gen 31:10-13). The Lord grants favour with Joseph as a slave, a prisoner and as vice-regent of Egypt. Moses encounters God in a burning bush while engaging in his shepherding work. Bezalel, a craftsman, is the only person in the Old Testament about whom it is said that he was "filled with the Spirit of God" for the purpose of his work (Exod 31:3). God selects Saul while he working,

---

10. Todd Steen and Steve VanderVeen, "Will There Be Marketing in Heaven?" *Perspectives* (November 2003): 6-11.

11. Steen and Vanderveen, 10.

looking for his lost donkeys. God provides a husband for Ruth in the marketplace as she gleans for her provision (Ruth 2).

In the New Testament the call to discipleship came to the fishermen, Peter, Andrew, James and John (Matt 3:18-22; Luke 5:1-11) while they were working in their aqua business. Peter is reinstated in his discipleship while he is again at work (John 21:15-23). The call comes to Matthew while collecting taxes for the federal government (Matt 9:9-12). Then there is the sermon of Stephen. After showing that the revelation of God has taken place mainly in places other than the sanctuary he says, "The Most High does not live in houses made by men" (Acts 7:48); he got executed for preaching this message! Most of the revelations of God did not take place in tabernacle, temple or church but right where people were working and living. It would be like God to do that![12] God originates and is involved in global blessing.

**The Marketplace in the Global Mission of God**

As mentioned above, in the Bible we even have an example of international trade in Solomon's exchange with Hiram king of Tyre, Hiram selling Solomon logs for the temple and Solomon selling Hiram wheat and oil. We are, of course, in a vastly more complex situation that obtained at the time of writing of Scripture. I replaced my stolen film camera with a "Japanese" digital, only to discover that the body is made in Thailand and the lens in China. Sitting on the rapid transit in Manila a young woman beside me struck up a conversation. "Are you a visitor?" "Yes." I ask why she is coming home from work so early (it was 2.30 p.m.). She explained that she has the night and morning shift for a call centre, answering inquiries for a telephone company is the eastern USA. "That must be a tough job,"

---

12. Additional Scriptures: Gen 23:5-20; 24:52; 39:3; 39:21; 40; 45:5; 50:20; Exod 1:11-14; 2:23-5; 3; Deut 8:3, 10-18; Judg 6:16; 1 Sam 9:1-10:27; 2 Chr 32:24-33; Neh; Job 24; Jer 18:6.

I offered. "I love it," she replied. "People usually start off rudely or even angrily, and I get to talk them down. By the end they are apologizing." CNN carries the news of the China—Africa conference in Beijing that will result in China having greater access to the raw materials, especially oil in Africa and African nations receiving both aid and increased trade. Unquestionably international trade plays a role in world peace for as someone has said Japan would be crazy to drop bombs (now) on its most important trading partner.

The Bible reveals the settled determination of God to bless all the nations. It starts with God: *missio Dei*. God is sender, sent, and sending. God calls Adam and Eve to "fill the earth." Then Abraham is chosen and empowered with a promise that includes family, the land and the "blessing the nations." Israel (Abraham's successors) is called to be a light to the nations which involves being a "demonstration plot" for how life is to be lived, how economic justice is to be effected and how the land is to be developed. This has led Michael Novak to propose that:

> From its very beginnings the modern business economy was designed to become an international system, concerned with raising the "wealth of nations," all nations, in a systematic, social way. It was by no means focused solely on the wealth of particular individuals.[13]

Whether cedar from Lebanon, olive oil from Israel, pencils or automobiles, coffee or telephones, most goods cannot be created through the work of an isolated individual and require cooperation of several, often many, towards a common goal.

Undoubtedly Israel failed to live up to this high calling, and the prophets railed against the injustices in the marketplace—selling the poor for the price of a pair of sandals, holding back wages (a matter raised in the New Testament book of James). But the intent

---

13. Michael Novak, *Business as a Calling: Work and the Examined Life* (New York: Simon & Shuster, 1996), 125.

of God was that God's mission would bring *shalom*, well-being and fruitful enterprise throughout all the nations. The coming of Christ did not change this mission, but rather "fleshed it out" in the life of God's Son. Jesus calls his followers to a fully incarnational mission: "As the father has sent me, so I am sending you" (John 20:21). The Gospel of the Kingdom is not merely soul-salvation but comprehensive renewal and transformation. Therefore we are doing Kingdom work when we create new wealth, alleviate poverty, bring well-being to people, embellish and improve human life, and as we engage powers resistant to God's coming *shalom*. James Luther Adams argues that since early Christianity 'rejected civil religion, allowed voluntary membership and transcended ethnic divisions' Christianity was in fact the first global corporation."[14] The first multinational, it is argued, is the Knights Templers, whose international business enterprises supported their action in the Crusades. And even William Carey, often cited as the founder of the modern mission movement (though he had many predecessors), believed that the kingdom of God would spread through international trade. Business is one way in which we are called, with Abraham and his seed, to bless the nations and to build unity interculturally and internationally, not as a tower of Babel, not homogenizing but with interdependence, albeit mixed with sin and deconstruction.

At the same time, there is conflict between the ages, between the worlds, a conflict which every kingdom person in the marketplace will experience. Mortimer Arias in this masterful study of the kingdom says:

> The coming of the kingdom means a permanent confrontation of worlds. The kingdom is a question mark in the midst of established ideas and answers developed by peoples and

---

14. Gordon Preece, "Business as a Calling and Profession: Towards a Protestant Entrepreneurial Ethic" (unpublished manuscript delivered at the International Marketplace Theology Consultation, Sydney, June 2001), 36.

societies. The kingdom is an irreverent exposure of human motivations and of the most sacred rules of human mores. The kingdom is an iconoclastic disturber of religious sacred places and customs and the most radical threat to temple altars, priestly castes, and the most protected 'holy of holies.' The kingdom is the appointed challenger of all sacralizing myths and systems and the relentless unmasker of all human disguises, self-righteous ideologies, or self-perpetuating powers.[15]

In the twenty-first century we are undoubtedly dealing with a global marketplace, more extensive that could ever have been envisaged by Jonah as he made his way to hinterlands of Spain instead of witnessing to Iraq (ancient Nineveh). In *Doing God's Business*, I cite Paul Williams, an economist, who says "Globalization is ... gradually undermining the nature of 'national places' and creating a borderless world in which everyone belongs equally everywhere but nobody is at home in community."[16]

In that same chapter I comment on the complexity of the problem.[17] There have been some benefits: the transfer of information technology, the provision of non-agricultural employment in countries formerly dominated by subsistence farming, and the creation of new industries and services in countries with stagnant economies. In the last ten years, by the 2003 reckoning of the World Bank, the percentage of people in the world living in poverty has dropped from 29.6 to 23.2 per cent. This means, it is estimated, that four hundred million people, while still desperately poor, are no longer facing starvation daily. Consumer purchasing power worldwide has nearly tripled. Infant mortality is down 42 per cent since 1970 and there has been

---

15. Mortimer Arias, *Announcing the Reign of God: Evangelization and the Subversive Memory of Jesus* (Lima: Academic Renewal Press, 1984), 46-7.
16. Paul S. Williams, "Hermeneutics for Economists: The Relevance of the Bible to Economics," (MCS Thesis, Regent College, Vancouver, 1995), 154.
17. The following two paragraphs are taken from R. Paul Stevens, *Doing God's Business: Meaning and Motivation for the Marketplace* (Grand Rapids: Eerdmans, 2006), 106-107.

a five-fold increase of access to safe water by rural families worldwide.[18] But there is another side to the picture.

There is loss of employment in both industrialized countries (through outsourcing) and in less industrialized countries. The damage to the biosphere is potentially catastrophic. It is well known that if the whole populated world were to adopt the high-consumption lifestyle of the West and North, it would take at least three planets of resources. Faced with globalizing cultures, people groups struggle to maintain their identity and perhaps some of the Balkanization of various nations around the planet can be attributed to this struggle for identity in an increasingly merged world order. One cannot belong to the whole human race. Economically the poor are getting poorer and the rich richer, even though there has been, overall, some lift in wealth world-wide. Jeremy Rifkin in *The End of Work* forecasts world-wide unemployment through technology, even in the so-called service sectors. "Just outside the new high-tech global village lie a growing number of destitute and desperate human beings, many of whom are turning to a life of crime and creating a vast new criminal subculture."[19] On top of this Third World debt is at a punishing level.[20]

The *New York Times* noted that the three richest people in the world have more than the GNP of the 48 poorest countries; that the richest 20% of the world's people consume 86% of all goods and services; that the poorest 20% consume 1.3 % of all goods and services; that Americans and Europeans spend 17 billion dollars a year on pet food,

---

18. World Bank, *Global Economic Prospects and the Developing Countries* (Washington, DC: The World Bank, 2003), 30, quoted in Steve Rundle and Tom Steffen, *Great Commission Companies: The Emerging Role of Business in Missions* (Downers Grove: InterVarsity Press, 2003), 47.
19. Jeremy Rifkin, *The End of Work: The Decline of the Global Work-Force and the Dawn of the Post-Market Era* (London: Penguin, 2000), xvii-xviii.
20. See James H. Ottley, "The Debt Crisis in Theological Perspective," in Max Stackhouse, Tim Dearborn and Scott Paeth, eds., *The Local Church in a Global Era: Reflections for a New Century* (Grand Rapids: Eerdmans, 2000), 39-47.

this being 4 billion more than what is needed to provide basic health care and nutrition for everyone in the world; and that Americans spend 8 billion a year on cosmetics, 2 billion more than needed to provide basic education for everyone in the world.[21] To this the Bible speaks especially on how to behave in the marketplace.

**Directions on how to Live in the Marketplace**

Sometimes this is done by an example without moral evaluation leaving us to assess the ethics of the action through its consequences. For example, Abraham lets Lot select the better resources—a description without moral comment except that God promises him everything afterwards (Gen 13). And later (Gen 14:23) Abraham says to the king of Sodom "I will accept nothing belonging to you...so that you will never be able to say, 'I made Abraham rich.'"—a refusal to exploit gratitude. Negatively, we see how the deceitful deal made by Jacob's sons in negotiating a bride price with Shechem for their sister Dinah resulted in their becoming a stench to the people and having to move on (Gen 34). Significantly, with regard to Jacob's somewhat deceitful negotiation with Laban to get the best of the flocks for himself and his family, Christian commentators tend to see this as evil, even though the text says that both Laban and Jacob saw the hand of God in this. Jewish commentators pass over the morality of this (and sometimes praise this holy shrewdness) and see only one fatal mistake made by Jacob, his delay in returning to Bethel as he had vowed, with the result that his daughter Dinah was raped.

Besides passages where people are described, usually without moralistic comment, there are many direct instructions about how we are to conduct ourselves in the marketplace. The Ten Commandments (Exod 20:1-17) deal with idolatry, the limits of work (Sabbath), sexual misconduct (adultery), stealing, truth-telling, and covetousness. Slaves are to go free after six years (Exod 21:1-6);

---

21. *New York Times* (September 27, 1998), 16.

interest is not to be charged "to one of my people" but you may take a pledge (a coat, but it must be returned by sunset); bribes are not to be accepted for they blind the eyes of those who see and twist the words of the righteous (Exod 23:8); the edges of fields are not to be harvested but to be left for the poor and the alien (Lev 19:9)—Is this a word about monopolies? Isaiah and other prophets cry for economic justice in the marketplace: "Is not this the kind of fasting I have chosen: to loose the chains of injustice and untie the cords of the yoke? To set the oppressed free and break every yoke? Is it not to share your food with the hungry and to provide the poor wanderer with shelter..." (Isa 58:6-7).

Accurate and uniform weights and measures are to be used. This is really not a reference to fair pricing (as suggested by Larry Burkett in *Business by the Book*)[22] but is about reliable currency, the medium of exchange.[23] "Do not use dishonest standards when measuring length, weight or quantity. Use honest scales and honest weights, an honest ephah and an honest hin" (Lev 19:35). Wages are to be paid promptly. "Do not hold back the wages of a hired hand overnight" (Lev 19:13, see also Jas 5:4). In the workplace and in the courts people are not to be treated with favouritism: "Do not pervert justice; do not show partiality to the poor or favouritism to the great" (Lev 19:15, see also Jas 2:1-13). A remarkable passage in Deuteronomy 17:14-20 describes the way a king is to behave. The king "must not accumulate large amounts of silver and gold" (17:17), a passage of particular import to CEO's who sometimes earn salaries two and three hundred times that of their entry level employees. Further, the king is "not consider himself better than his brothers" (17:20). Deuteronomy also has what could be the earliest

---

22. Larry Burkett, *Business by the Book: The Complete Guide of Biblical Principles for Business Men and Women* (Nashville: Nelson, 1990).
23. Peter McCarroll, "Accurate Weights and Measures," an unpublished academic paper for the Marketplace Ministry course, Regent College, 2003.

recording building code: build a parapet around your roof to keep people from falling off (22:8).

In the New Testament Paul writes to the Romans: "Give everyone what you owe him. If you owe taxes, pay taxes; if revenue, then revenue; if respect, then respect; if honor, then honor" (13:7). Slaves are to obey their masters, serving wholeheartedly as they are serving the Lord; masters are to treat their slaves the same way because they are serving the master. The slave is free and the master is a servant (Eph 6:5-9; Col 3:22-4:1; 1 Peter 2:18-21). Dealing with the moral sloth of some workers in Thessalonica, Paul warns against idleness (and not following Paul's example, 2 Thess 3:6-13). He exemplifies that it is more blessed to give (his ministry free of charge) than to receive (Acts 20:35) and thus by his example of hard work he helps the weak. The love of money, and not money, is the root of many and all kinds of evil (1 Tim 6:3-10). And so Paul warns the rich who have special temptations: "Command those who are rich in this present world not to be arrogant nor to put their hope in wealth... to be rich in good deeds... In this way they will lay up treasure for themselves as a firm foundation for the coming age, so that they can take hold of life that is truly life" (1 Tim 6:17-19). This all has to do with security, or what Jesus called "Mammon" (a word that derives from the Aramaic, "Amen"—let it be definite, Luke 16:13). Thus we are not to boast about tomorrow: "'We will go to this or that city, spend a year, carry on business and make money.' Why you do not even know what will happen tomorrow" (Jas 4:13-17).[24]

Undoubtedly there are terrible inequalities in the world, with the rich getting richer and the poor poorer. How do we show love in the global marketplace and in the context of global poverty? One certain

---

24. Additional Scriptures: Exod 23:10-12; 20; 31:12-17; Lev 19:3; 19:30; 23:3; Lev 19:9; 23:9-10; 25:1-55; 26; 27:30; Deut 5:7-21; 6:3; 15:1-8; 23:19; 24:10, 14-15, 19-21; 25:13-16; 26:1-15; 28:1-14, 15-68; Ps 15:5; 25:13; Prov 3:9-10;16:11; 20:10;22:9;23:4; Eccl 11:14; Isa 58:13-14; Jer 17:19-27; Joel 3:3; Amos 2; 6:4-6, 11; Micah 6:11; Matt 12:1-14; Luke 6:1-11; Jas 5:1-6.

and creative way is through micro-economic enterprise, enabling the poor and marginalized to become creators of new wealth. This is entirely in line with God's original calling to Adam and Eve and their descendents, and with the goodness of work in the marketplace. The medieval Jewish theologian Maimonides (1135-1204) defined charity's eight degrees by ranking them. At the bottom he notes that a person gives, but only when asked by the poor. But the highest is this: Money is given to prevent another from becoming poor, such as providing him with a job or by teaching him a trade or by setting him up in business and not be forced to the dreadful alternative of holding out his hand for charity. This is the highest step and the summit of charity's golden ladder.[25] So the global marketplace is a location for service to God and neighbours, near and far.

## The Marketplace as a Place of Ministry

As previously mentioned ministry (in the sense of serving God and God's purposes) took place in the marketplace with Joseph (in Egypt), with Esther (in the king's palace), with Nehemiah (in a foreign palace and then in a building project), with Daniel, who witnessed and prayed for the king and kingdom in a pagan environment, conducting himself with integrity, with Jonah, so that the sailor's workplace was the place of a great religious revival (Jonah 1:16), and with Paul in Ephesus in the hall of Tyrannus for two years (Acts 19:9-10). Paul ministered in the context of his tent-making business. Tentmaking was not merely a way of "getting bread" or "gaining access" to a restricted situation but was taken up into his apostolic ministry.[26] Paul's ministry in the marketplace of Ephesus

---

25. Quoted in William E. and Judith Ruhe Diehl, *It Ain't Over Till It's Over: A User's Guide to the Second Half of Life* (Minneapolis: Augsburg Press, 2003), 129-30.
26. See R.F. Hock, "Paul's Tentmaking and the Problem of his Social Class," *Journal of Biblical Literature* 97 (1978): 555-64. See also R. Paul Stevens, "Tentmaking" in Robert Banks and R. Paul Stevens, eds., *The Complete Book of Everyday Christianity* (Downers Grove: InterVarsity Press, 1997), 1028-34.

in the rented hall of Tyrannus, over a two year period in the siesta time of day resulted in "all Asia hearing the Word of God." The spreading Christian faith in Ephesus threatened the image-making business of Diana-worshippers and caused a riot (19:9). Finally, in the little letter of Paul to Philemon, Paul persuades Philemon to take back his runaway employee who has now become a brother to his patron. So much for the direct references to work in the marketplace. But when Jesus wants to find a way to express truth about life in the kingdom of God he turns to images from the marketplace.

**Marketplace as a Metaphor of the Kingdom of God**

A metaphor carries meaning from one reality to another and so deepens our engagement with truth. Significantly many words about life in the kingdom of God are commercial terms: "inheritance" (Ps 16:6: Eph 1:18); "profit"; "exchange"; "sell"; "buy"; "gain"; "redemption" (Ps 49:7-8); "refine" (Ps 66:10); "wages" (of sin). Here are some other examples of marketplace metaphors: "The words of the Lord are flawless, like silver refined in a furnace of clay, purified seven times" (Ps 12:6). "The stone the builders rejected has become the capstone; the Lord has done this and it is marvelous in our eyes" (Ps 118:22). "Unless the Lord builds the house, its builders labor in vain" (Ps 127). In Ecclesiastes 11:1-4 the Professor says, "Cast your bread upon the waters" (a reference to the grain trade in the Mediterranean) "for after many days you will find it again. Give portions to seven, yes to eight, for you do not know what disaster may come upon the land....Whoever watches the wind will not plant; whoever looks at the clouds will not reap...." This is potent metaphor for risk-taking but, at the same time, encouragement to divide the risk so that "not all the eggs are in one basket" (another common metaphor today).

In Isaiah 5 the Song of the Vineyard compares the nation of Israel to a business that was well nurtured but yielded bad fruit. Also in Isaiah there is a prophecy about the future expansion of God's kingdom that William Carey found as a text for world evangelization carried on through international trade (read "multinationals"): "Surely the islands look to me; in the lead are the ships of Tarshish, bringing your sons from afar, with their silver and gold, to the honor of the Lord your God....Your gates will always stand open...so that men may bring you the wealth of the nations—their kings led in triumphal procession" (Isa 60:9-11). In similar manner Jeremiah is instructed to buy a field while Nebuchadnezzar was besieging Jerusalem as a prophetic sign of hope of the restoration: "Houses, fields and vineyards will again be bought in this place" (32:15).

The ministry of Jesus is rich in marketplace metaphors: the "wise and foolish builders" is a metaphor for two ways of responding to the message of the kingdom. Hearing Jesus' words and doing them is like building one's house on a rock (Matt 7:24-27; Luke 6:46-49). The kingdom is like a pearl merchant who, finding one of great value, sells everything to obtain it (Matt 13:45-6).

The parables often throw down marketplace images to evoke faith in God's coming and present rule: In the Parable of the Unmerciful Servant, an employee would not forgive a small debt after he had been forgiven a huge debt—so we, the forgiven, are to forgive our brothers and sisters (Matt 18:21-35). The Parable of the Workers in the Vineyard is not about fair wages. Day-labourers employed at various times of the day all got the same pay, as does the grace of the kingdom come equally to those who come into the kingdom early or late (Matt 20:1-6). In the same way the Parable of the Tenants is not about inheritance or fair pay. The tenants seized the son and killed him to get his inheritance—a parable Jesus used to expose the death-threat against him (Matt 21:33-46; Mark 12:1-12; Luke 20:9-19). The Parable of the Talents shows that we must and may risk in the kingdom, just as a person must risk to make money, and we do this because we have a God who is not hard and unforgiving (Matt 25:14-30). The Parable of the Rich Fool uses the picture of a greedy business person to show how a fool stores up things for himself and is not rich towards God (Luke 12:13-21). The Parable of

Not Counting the Cost of building a tower shows how important it is to count the cost of being a disciple (Luke 14:28-30). The Parable of the Shrewd Manager contains the outrageous advice that we are to make friends for ourselves by means of unrighteous mammon (Luke 16:1-15) just as the shrewd manager saw to his own needs. Shrewd faith is encouraged. The Parable of the Ten Minas is a parable about investments, risking for the kingdom (Luke 19:11-27). Most of these images originated in the Middle Eastern agrarian society of Jesus with village marketplaces and small businesses. But how can we relate these to our contemporary situation –a global marketplace with multinational corporations? How can we read the Bible in *this* context?

**How then Shall We Read?**

Mostly the Bible is "read" ecclesiastically—in the church and for it. Therefore we "see" and interpret the book as essentially dealing with ministry defined by those we call "ministers" and spiritual life understood as private piety or corporate worship. Life in the Spirit, when so read, has to do with religious services, relationships within the people of God and declaring the good news of the kingdom. Admittedly, the New Testament is mainly concerned with life in the church, especially in the letters of Paul, Peter and John. By and large preachers skip over the numerous passages in both testaments that deal with work, economic life, enterprise and creativity in the world, and concentrate on personal devotion. I often ask my classes how many have heard a sermon on work in the last year. In a class of fifty there might be one or two. How is it possible to miss so much of the Bible? As I have indicated above, we see something quite different when we read the Bible in or for the marketplace. But it is not merely enough to discover marketplace data in the Bible.

Eugene Peterson warns against using the Bible for our own purposes, for validating our work in business or catering to what

Peterson calls "my Holy Trinity"—my holy wants, my holy needs and my holy feelings.[27]

It is entirely possible to come to the Bible in total sincerity, responding to the intellectual challenge it gives, or for the moral guidance it offers, or for the spiritual uplift it provides, and not in any way have to deal with a personally revealing God who has personal designs on you.[28]

Reading the book spiritually, "eating it" to use the metaphor of Revelation 10:9, means coming into submission to the God revealed in the marketplace. It demands a reversal: seeing how our stories taken up into God's great story rather than the other way round—trying to fit God's story into ours. If we read the Scripture contemplatively, along the lines of *lectio divina*, absorbing it, chewing it, brooding on it and praying it back to God, we must conform our life to it. In so doing we cannot prevent becoming nonconformists to the world even while being involved in that same world in a transformative work. We discover our daily work to be a ministry to God and our neighbour, albeit shot through with sin and struggles with the principalities and powers.

This, however, is not quite the same thing as "using" our faith in God to find meaning in work, the current work heresy that is promoted by the spate of books today on how to love Monday and develop a nine-to-five spirituality that results in more productivity. Spiritual reading of the text with its marketplace orientation means something truly revolutionary: we will find our meaning in God, not in the work we do, but we will discover our meaning in God in the context of our work. That seems to be one of the conclusions of the inductive research undertaken by the Professor in the book of Ecclesiastes. This business and social leader engages in first-hand examination of life "under the sun" without reference to a transcen-

---

27. Peterson, *Eat This Book*, 31.
28. Peterson, *Eat This Book*, 30.

dent personal God and draws a jolting conclusion in chapter two. Considered by itself, outside of the "fear of God" (Eccl 11:13), work is meaningless—it is pain and grief, overly demanding, and we will be followed by a fool. Work itself then turns out to be an evangelist to take us to God, in whom and through whom alone we find satisfaction. But that is exactly where Scripture proposes to take us. But it will not lead us to this conclusion unless we are contemplative, even while being active.

Theologian Hans Urs von Balthasar, a Roman Catholic, who devoted his life to contemplation, refused to disconnect contemplation from worldly action: "The life of contemplation is perforce an everyday life, of small fidelities and services performed in the spirit of love, which lightens our tasks and gives to them its warmth."[29] It is through the contemplative reading of the Bible that we can put the marketplace and our own participation in it into proper perspective. This will inevitably involve discernment of injustice (along with the prophets) and even repentance of our own sins (daily). Further, this calls us to work globally for the "filling of the earth" so that all human beings are given their daily bread. For this we pray—as we might as a result of reading the Bible spiritually in the global marketplace, that God's kingdom will come and God's will done on earth as it is in heaven. As we pray and live this word we will be rich toward God, unlike the rich fool in Jesus' parable (Luke 12:13-21).

---

29. Hans Urs von Balthasar, *Prayer* (A. V. Littledale, trans. London: Geoffrey Chapman, 1963), 111, quoted in Peterson, *Eat This Book*, 110.

15

# The Heart of Leadership is Asking the Right Questions

## PETER SHAW CB

We live in a world full of information. We are drowned by facts, figures, pictures and opinions. How does a leader make sense of this myriad of information? Do we just soak it up like a sponge and wait for it to be squeezed out of us?

The ability to ask the right question in the right way at the right time can bring clarity to an otherwise confused world. The ability to ask the right question can bring a new focus leading to enlightenment about next steps. This article looks at the way Jesus used questions and how his use of them is relevant for the way we as leaders use questions today.

### Jesus' Use of Questions

In his book *Jesus Asked: What He Wanted to Know*, Conrad Gempf highlights that the first recorded event in Jesus' life after his birth was at the Temple in Jerusalem when he sits with the Jewish teachers listening to them and asking questions.[1] In Mark's Gospel

---

1. Conrad Gempf, *Jesus Asked: What He Wanted to Know* (Grand Rapids: Zondervan, 2003).

there are 67 episodes where there is a conversation: these episodes include Jesus asking 50 questions.

Jesus used a wide range of different approaches. He would assert truth, use parables, paint word pictures, but fundamental to his approach was the use of questions of many different types. Conrad Gempf comments,

> He doesn't ask primarily because he wants to acquire knowledge, nor does he ask to help people realise they already have the knowledge. He asks to help people realise where they stand; he asks questions in order to give an occasion for a reply, in order to initiate a conversation.

In this article I draw from four types of approaches that Jesus used, namely, the innocent question, the absurd question, responding to a question with a question and the challenging question.

**The Innocent Question**

Not all Jesus' questions were full of symbolism. Some were part of daily life. In a story about healing, Jesus asked, "How long has he been like this?" Before the feeding of the five thousand he asked, "How many loaves do you have?" As he walked with the disciples after the Resurrection on the road to Emmaus he asked "What are you arguing about on the road?" Jesus used innocent questions as a means of building understanding and generating trust in a conversation. The innocent question was part of life for Jesus and enabled him to build rapport, empathy and clarity.

**The Absurd Question**

Gempf talks of the way Jesus seems to delight in using questions to conjure up absurd situations as a mean of encouraging individuals and the disciples to re-evaluate their way of thinking. He comments on the words of Jesus, "If the salt loses its saltiness, how can it be made salty again?" as follows:

## THE HEART OF LEADERSHIP IS ASKING THE RIGHT QUESTIONS

This apparently silly little sentence shakes up the religious people of his day as well as Jesus' contemporaries. If your whole identity is tied up in being the salt of the earth, and you are found not to be salty, it's a pretty fundamental problem.

Other examples of the absurd question from Jesus are, "Do you bring in a lamp to put it under a bowl or under the bed? Instead don't you put it on a stand?" Perhaps the best known of the absurd questions which many people use without knowing its biblical origin is, "Why do you look at the speck of sawdust in someone else's eye and pay no attention to the plank in your own eye?"

Jesus' use of the absurd question works superbly in terms of individuals seeing how their behaviour can be interpreted as myopic or ridiculous. It is a technique he uses with powerful effect once his hearers are engaged with him.

### Responding to a Question with a Question

The best known example of this approach of responding to a question with a question is when Jesus is asked whether taxes should be paid to Caesar or not. His first response is with a question, "Why are you trying to trap me?" He then asks to see a silver coin and follows with another question, "Whose face and name are these?" After his hearers said it was the emperor's face on the coin Jesus responds with the statement, "Well, then pay the emperor what belongs to the emperor, and pay God what belongs to God."

Jesus uses questions to draw out the real concerns of those with whom he is in discussion. He uses questions to get to the root of their concerns and also as a means of not falling into the traps they are trying to set for him.

### The Challenging Question

Jesus often takes the disciples to one side to explain to them the meaning of some of his teachings. Sometimes he can be quite challenging with his disciples with such questions as, "Do you still not see or understand?" "Are your hearts hardened?" "Do you have eyes but fail to see?" and "Do you still not understand?"

Jesus had a remarkable skill of provoking people into thinking in new ways. Gempf uses the phrase, "He was not in the convincing business, he was in the provoking business." But the provoking was done in a purposeful way. With the disciples it was in the context of a relationship built up over some years together. With the Pharisees and secular leaders it was his way of challenging them to break out of their rigid perspectives.

**The Relevance of Jesus' Approach to Questioning Today**

Looking at the questions Jesus asked afresh has reinforced for me the relevance of his approach in a range of different spheres. Questions have been a key tool for me in different leadership roles.

- As a Director General within the UK Government with 800 plus staff, and in one role with responsibility for over £40 billion expenditure, I had to be able to ask questions that led to the best possible use of resources and searched out inefficiencies.
- As an executive coach asking the right question is crucial to enable an individual to clarify their own thinking about next steps.
- As a Non-Executive Director at a University College and a Sixth Form College I am there to ask the key question from an independent perspective.
- As a writer in the area of leadership and spirituality I need to understand the key questions in individuals' hearts as they take on bigger leadership roles.
- As a Christian lay minister I need the ability to understand the key questions in a congregation's mind and will often start with a question which I trust resonates with members of that congregation.

THE HEART OF LEADERSHIP IS ASKING THE RIGHT QUESTIONS

There are occasions when a question is the least appropriate way of acting. Sometimes it is being with somebody that matters with no questions asked. With one's own children questions are often best avoided! They will tell us what they want to tell us at the time of their choosing! Questions to the recalcitrant teenager are probably the least effective way of building a relationship.

It is worth asking yourself the following questions:

- How well do you use questions to build and grow relationships?
- Is there a pattern about your use of questions?
- Could you use questions more effectively varying your repertoire more?
- Are your questions entirely random, do you pre-plan where you are going to use certain types of question?
- Are there ways in which you can build into your repertoire the types of approaches Jesus used in his questioning?

**Innocent Questions**

The innocent, open-ended question is crucial for building relationships and building a clear picture about any situation. If the questioner looks as if they are taking a particular perspective that will influence the hearer's response. The most honest responses will come as responses to innocent questions. As an executive coach my main tool is the open-ended question that enables an individual to develop their strategy for tackling a difficult issue. It is never right for me to impose a solution, it is through the use of innocent questions that I enable my client to work out a plan for their next steps.

As one of the first four full-time students at Regent College in 1970, I long remember a young, energetic Old Testament professor called Carl Armerding who had a great gift of posing questions to students about the book or text we were looking at. The questions were always put with energy and a positive approach which encouraged us to think through the issues and articulate clearly our level of understanding. Carl's ability to be both positive and searching in his use of questions was for me a brilliant role model that I have tried to aspire to ever since.

**Absurd Questions**

The ability to describe or draw attention to the absurd in any situation can bring shared humour as well as a strong dose of reality. Questions which enable individuals to see the logical consequence of their behaviours or actions can be powerful. I might reframe the question about, "is there a moat in your eye" to "Are there ways in which you are blinded to reality?" I might ask a sequence of "What if" questions which would enable an individual to take a particular set of actions to their logical finishing point to see if they ended in success or absurdity.

**Responding to a Question With a Question**

As an executive coach I am often asked questions that seek my perspective based on my experience as a Board Member and as a Director General within the UK Government. Sometimes I will draw from my personal experience directly. But more often I will use my experience in order to ask follow up questions which enable the individual to work out their own response to the problem they are dealing with. When an individual develops their own answer to their question they are much more likely to be committed to it than if they take an off-the-shelf answer that somebody else has provided.

The skill of asking the right supplementary question comes from being able to sit inside the shoes of the questioner. As a coach I spend a lot of time thinking about what it must be like to be in the shoes of one of my clients. What are the issues and pressures they are facing? What are the options that they are most likely to go for?

## THE HEART OF LEADERSHIP IS ASKING THE RIGHT QUESTIONS

Having sat myself in their shoes I am in a better position to ask the supplementary questions which will enable them to move forward. For example if their presenting question is about what should their next step be in their job I may well respond by inviting them to think about questions such as, "what gives you greatest joy in your work," "where is the place of fulfilment in your work," "what next step would resonate best with your values," or "where do you want to be in five years time?" Responding to a question with a question is often such a good way and moving more deeply into understanding a difficult issue.

### Challenging Questions

By challenging questions I do not mean haranguing questions. As soon as I feel that I am being lectured at, I turn off. The preacher who tries to browbeat me into submission tends to be dismissed in my mind as someone who has lost the plot.

The good challenging question goes to the heart of the matter and forces you to think. But the successful challenging question takes account of the context. Ideally it is done within a relationship where trust already exists and where the individual does not feel threatened by the tone of a challenging question. The most effective challenging questions flow out of a robust, trusting relationship. As a coach there is no point in asking a challenging question until you have built up a strong rapport with the client. Then once the ground rules are clear the challenging question can help an individual to develop a measure of resolve and courage to take difficult decisions that they had never conceived as possible before.

As a Non-Executive Director of two major educational institutions my job is to ask challenging questions. The non-executive brings a wider perspective with a clear brief of both supporting and challenging the executive leaders. In church life we are often surprisingly unwilling to be challenged by an independent person looking at the way we do things. Jesus challenged the religious and civic leaders of the day. We expect our schools, hospitals and governmental organisations to be externally challenged. But sometimes we are reluctant to apply the same discipline to our Christian and church organisations.

**Next Steps**

I invite you to:

- Observe someone you know who asks questions well to see how they do it and what sort of response they get.
- Reflect on how you use questions, when you use them well and when does it provoke an unhelpful response.
- Reflect on the extent to which you can adopt some of the approaches Jesus used in asking questions.
- Consider whether you can more often use innocent questions, absurd questions, responding to a question with a question, and challenging questions.

Just as Jesus used questions effectively, the more we can use questions in a well planned and thoughtful way the more influential we can be in the various contexts in which we live. Being influential is not to be measured in imposing our views but in enabling others to become more effective leaders, teachers, citizens and Christians.

16

# The Named Human and the Question of 'Being' Christlike

## Revisioning Evangelical Spirituality through Renewing the Communicatio Idiomatum

DARRELL COSDEN

**Abstract:**

Many evangelicals find it almost instinctive to equate humanness with sinfulness. Human finitude, genuine creaturely limitation, and weakness are often seen as spiritual problems to be overcome through becoming "more Christlike." This tendency reveals a deeply seated Nestorian logic within evangelical theology and piety that stems, through not exclusively, from a failure to grasp the function and logic of the doctrine of the communication of the attributes developed within classical Christology. After reappraising the Cyril—Nestorius debate in the context of Chalcedon, and examining the *communicatio idiomatum* as understood by Wayne Grudem—as a case study in evangelical theology—this article proposes a way to re-appropriate the doctrine in a post-metaphysical form for the purpose of rehabilitating evangelical spirituality. This proposed renewal makes use of Richard Bauckham's Christology of "divine identity" and Stanley Grenz's proposal for an *"Imago Dei Christo-Anthropology."*

## A Tendency in Evangelical Spirituality

Spirituality is the new fashion accessory. Secular spiritualities of all shapes and varieties have spawned a multi-million dollar infomercial, publishing and consultancy industry.[1] Titles showcasing spiritually in touch celebrities and promoting spiritual remedies to life's ordinary problems are now best-sellers. What used to be simple self-help guides have evolved into philosophies of life incorporating a smorgasbord of spiritual practices which promise to transform us. A new level of therapeutic experience is on offer which is guaranteed to help us rise above the limitations and ordinariness of life. The realm of "spirit" or pure transcendence is what many consumers now crave.

Likewise, for an increasing number of evangelical Christians, words like "spirituality" and "spiritual-formation" have become fashionable. They have become buzz-words signalling what are seen as new vistas within the Christian life.

For those of us coming from an evangelical tradition used to speaking of "spiritual growth" primarily in terms of discipleship—and this often perceived along activist and pragmatic lines—the notion of spiritual formation and spirituality is new, fresh and exciting. Many of us have found ourselves on a journey to rediscover and reconnect with established, ancient, and even mystical Christian spiritual practices. We argue that before being shunned by the more pragmatic and activist evangelicals, and before being turned into a consumer commodity by secular and pop-culture gurus, spirituality in the form of Christlikeness was understood

---

1. Jeff M. Sellers, "The Higher Self Gets Down to Business," *Christianity Today* (February 2003): 34-40.

both by historic evangelicalism and wider Christianity to be the purpose of the Christian life.

But what does evangelical Christianity typically understand this spirituality, or Christlikeness, to look like? Are we seeking the same kind of experience as our secular counterparts, only mediated to us, of course, by Jesus?

Unfortunately, I think that this is often the case. Today within popular western culture (Christian and secular) there is a growing and deep dissatisfaction with the perceived inadequacies of an "ordinary life." Advertising tells us that ordinary is sub-standard and can be transcended with the right products. Likewise, an increasing number of Christian churches offer "spiritual power" as a means to overcome ordinary frailty and finite existence. Overall there appears to be a growing assumption that merely to be human is substandard, and that to transcend our material human existence is the goal of the spiritual life.

The desire is for some sort of spiritual and therapeutic experience that will transform our limited human condition, thus enabling us to live on a plane that we mistakenly believe to be "life in the Spirit." For evangelical spirituality, this tendency is expressed in the inclination to marginalize or subordinate our humanness so that, in the name of becoming Christlike, we for all practical purposes seek to become divine. This I call "evangelical deification"; a version of the "I must decrease that he might increase" spirituality.

Within a good deal of popular evangelical Christianity there is a tendency to view our humanness as actually an encumbrance to true spirituality—here I mean our being physical and finite creatures. In popular evangelical teaching, for example, our salvation hope is often pictured as the soul or spirit upon death leaving human bodily limitations behind and going to heaven where we will then become truly spiritual beings "like the angels."

Let me illustrate further. In 1994, in a course at the Schloss Mittersill Study Centre in Austria, Carl Armerding raised a most basic question about the purpose of spiritual formation.[2] He suggested that our goal as Christians should be to become more genuinely human and that we should evaluate our spiritual growth and maturity accordingly. This suggestion by Carl excited me. Although I had come to faith as a child, been immersed in evangelical spirituality from that time, been through an evangelical college and seminary, and had spent several years in ministry, this was the first time I can remember hearing that to become more spiritual I need to become more human.

Another class member, however, reacted to this in the strongest possible way. He was absolutely appalled by the suggestion. As he argued his point it became clear that to him his finitude (his humanity) was precisely what he wanted spiritual growth to enable him to overcome, both already now and ultimately in eternity. He explained that he didn't want to become more human, he wanted to become Christlike. Both his theological anthropology and Christology could not have been expressed any more clearly.

He, like many evangelicals, found it almost instinctive to equate humanness with sinfulness. Yet, even when realizing that this is a theological mistake, many of us live with a deep sense of frustration and even guilt for the fact that we are limited rather than omni-competent beings. We feel that there is something wrong with us since we cannot anticipate and solve all problems before they happen, successfully accomplish all the tasks that life throws at us, be in two places at once, and have all the answers. Many of us

---

2. Importantly, I am completely indebted to Carl for this course for at least two reasons. First, it was here that Carl introduced me to an idea that has decisively shaped and guided my teaching and research on Christology since; the necessarily link between Christology and spiritual formation. Secondly, it was with this course that Carl introduced me to the notion, and importance, of a theology of work, the topic that since has shaped my life by becoming both the subject of my doctoral research at St. Andrews and subsequently the subject upon which I have written to date two books and several articles.

## THE NAMED HUMAN AND THE QUESTION OF 'BEING' CHRISTLIKE

believe deep down that if we were just more "spiritual" we would overcome such limitations. If we were more like Christ and filled more with the Spirit, rather than more our human selves, we are sure we could overcome these negative restrictions and live successfully God's will for us.

But what do we mean by "spiritual" here? This is where things start to get a bit muddled. In popular thinking we often associate "spiritual" with the notion of "a spirit" so we understand it to be different from or even opposite to bodily and material. And when we do think of the "human spirit" it is often as our "higher" part, an immaterial substance in ourselves that transcends our normal human realities and through which we connect with and become like God.

Hence, in our spirituality we often tacitly live as if the goal were to subjugate the "non-spiritual"—physical or finite aspects of ourselves, the overtly human, so as to let come to the fore the "spirit-ual" dimension—the bit we associate most closely with infinitude or divinity (Christ or the Holy Spirit).

It is not uncommon to hear evangelicals expressing this kind of spirituality by referring to John the Baptist, where he is interpreted to be saying that "I [who am but human] must decrease and get out of the way so that he [the divine Christ] might increase." This, translated into a "more of God less of me" spirituality leads us in turn to feel the need to suppress our unique human selves so that God alone, or Jesus, will shine through instead of me.

Although we would never allow ourselves to say it this way, what this leads to is the desire to purge our humanness (our "fleshly limitations") as God makes us Christlike. Or at least we hope that he might for all practical purposes transform our frailties, limitations and finitude (our humanity) into a kind of transparent and incidental receptacle for spirit / divinity. We seek a kind of deification.

Yet when this does not happen to the degree we think it should, we internalize the problem and blame ourselves for being human and thus for "getting in God's way." And deep within this can lead to frustration with God for not making us "in Christ" less human and more like Jesus—meaning divine. Or maybe this will go even further to resenting God for not making us divine in the first place—an "Adam syndrome." And it is from such angst that either in desperation or rebellion we begin, in the guise of an evangelical spirituality, to work harder to try and accomplish for ourselves what God has not and seemingly will not do, which is to make us Christlike—by which we mean to deify us.

This tendency surfaces throughout our evangelical practice. Our sermons notwithstanding, over the years I have begun listening quite carefully to how we pray. I have been struck by how so much of our intercessory and petitionary prayer for help or success is actually a latent plea for God to overcome our humanness, or at least for God to minimize or bypass it. Likewise, I have found in my own and in others' prayers for repentance what often amounts to little more than apologies for finitude, frailty, or the failure not to overcome our human limitations and so be like God. And either within such prayer, or at least close by in our worship songs, often lies the plea to be more like Christ.

But, of course, the issue here is our theological understanding of who Christ is. For who we think he is determines what we think "being" Christlike involves. Obviously if we get this wrong, we will be moving toward a deformed spirituality.

Although there are doubtless many cultural, psychological, and other theological reasons contributing to this desire to suppress or transcend our humanness, at the heart of our problem is often a deficient Christology.

### The Communication of the Attributes

In *Theology for the Community of God* Stanley Grenz points out how our understanding of who Jesus is can easily go astray, even when we think we are being biblically orthodox. In rehearsing some general criticisms of classic metaphysical, or what he calls the traditional understanding of incarnational Christology, he says:

> Implicit in the traditional position is an incipient Docetism, or at least overtones of Apollinarianism. Although proponents of incarnational Christologies generally have no desire to deny Jesus' full humanity, in practice they often picture the incarnate life in terms of the eternal Son [divinity] hidden in a human body. In this manner Jesus becomes a divine being who functioned during his earthly sojourn through a human exterior.[3]

Grenz takes us to the root of the problem. In practice, classical incarnational Christology has often led to an ambivalence about Jesus' humanness, which is understood as either effectively transparent, or, a receptacle subordinated to his divinity—"his higher nature." But how can this happen, especially since the church historically has tried so hard to avoid such implications?

Grenz, along with many contemporary voices, suggests that it is incarnational theology itself, or at least its traditional metaphysical method, that inevitably leads to this problem. But is this so? Yes, admittedly there is this tendency with many whose Christology is built with traditional incarnational / two-nature metaphysical categories. But no, it need not inevitably lead here. As Grenz himself shows in a later work, *The Named God and the Question of Being*, the role of philosophy in theology, particularly metaphysics, is complex. It may of course lead us astray, but this is not the case inevitably.[4]

So why does metaphysical Christology often lead to a subordination or marginalization of Christ's, and then by extension our humanity? I suggest that the tendency rests with those (including

---

3. Stanley J. Grenz, *Theology for the Community of God* (Nashville: Broadman & Holman Publishers, 1994), 402-403.

4. Stanley J. Grenz, *The Named God and the Question of Being: A Trinitarian Theo-Ontology* (Louisville: Westminster John Knox, 2005).

but not limited to Reformed and evangelical believers) who fail to grasp the deeper logic and function (beyond the formulation and common use) of what just might be a linchpin of incarnational two-nature theology, namely the communication of the attributes.

Nevertheless, traditional metaphysical Christology cannot be let off the hook too easily either. As the Reformed tradition has quite rightly argued, and as we will see shortly, typical metaphysical formulations and uses of the *communication idiomatum* do produce some quite problematic theological and practical side-effects.

Must the remedy, however, be to reject the doctrine because of these, which by and large has been the Reformed response?[5] Not necessarily, but to argue this we must distinguish between the way many have understood, formulated and used the doctrine, and, what will be argued is its deeper and necessary function and purpose. With this distinction the way is then cleared to offer a direction for retaining but recasting the doctrine with a return to explicitly scriptural categories, what Richard Bauckham proposes as "divine identity" Christology, supplemented by what Grenz has called the biblical ontology of the divine name, or a Trinitarian "theo-ontology."

To get to that point though, we need first to carefully reconsider the communication of the attributes doctrine within its developmental context, including its function within Christology, its implications practically, and how the doctrine came to fall on hard times.

Although the technical and classical formulation of the doctrine that we call the *communicatio idiomatum* is bound up with the 451

---

5. A notable historical exception to this is John Owen. See for example Stephen Holms "Reformed Varieties of the *Communicatio Idiomatum*" in *The Person of Christ*, eds. Stephen Holms and Murray A. Rae (London: T&T Clark/Continuum, 2005), 70-86. For a contemporary Reformed example which, through rejecting the doctrine, nevertheless tries to preserve its deeper intent see; Bruce McCormack "Karl Barth's Christology as a Resource for a Reformed Version of Kenoticism," *International Journal of Systematic Theology* 8/3 (July 2006): 243-251.

## THE NAMED HUMAN AND THE QUESTION OF 'BEING' CHRISTLIKE

Chalcedonian Definition of the Niceno-Constantinoplian Creed, something like the doctrine was perceived by the Fathers to be operating in the New Testament itself. Put simply, in the biblical testimony something like what was to become the metaphysical formulation of the "communication of the attributes" was operating at least tacitly whenever the newly formed Christian communities ascribed to Jesus (a named human) those distinguishing characteristics or attributes that belong exclusively to the technically unnamed God of Abraham, Isaac and Jacob. And conversely, it also appears whenever we find attributed to the Son or Logos those experiences properly belonging to the human. ["God purchased the Church with his blood" (Acts 20:28), "the Lord of Glory was crucified" (I Cor 2:8), Jesus forgives sins.] But to this New Testament dynamic we will return later.

The Patristic development of the doctrine centers around how the Fathers, in the context of Greek metaphysical thought, came to talk about Jesus the man embodying in his own person the attributes or properties exclusive to divinity for the purpose of our healing, our salvation. Likewise, and arguably more reluctantly and paradoxically, it also centers on how they came to speak of the divine Logos embodying human attributes and experiencing full humanness in Jesus, thus securing God's full presence or participation with us in creation. (Jesus was born and did die *and* was *homousias* with the Father and thus Cyril hesitantly speaks of the "impassible suffering of God.") That these two "natures," metaphysically speaking, don't mix or blend and thereby change in themselves, but do interpenetrate and reciprocally share properties with and within each other (perichoresis), is the doctrine of the *communicatio idiomatum.*

The occasion for the fuller articulation of this doctrine was the controversy between Cyril of Alexandria and Nestorius, archbishop of Constantinople, over whether in worship (a practical activity of all believers) it was appropriate to refer to Mary as the mother of God, or God bearer. Against accepted practice, Nestorius began to teach that it was improper to call Mary the mother of God for by definition divine nature cannot be born. He reasoned that it was better to call her the Christ bearer, for it was not his divinity that was born but rather his humanity. Cyril understood such a pulling apart of the one person of Christ to be tantamount to undermining and thus denying the fullness of the incarnation and therefore salvation. This he perceived would unwittingly lead the Church back into Arianism by denying the whole of Jesus' life as fully divine, thus undermining the Trinity and our salvation.

It is common to read this controversy as the attempt by Cyril to emphasize the divinity of Christ to the neglect or even undermining of his humanity, which incidentally is the spiritual problem I have outlined and the problem Grenz identified. (Given that Apollinarius was also from Alexandria such an interpretation might appear at first plausible.) Together with this, it is common to see Nestorius as simply trying to safeguard the humanity of Jesus against such subordination.

However, this modern interpretation has recently and increasingly been called into question by Patristic scholars, who are developing what is in effect "a New Perspective on Cyril."[6] John J. O'Keefe for example has argued that the real question at issue was not over the humanity of Christ at all, although it may have seemed to be for many then and subsequently. Rather, the real question he argues is over the fullness of the incarnation, over whether God or divinity can actually suffer. The debate is over the impassibility of God, which is really the question of whether God can be said to fully go through human experiences. Says O'Keefe; "In order to understand the christological debate, we must recognize that

---

6.   John J. O'Keefe, Paul L. Gavrilyuk, and Donald Fairbairn are among a growing number of patristic scholars contributing to this reinterpretation of Cyril. See Donald Fairbairn, *Grace and Christology in the Early Church* (Oxford Early Christian Studies; Oxford: Oxford University Press, 2003), Paul L. Gavrilyuk, *The Suffering of the Impassible God: The Dialectics of Patristic Thought* (Oxford Early Christian Studies; Oxford: Oxford University Press, 2004).

concern about God's impassibility goes to the heart of the controversy itself."[7]

In this understanding, Nestorius' motivation in arguing for something like two distinct persons in the one Christ, one exclusively divine and the other exclusively human, was to make sure that in Christ the divine *ousia* or substance would not be "tainted," polluted, or demoted by "contact" with the changeable and suffering human *ousia* or substance.

Nestorius' goal was not then to protect Christ's humanity or human substance. Rather it was to promote, keep pristine or protect the divine *ousia*. To do this he thought it necessary to keep Jesus' divine essence removed from his humanness and, given his view of impassibility, arguably set over it. What we have here is the logic of asymmetry and keeping separated the human substance and divine substance in Christ, whether these are called persons or natures.

This is why the hypostatic union (conceptually *perichoresis*) of the natures was such a problem to Nestorius. Cyril argued that it was necessary for salvation for the divine Logos, God himself, to assume full humanity (not an existing human or simply a human outer existence) and so experience a fully human life. Thus the specifically metaphysical metaphor eventually emerged picturing two natures in one person of Christ that "touch" completely and at every point, and share their unique properties with each other—the hypostatic union. For any aspect of humanity that fails to be assumed (including a human soul life) and brought into contact at every point with the divine life fails to be healed. Salvation is then either incomplete or undermined. For Cyril the divine life heals the human rather than being compromised by it. The divine needed to experience / assume genuine humanness. This led Cyril reluctantly to affirm that in Christ we have the paradox of the "impassible suffering of God."[8]

---

7. John J. O'Keefe, "Impassible Suffering? Divine Passion and Fifth-Century Christology" *Theological Studies* 58 (1997): 41.

8. O'Keefe, 45.

In the subsequent understanding of the doctrine of the communication of the attributes throughout the church however, the two-nature metaphor was misapplied by many to suggest or imply that when the two natures touch, or unite, the divine transforms the human even at the level of substance—deification of even the flesh. It is unfortunate that the metaphysical metaphor came thus to be over extended. And rightly this is where many objections to the doctrine, particularly those of the Reformed, begin to arise.

However, back to Nestorian logic for a moment—if the natures/substances (or persons) were hypostatically united or "touched," then the divine by receiving the attributes of the human becomes dragged down, even to the point of experiencing suffering. Yet according to Greek philosophical assumptions, by definition divinity is not able to suffer. To be somewhat fair to Nestorius, his reasoning suggests that if the attributes were communicated to each other in the one Christ, and if the divine by definition cannot suffer, and if Jesus suffered and died, then unless some creative solution emerges (which he thought he had found) we would end up denying Jesus' divinity—something he too wanted to safeguard.

But Chalcedon agreed with Cyril and argued for the hypostatic union of the natures, where the natures remained themselves, and were neither mixed nor blended. They were nevertheless "communicated" completely, sharing themselves as themselves with each other in order to safeguard the full healing brought to humanity and creation by the full touch of God in Jesus. Thus in Christ the attributes of divine nature were communicated to or experienced by human nature. And, accepted somewhat reluctantly (e.g. impassible suffering), this communication had to be reciprocal for Christ's death to effect salvation (hence the notion of *perichoresis* was developed). In fact unlike Nestorius' understanding, what Cyril's view and this doctrine of the communication of the attributes (the meaning of the hypostatic union) did, contrary to standard interpretations, was to protect the integrity of human nature in Christ and keep it from getting subordinated to the divine and thus practically obliterated.

However, it is important to underline, if one is too reluctant to emphasize the two-way communication of the attributes between each other, if one over-emphasizes the "divine to the human direction" (as with much metaphysical incarnational Christology), and if one downplays or even denies the "human to the divine direction," then we end up with the problem Grenz pointed out earlier—we in thought and practice end up seeking an asymmetry and thus subordinating or even eradicating (through divinization) the human. How? If not denied altogether (Docetism), the human will be thought of as primarily a shell or receptacle for that which really matters—the divine nature (Apollinarianism). Or the divine will by contact so heal or divinize the human (one way communication in the incarnation) that the human nature will be metaphysically eradicated. Thus the two-way communication of the attributes turns out, especially in this metaphysical formulation, to be a linchpin to preserve the integrity and non-subordination of humanness. It is therefore the safeguard that the incarnation really is God's "yes" to a corporeal creation which is genuinely something other than God.

Yet as we have said, the Reformed tradition has been right to detect within the metaphysical tradition and method a tendency or gravity pulling toward the divinization of the human. Therefore by and large the Reformed have come to reject the doctrine as classically defined, the two-way communication of the attributes between the divine and human natures in the one Christ. Some Reformed however, have attempted to recast the doctrine, usually along the lines of the two mutually exclusive natures communicating attributes, not to each other, but rather to the one person of Christ.[9]

---

9. See again Stephen Holms "Reformed Varieties of the *Communicatio Idiomatum*": 70-86.

Sometimes the Reformed motivation comes across as rather closely resembling Nestorius'; an attempt to exalt God's divine holy nature above the human and created thus ruling out of hand the idea that a sovereign being could be vulnerable, weak or suffer. More often though, the rejection seems motivated by a practical concern related to discipleship. For the way of life offered by a Jesus whose flesh was perfected / divinized in the incarnation would be a way of life we could never follow.

The focus of the Reformed opposition to the doctrine, however, has traditionally been bound up with the rejection of how Lutherans practically have used this doctrine in worship. That is, as the basis for the Lutheran understanding of consubstantiation in the Eucharist, where Christ's physical presence everywhere (ubiquity) includes his physical presence in the bread. And incidentally, this has basically been the only direct practical "application" of the doctrine within most of the western Church tradition.

In one sense the Reformed tradition has been right to reject the doctrine, for they have grasped rightly that if it implies a divinized humanity, Jesus would be quite different from us and thus of limited value for discipleship. They have indeed been right to want to avoid the loss, through divinization, of the humanness of Jesus Christ.

Yet, have they been entirely correct to reject the communication of the attributes between the divine and human natures? Or have they been successful in their attempts to reformulate the doctrine along the lines of two naturally opposing natures contributing separately what is exclusive to each to the one person Jesus Christ? I don't think so. For what they have rejected in order to avoid Apollinarianism and the divinization of the humanity of Christ is not, I believe, the most careful understanding of the doctrine, but rather a skewed one-directional version of it (albeit the tendency of many in the tradition).

But more worrisome is that in attempting to avoid the Apollinarian tendency to undermine Christ's humanity, Reformed orthodoxy has never fully demonstrated an avoidance of at least the theological logic of Nestorianism.[10] And if they have not, it is at least possible they have not managed theologically to safeguard genuine humanness, and thus have paved the way for landing us in exactly the place they have rightfully tried so hard to avoid.

But how does this relate to distinctively Evangelical theology and spirituality? By and large—mainstream—what is termed post World War II as neo-evangelicalism both in the US and Great Britain, has followed in the Reformed tradition. However, since the Eucharistic debate with Lutherans has not been the issue, pragmatically oriented neo-evangelical theology, it would seem, has not often perceived a need to engage with, let alone deeply engage with, the doctrine of the communication of the attributes.[11] Thus, what we find or fail to find is not so much a reasoned rejection of the doctrine, but simply ambivalence toward it.

**An Evangelical Case Study**

Nevertheless, one widely read theologian operating within this tradition, Wayne Grudem (while clearly still working within the Reformed tradition) does propose a version of the doctrine. And, if the doctrine becomes accepted at all by the average evangelical, his understanding of the communication of the attributes as presented in *Systematic Theology* will possibly become a default neo-evangelical understanding. At least this will be so among many pastors and those from student movements like IFES who often use this text for their basic theology.

---

10. See Robert W. Jensen "Christ in the Trinity: *Communicatio Idiomatum*" in *The Person of Christ*, eds. Stephen Holms and Murray A. Rae (London: T&T Clark/Continuum. 2005), 61-69.

11. For example, in the whole of Millard Erickson's *Christian Theology* there is only one oblique reference to anything like the doctrine of the communication of the attributes. Millard Erickson *Christian Theology* (Grand Rapids: Baker, 1983-1985), 738. Note also the lack of the discussion by the premiere neo-evangelical theologian, Carl Henry.

However, in his handling of the doctrine we can detect not far below the surface the various problems we have been discussing.[12]

Before Grudem reaches his discussion of the Trinity or of Christology, the place where we expect to find both the revelation of who God is and what it means to be human, he has already concluded—he claims biblically—what the divine attributes are, and which of these attributes are and are not communicable to humanity.[13] Having in this way determined *a priori* the natures of divinity and humanity, when he comes to explore Christ as one person in two natures (and the communication of the attributes) he begins with a problem or dilemma. This is the quandary of how these two already decided to be mostly opposing natures can be united in one person. Let us explore this.

Grudem's treatment of Nestorianism is most revealing. He suggests that the real issue is whether we can use the language "two persons" when describing Christ. He states that we cannot since the Bible never says this. And this is about as far as his reasoning goes—such language is not biblical. Of course, this is a rather shallow understanding of both Nestorianism and the debate. In fact, Grudem has altogether missed the logic of Nestorianism and the real point of its opponents. Although correct in saying that a Nestorian two-person model is unbiblical and inadequate, he fails to see where the real danger lies, namely in its metaphysical assumptions about the incompatibility of divine and human natures, which in turn undermine the incarnation as God's full presence with us. Thus, Grudem's discussion of the Chalcedonian definition that follows likewise lacks depth. He simply fails to grasp what the hypostatic union is about. Stating that it "means the union of Christ's human

---

12. Wayne Grudem, *Systematic Theology: An Introduction to Biblical Doctrine* (Leicester, UK: IVP, 1994), 529-563.
13. Grudem, chs. 11-13.

and divine natures in one being" is simply too imprecise and obscures the deeper point—even in an introductory text.[14]

Yet it is from this imprecision that he proceeds (strangely having earlier claimed that such is not possible) to suggest that we must do as "Evangelical theologians in previous generations" and not hesitate "to distinguish between things done by Christ's human nature but not by his divine nature, or by his divine nature but not his human nature."[15] As Grudem unpacks this he appears to use a Nestorian logic, and essentially for the same reason as Nestorius —as an attempt to keep pristine the divine nature. All Grudem seems to have done is substitute the words "natures"—he oddly sees as biblically acceptable—for "persons" which he sees as not.

Somewhat surprisingly then, Grudem in the end does state that there is a communication of the attributes between the natures, and with this he distances himself from his Reformed tradition. But what he presents is little more than a muddle. It has the outward appearance of the classical view but clearly misses the deeper point since it is predicated on a commitment to keep apart the actions and attributes of the natures.[16] What Grudem then understands the function of this doctrine to be remains unclear.

And this is my larger point. Grudem fails to offer an argument for how the natures communicate while remaining uniquely themselves (e.g. something like a mutual interpenetration of each other). Thus, while maybe technically avoiding Nestorianism verbally, what Grudem presents with his version of the communication of the attributes is an understanding of Christ using an essentially Nestorian logic. Therefore, while being orthodox in language in order to preserve the integrity of the humanity of Christ, his proposal in no way safeguards it. For by inadvertently using a Nestorian tactic he in fact leaves open the possibility, or even points toward the conclu-

---

14. Grudem, 558
15. Grudem, 558
16. Grudem, 563

sion that in Christ, humanity is lesser the subject than divinity, or we might even say, subordinated to it. This, again as in Nestorius, is not because Grudem wants to marginalize humanness, for he does not. Rather it is because he is so intent in earlier chapters to show that the divine nature, at least with respect to the more properly exalted attributes, is the opposite of human nature. (Of course, whether his argument is more biblically or philosophically driven remains the question.) Thus the two natures in Christ are inherently in tension. We might even say they compete with each other, and in this scenario practically the human will be prone to marginalization.

So what has been the point of our whole discussion on the communication of the attributes? It has been to argue that without some kind of doctrine suggesting a two-way communication of the attributes between divinity and humanity we end up, whether by subordinating humanity directly or exalting divinity over it, marginalizing Christ's humanity and thus ours within spiritual formation. But as we have seen, the classical metaphysical approach to the doctrine in the hands of those lacking extraordinary care to be "two-way" will also lead us to the same place. There are however, other ways to redevelop the communication of the attributes doctrine that are not dependent, as these ways have been, on a Greek ontology or understanding of "being."

### Jesus and *Imago Dei* Christology: The Identity of the Named Human who is God (and vice-versa)

In this all too brief section I shall now suggest a way forward for preserving the meaning and deeper function of the communication of the attributes while at the same time avoiding some of the troublesome tendencies associated with it as classically developed within a specifically substance metaphysic. This could be seen as providing a parallel to supplement the metaphysical metaphor, or as finding a different way altogether doctrinally to achieve the same end. But either way, the goal is to give us a tool to help us overcome

## THE NAMED HUMAN AND THE QUESTION OF 'BEING' CHRISTLIKE

the problem we give ourselves spiritually when we pit the humanity and divinity of Jesus against each other so that the humanity becomes marginalized.

I will begin with Richard Bauckham's Christology of "divine identity," and this will then lead into an *Imago Dei* Christology (Jesus the named human and the named God) as developed by Grenz.

Bauckham in his small but important book, *God Crucified: Monotheism and Christology in the New Testament,* argues that in the New Testament we find a high Christology but one stemming from an ontology that is decidedly different from the later Greek metaphysical Christology. He calls this a biblical Christology of divine identity and says that "this is not a mere stage on the way to the patristic development of ontological Christology in the context of a Trinitarian theology… [but] is already a fully divine Christology, maintaining that Jesus Christ is intrinsic to the unique and eternal identity of God."[17] As he explains: "When we think in terms of divine identity, rather than divine essence or nature, which are not the primary categories for Jewish theology, we can see that the so-called divine functions which Jesus exercises are intrinsic to who God is."[18] He argues that "not only the pre-existent and exalted Jesus but also the earthly, suffering, humiliated and crucified Jesus belong to the unique identity of God and reveals who God truly is—in humiliation as well as exaltation, and *in the connection of the two.*"[19] He reasons further: "While the Fathers successfully appropriated, in their own way in Nicene theology, the New Testament's inclusion of Jesus in the identity of God, they were less successful in appropriating this corollary, the revelation of the divine identity

---

17. Richard Bauckham, *God Crucified: Monotheism and Christology in the New Testament* (Carlisle: Paternoster, 1998) viii.
18. Bauckham, viii.
19. Bauckham, viii. [ital. added]

in Jesus' human life and passion."[20] (In my terms, they more readily spoke of a one-way communication of the divine to human attributes, but were less ready to speak of the human to the divine.)

While not addressing directly the question of the communication of the attributes, what we find Bauckham arguing for in the "connection of the two" is a doctrine very much like it. But this is by way of a Jewish "ontological category," divine identity, which is derived from the scriptural narrative itself. Throughout his argument Bauckham reflects on two examples of primary importance that show this "connection of the two," or that human attributes and divine are "shared" by way of divine identity. These are New Testament believers directing their worship to Jesus (not to the divine in Jesus), and, the cross—where God sheds his blood for us.

Yet how could Jews come to worship a man named Jesus? The earliest followers of Christ, Second Temple Jewish monotheists, knew that Jesus was a human. But they nevertheless came to believe that it was appropriate and necessary to direct their worship to him. According to Bauckham, these believers recognized in this man Jesus aspects of the divine identity belonging properly to God alone—that God is sole ruler and sole creator of all things.[21] Or to state it the other way round, they recognized that the identity of this human named Jesus was included within the identity of the God of Israel in such a way that what truly characterizes God likewise truly characterizes the human Jesus and what truly characterizes the human truly characterizes God.

But why? How could they justify being this radical, and thus in their worship seemingly tarnishing the identity of the exalted God of all creation by suggesting that he experienced the weakness of human pain and suffering, particularly the cross? Because what was at stake was no less than our salvation, for what was at stake

---

20. Bauckham, viii-ix.
21. Bauckham, 25

was no less than the fullness of the incarnation itself. Here is the reasoning.

They knew from their Jewish faith that our plight is so severe that only God can save us. They likewise had experienced in the Holy Spirit the salvation that Jesus provided on the cross. Therefore they knew, and expressed in a Second Temple Jewish way, that Jesus must be God (included uniquely in the divine identity). Thus, it is entirely appropriate to worship the man, the "named" Jesus, regardless of how scandalous it might be to suggest that in Jesus God is named as the one who suffered and died for us on the Cross.

Thus, when knowing full well that Jesus was human, the New Testament believers came to see divine activities / characteristics as belonging to this named human; and when they saw this divine Christ experience the full spectrum (without sin) of human life in the named person / identity of Jesus, they were in their own way suggesting what the Chalcedonian Fathers would later articulate differently and with recourse to the hypostatic union of two natures or substances; that is, the communication of the attributes.

The main difference however, is that the New Testament believers began with a Jewish theological category, or ontology, which was itself amenable to such "innovations," rather than Greek ontology that set up the question of the identity of Christ as a dilemma needing to be solved. That is, by using this ontology of divine identity so labeled by Bauckham, or what Grenz labels a Trinitarian "theo-ontology" / "ontology of the divine name," while maintaining the distinction between the divine and human they avoided starting with the assumption philosophically that humanity and divinity are opposites and thus by definition either incompatible or in competition with each other.[22] Rather, they started with the idea that to know what it means to be truly human (created to image God), and to know who God really is, we look to the named God

---

22. Grenz, *The Named God*, ch. 8.

Jesus or to what Grenz called an *"Imago Dei* and Biblical Christo-Anthropology."[23]

With Jesus named as the *Imago Dei* we find uniquely the picture of divinity and humanity united and sharing identity simultaneously without an inherent tension or the tendency to subsume the latter. We see that humans are creations who are genuinely other than God, but that humanity or humanness is not the opposite of divinity / God. Rather, humanness is indeed the only identity that by being fully itself (in relational union with God) can fully reflect and represent who God is. In Jesus we see that humanity is a characteristic embodied by God.[24] We see therefore in Jesus, who shares both in humiliation as well as exaltation, what is the named human identity of the unnamed "I am who I am" God. To be human "in Christ" by the Spirit is thus to be able to share relationally with God and with each other the divine triune personal identity without having one's own properties or "substance" transformed into that divine nature or swallowed up and overpowered by it.[25]

This is a version of deification, but neither the negative evangelical one presented earlier nor the common Orthodox one. It is as Grenz describes, our being included relationally in Christ by the Spirit and thus our being gifted by the Spirit with the fulfillment of our God-named identity—fully human, the *Imago Dei* realized.[26] It is, as Grenz borrows from Orthodox theologian Panayiotis Nellas, our "Christification," our being Christlike.[27]

---

23. Grenz, *The Named God*, ch. 9. and *The Social God and the Relational Self: A Trinitarian Theology of the Imago Dei* (Louisville: Westminster John Knox Press, 2001), ch.5.

24. See also Karl Barth, *The Humanity of God*, (Atlanta: John Knox Press, 1956 [1982 14th printing]).

25. Grenz, *The Named God*, 364-365.

26. Grenz, *The Named God*, 364-369.

27. Grenz, *The Named God* , 365.

This conception of deification with recourse to the *Imago Dei* does not conflate or mix divinity and humanity. Nor does it hierarchically order the two either in Jesus or in the spirituality of those whose identity is now in Jesus. Rather the *Imago Dei* brings mutually together divinity and humanity and is the way to find Jesus' divinity, thus God's name and identity. But this is found through and only through Jesus' humanity.

In terms of our discipleship the way to most appropriately be human is to image God. And the way most appropriately to image God and thus participate or share in his very way of being is, in Jesus, to ever increasingly become more genuinely human—which is to become more Christlike. Paradoxically, the more "in Christ" we come to terms with and embrace our finitude, frailty and otherness, the more we image (become like rather than become) God in our own "being." Our humanity itself, now in Christ, brings us through his own "communication of the attributes" into a full participation or sharing in the divine life itself. Thus, to become more spiritual we need to become more human. This is our destiny.

# Carl Edwin Armerding

*Curriculum Vitae*

## Academic Qualifications

1957      AB (European History), Gordon College, Boston

1965      BD (Theology), Trinity Evangelical Divinity School, Chicago

1966      MA (Old Testament), Brandeis University, Boston

1968      PhD (Ancient Near Eastern History and Culture), Brandeis University, Boston, awarded for a thesis entitled, "The Heroic Ages of Israel and Greece; a Literary-Historical Study" (H. A. Hoffner, supervisor)

## Professional Career

1957–61      Officer, United States Navy. Retired from Reserve, 1990, as Captain, Chaplain Corps, USN

1961–2      Traveling Secretary, Officers" Christian Union (European)

1969–70      Wheaton College, Illinois, USA
               Instructor, Old Testament

1970–91        Regent College, Vancouver, BC, Canada. Assistant Professor (1970–74), Associate Professor (1974–77), Professor of Old Testament (1977–1991), Principal (President) (1977–88), various visiting teaching events (1991–present).

1991–present   Schloss Mittersill Study Centre, Austria. Director 1991–2005. Professor Emeritus

1995–present   Oxford Centre for Mission Studies, Oxford, UK. Fellow.

Various dates  Visiting Professor of Old Testament/Archaeology: University of British Columbia; Hong Kong Baptist College; Singapore Bible College; Evangelical Theological Seminary, Osijek, Croatia; Biblical Seminary, Wroclaw, Poland; Emmanuel Bible College, Oradea, Romania; St. Petersburg Christian University, Russia; Sichuan University, China; Wuhan University, China; Azusa Pacific University

Supervisor/examiner of completed research at both MA and PhD level, in various British, Canadian, Croatian, and Russian universities. External PhD, MA examiner in various British universities.

**Professional Activities**

Member, Society for Old Testament Study; Evangelical Theological Society; Society of Biblical Literature; American Schools of Oriental Research; Canadian Society for Biblical Studies; Near East Archaeological Society; Institute for Biblical Research; Tyndale Fellowship for Biblical Research

CURRICULUM VITAE

President, Society of Biblical Literature, NW Region (1975–76)
Secretary, Institute for Biblical Research (1977–82)
Special lectureships: various universities and theological schools in North America, Asia, Latin America and Europe.

**Select Publications**

"Fruitful year in the Old Testament field," *Christianity Today* 14 (13 Feb. 1970): 3–6.

"Old Testament as a whole," *Christianity Today* 15 (18 Dec. 1970): 17–19.

With W. Ward Gasque, "Bible as a whole," *Christianity Today* 15 (6 Nov 1970): 18–21.

"Books on the Old Testament 1970," *Christianity Today* 15 (26 Feb. 1971): 11–17.

"Ancient Israel and her neighbors," *Christianity Today* 15 (12 Feb. 1971): 21–22.

"Religion and theology of Israel," *Christianity Today* 15 (21 May 1971): 27–29.

"Bibliography for Christians," *Christianity Today* 16 (4 Feb. 1972): 10–12.

"Some significant books of 1971: IV. The Old Testament," *Christianity Today* 16 (3 Mar. 1972): 12–16.

With W. Ward Gasque, "Some significant books of 1971: I. The Bible as a whole," *Christianity Today* 16 (18 Feb. 1972): 8–12.

"Bibliography for Christians," *Christianity Today* 16 (21 Jan. 1972): 9–11.

"Biblical Perspectives on the Ecology Crisis," *Journal of the American Scientific Affiliation* 25, 4–9.

With W. Ward Gasque, "Significant books of 1972: The Bible as a whole," *Christianity Today* 17 (2 Mar, 1973): 4–7.

"Significant books of 1972: the Old Testament," *Christianity Today* 17 (2 Mar. 1973): 7–13.

With W. Ward Gasque, "Significant books of 1973: The Bible as a whole," *Christianity Today* 18 (1 Mar. 1974): 30–33.

"Significant books of 1973: the Old Testament," *Christianity Today* 18 (1 Mar. 1974): 45–46.

With W. Ward Gasque, "Significant books of 1974: The Bible as a whole," *Christianity Today* 19 (14 Mar. 1975): 7–9.

"Significant books of '74: the Old Testament," *Christianity Today* 19 (14 Mar. 1975): 10–11.

"Were David's sons really priests," *Current Issues in Biblical and Patristic Interpretation*. Grand Rapids: Eerdmans Pub Co, 1975. pp. 75–86.

With W. Ward Gasque, "Significant books of 1975: The Bible as a whole," *Christianity Today* 20 (12th Mar. 1976): 9–11.

"Significant books of '75 : The Old Testament," *Christianity Today* 20 (12 Mar. 1976): 11–15.

Carl E. Armerding & W. Ward Gasque, "Key books of '76: Both Testaments," *Christianity Today* 21 (18 Mar. 1977): 12–13.

"Key Books of '76: The Old Testament," *Christianity Today* 21 (18 Mar. 1977): 17–19.

"Exodus and Liberation," C. E. Armerding, ed., *Evangelicals and Liberation*, Presbyterian and Reformed, 1977.

Carl E. Armerding & W. W. Gasque, eds., *Dreams, Visions and Oracles*. Grand Rapids: Baker Book House, 1977. Reissued as *Handbook of Biblical Prophecy*, 1980. 3rd ed., 1989 (Hendrickson Publishers).

"Old Testament Prophecy", C. E. Armerding & W. W. Gasque, eds., *Dreams, Visions and Oracles,* Baker, 1977.

Carl E. Armerding & W. Ward Gasque, "Key Books of '78 : Both Testaments," *Christianity Today* 23 (2 Mar. 1979): 20–31.

"Judges," in *The New Layman's Bible Commentary*. G. C. D. Howley, gen. ed., Paternoster and Zondervan, 1979. Reissued as *The International Bible Commentary*, F.F. Bruce, ed.

"Structural Analysis," *Themelios* 4.3 (April 1979): 96–104.

With W. Ward Gasque, "Whole Bible Book Survey 1979," *Christianity Today* 24 (7 Mar. 1980): 26–27.

"The Old Testament," *Christianity Today* 24 (7 Mar. 1980): 28–31.

CURRICULUM VITAE

*The Old Testament and Criticism.* Eerdmans. (Translated into various languages). Reprinted (1998) by Paternoster in Contemporary Christian Classics series.

"Obadiah, Nahum, Habakkuk," F.E. Gaebelein, editor, *Expositors' Bible Commentary,* Vol. 7. Grand Rapids: Zondervan, 1985. (Revision in preparation).

"Meaning of Israel in Evangelical Thought," Marc C. Tannenbaum, et al., eds. *Evangelicals and Jews in Conversation.* Grand Rapids: Baker, 1987.

"Charismatic Theology of Judges," M. Bockmuehl & H. Burkhardt, eds., *Gott Lieben, und Seine Gebote Halten: in Memoriam Klaus Bockmuehl,* Giessen/Basel: Brunnen Verlag, 1991.

"Images for Today: Word from the Prophets', R.L. Hubbard Jr., R.K. Johnston and R.P. Meye, Eds., *Studies in Old Testament Theology: Historical and Contemporary Images of God and God's People,* Festschrift D.A. Hubbard. Dallas: Word, 1992.

"When the Spirit Came Mightily: The Spirituality of Israel's Charismatic Leaders," J.I. Packer & L. Wilkinson, eds., *Alive To God: Studies in Spirituality* (presented to James M. Houston). InterVarsity Press, 1992.

"Confessions of a Failed Archaeologist," *Navy Chaplains Bulletin* 1992; reprinted in Crux.

"Spiritual Gifting and the Leadership of the Laity," *Context,* 1993.

"Faith and Method in Old Testament Study: Story Exegesis," P.E. Satterthwaite and D.F. Wright, eds., *Pathway into the Holy Scripture.* Grand Rapids: Eerdmans, 1994. 31–49.

"Reflections of a Canadian Theological Educator: A Personal History," Kevin Quast and John Vissers, eds. *Studies in Canadian Evangelical Renewal; Essays in Honour of Ian S. Rennie.* Markham, Ontario: FT Publications, 1996.

"The Child at Risk: A Biblical View," *Transformation* 14 (April–June 1997): 25–27, 30–31.

"Judges 8–13," *Encounter with God.* Milton Keynes: Scripture Union, 2000.

"Stewardship of the Land: a Christian Mandate' P. Walker and P. Johnston, eds. *The Land of Promise in the Purposes of God.* Leicester: Inter-Varsity Press, 2000.

"Judges," in *New Dictionary of Biblical Theology.* Leicester, Downers Grove, IL: Inter-Varsity Press, 2000.

"Borrowing and lending: is there anything Christian about either?" *Transformation* 18.3 (July 2001): 146–154.

"Feasts," in *Dictionary of the Old Testament: Pentateuch*, Leicester, Downers Grove, IL: Inter-Varsity Press, 2003.

"Did I Ever Ask for a House of Cedar? The Contribution of 2 Samuel 7 and 1 Chronicles 17 to the Theology of the Temple," T. D. Alexander & S. Gathercole, eds., *Heaven on Earth; the Temple in Biblical Theology.* Carlisle: Paternoster, 2004.

Notes on Obadiah, Judges in *New Living Study Bible*, Tyndale House Publishers.

"Habakkuk, Obadiah, Nahum' in revised *Expositors Bible Commentary* (Forthcoming)

www.ingramcontent.com/pod-product-compliance
Lightning Source LLC
Chambersburg PA
CBHW020944230426
43666CB00005B/166